NATURE WALKS
IN AND AROUND
NEW YORK CITY

AN AMC NATURE WALKS BOOK

SHEILA BUFF

APPALACHIAN MOUNTAIN CLUB BOOKS
BOSTON, MASSACHUSETTS

Cover Photograph: Hal Korber
All photographs by the author unless otherwise noted.
Cover Design: Elisabeth Leydon Brady
Book and Map Design: Carol Bast Tyler

Distributed by The Globe Pequot Press, Inc., Old Saybrook, CT

Published by the Appalachian Mountain Club. No part of this publication may be reproduced or transmitted in any form or by any means, electronic or mechanical, including photocopying and recording, or by any information storage or retrieval system, except as may be expressly permitted by the 1976 Copyright Act or in writing from the publisher. Requests for permission should be addressed in writing to Appalachian Mountain Club Books, 5 Joy Street, Boston, MA 02108.

Library of Congress Cataloging-in-Publication Data
Buff, Sheila.
   Nature walks in and around New York City / Sheila Buff.
     p.   cm.
   "An AMC nature walks book."
   Includes index.
   ISBN 1-878239-53-8 (alk. paper)
   1. Walking—New York Metropolitan Area—Guidebooks. 2. Nature study—New York Metropolitan Area—Guidebooks. 3. New York Metropolitan Area–Guidebooks. I. Title.
GV199.42.N65B84   1996
796.5'1'097471—dc20   96-9738
                                                         CIP

The paper used in this publication meets the minimum requirements of the American National Standard for Information Sciences—Permanence of Paper for Printed Library Materials, ANSI Z39.48–1984.∞

**Due to changes in conditions,
use of the information in this book
is at the sole risk of the user.**

Printed on recycled paper using soy-based inks.
Printed in the United States of America.

10 9 8 7 6 5 4 3 2 1   97 98 99 00 01 02

Contents

Orange and Rockland Counties

Connecticut

Northern New Jersey

To the memory of my father,
guide and companion on
the walk through life.

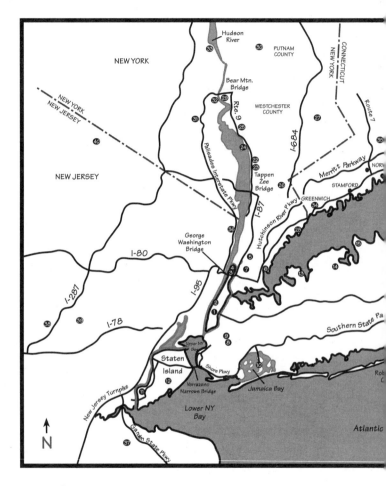

Walks Locator Map

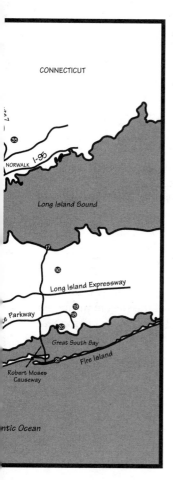

1. Central Park
2. Riverside Park
3. Fort Tryon Park and the Cloisters
4. Inwood Hill Park
5. Van Cortlandt Park
6. Pelham Bay Park
7. New York Botanical Garden
8. Prospect Park
9. Brooklyn Botanic Garden
10. Jamaica Bay NWR
11. Clay Pit Ponds State Park Preserve
12. High Rock Park Conservation Center
13. Sands Point Preserve
14. Planting Fields Arboretum
15. Caumsett State Park
16. Caleb Smith State Park Preserve
17. Sunken Meadow State Park
18. Bayard Cutting Arboretum
19. Connetquot River State Park Preserve
20. South Shore Nature Center
21. Fire Island National Seashore
22. Teatown Lake Reservation
23. Rockefeller State Park Preserve
24. Croton Point Park
25. Brinton Brook Sanctuary
26. Cranberry Lake Park
27. Ward Pound Ridge Reservation
28. Marshlands Conservancy
29. Anthony's Nose
30. Clarence Fahnestock State Park
31. Harriman State Park
32. Bear Mountain State Park
33. Black Rock Forest
34. Audubon Center in Greenwich
35. L. Pond Ordway Preserve–Devil's Den
36. Palisades Interstate Park
37. Cheesequake State Park
38. Scherman-Hoffman Sanctuaries
39. Great Swamp NWR
40. Wawayanda State Park

Acknowledgments

I'd like to thank the many friends who shared their favorite places and accompanied me on the walks in this book. They were all cheerful and very forbearing companions. I am grateful to my husband Joe and our dogs, Dagmar and Leopold; Sue Andrews; Susan Farenci; Patricia Godfrey; Ann Guilfoyle; Martin Kohl; Laurie Lewis; Greg Ludwig; Phyllis Rosenzweig; Leslie Sharpe; Carolyn and Guy Smith; and Ralph Weiss.

David Emblidge got me into this project, and Gordon Hardy at the Appalachian Mountain Club saw it through. Thanks to them both.

Finally, I'd like to thank the many dedicated rangers, naturalists, and other employees at the sites in this book. I could never have written it without their lively interest and valuable help.

Introduction

As a result of far-sighted thinking well over a century ago, the metropolitan New York area contains an astonishing amount of open space. Within the five boroughs of New York City alone are 26,369 acres of park space—13 percent of the city. The Palisades Interstate Parks system in northern New Jersey and Rockland and Orange Counties now encompasses more than 80,000 acres. Elsewhere in New Jersey, in Connecticut, in Putnam and Westchester Counties, and on Long Island, extensive state and county parks cover many thousands of additional acres. In addition to local, county, and state parks, the metropolitan region contains several national wildlife refuges and parks and numerous sites protected by nonprofit conservation organizations such as The Nature Conservancy.

Such an abundance of parkland made for some tough choices in this book. The first step was to eliminate places that were beyond a ninety-minute off-hours drive from my home in Brooklyn Heights. Next, I eliminated parks that are managed primarily as recreation sites, even though that meant ignoring such well-known parks as Jones Beach, and places that were too rugged for the average walker. Even so, I was left with a lot of sites. I then tried to select sites that presented interesting natural features—wildlife, birds, plants, geology, and so on—or were particularly scenic. I also tried to cover a range of terrains. The walks in this book take you from Atlantic beaches to mountaintops in the Hudson Highlands. Along the way are salt marshes, bogs, swamps, ponds, lakes, rivers, meadows, forests, and cliffs, to say nothing of arboretums and botanical gardens. In the end, of course, the final choices became a little arbitrary. Some places are included because they are my personal favorites.

Personal safety may be a concern for people walking in some of the areas described in this book. I should point out that I often walk alone in such allegedly dangerous places as Prospect Park in Brooklyn and have never encountered any sort of real threat. Incidents do occur, however, even in places that are far from the confines of New York City. Be aware of your surroundings and leave quickly if you feel uncomfortable.

There is also safety and companionship in numbers. Many of the places in this book offer guided group walks with a ranger or naturalist on weekends. An unusually large number of walking groups are active in the New York metropolitan area—you need never walk alone. The New York–New Jersey Trail Conference, an all-volunteer organization that maintains many of the trails in this book, is a federation of eighty-five hiking and outdoor groups with more than 8,500 members. Other large and active groups in the area include the New York–North Jersey Chapter of the Appalachian Mountain Club, the New York City Audubon Society, and the Long Island Greenbelt Trail Conference. On any given weekend day (and often during the week as well), you can go on interesting walks with friendly people. Car pools are often available to distant areas—a major advantage for the many New Yorkers who don't have cars (or even licenses).

Going for a nature walk is not very complicated, but you should be sure to wear appropriate shoes and dress for the weather where you're going. Sturdy, comfortable walking shoes or sneakers will be adequate for the hikes in this book. Beginning walkers often are shockingly unprepared for cold weather. Beaches and elevated areas are generally much colder and windier than your starting point at home. Wear warm socks, several comfortable layers, and a hat. You can always shed layers if you get hot. It is far, far better to get to your destination and be too warm than it is to be cold without recourse. To avoid ticks, mosquitoes, poison ivy, and scratches from shrubbery, wear closed shoes, socks, and long trousers even in warm weather. Insect repellent will help keep noxious bugs away. (Be sure to read the health caution below.)

Environmental education is an important mission for many of the places in this book. They offer a wide range of programs for both adults and children, from nature walks to full-scale evening courses. Most are free or charge only nominal fees. Almost every site offers at least some activities.

The following areas offer particularly good programs for kids:

- Audubon Center in Greenwich

- Central Park

- Cranberry Lake Park

- Marshlands Conservancy

- New York Botanical Garden
- Rockefeller State Park Preserve
- Scherman-Hoffman Sanctuaries
- Sands Point Preserve
- South Shore Nature Center
- Teatown Lake Reservation
- Ward Pound Ridge Reservation

Health Precautions

Two serious tick-borne illnesses are hazards to hikers in the New York metro area: Lyme disease and erlichiosis. Both illnesses are carried by the tiny deer tick *(Ioxides dammini)*; infected deer ticks are widespread in the area. Lyme disease is usually characterized by a red, bull's-eye rash at the site of the tick bite, followed days or even weeks later by aching joints and muscles, fever, flulike symptoms, and headaches. In more severe cases, permanent nerve damage and even death can result. Erlichiosis is even more serious than Lyme disease, although so far it is considerably less common. Victims develop a rash all over the body, along with high fever, muscle and joint pain, sleeplessness, sore throat, chills, headaches, and low white cell and platelet counts.

Fortunately, both Lyme disease and erlichiosis respond extremely well to conventional antibiotics. The chances of a complete cure are excellent, especially if you are diagnosed early. On the other hand, the symptoms of these diseases often begin days after the tick has dropped off. In addition, the symptoms can vary among individuals. In the case of Lyme disease, for example, the characteristic rash may not be present. If you become ill with flulike symptoms or seem to develop arthritis within a month of visiting a natural area, be sure to tell your doctor that you have been exposed to ticks. A simple blood test usually can detect the presence of spirochetes from Lyme disease or erlichiosis.

Prevention is the best way to avoid tick-borne disease. Particularly in the late spring and early summer when ticks are most common, wear ankle-high footgear, long sleeves, long trousers, and a hat. Tuck your trouser ends into your socks, tuck your shirt into your trousers, and button your cuffs. Select light-colored clothing so that ticks can be easily spotted. Stay on and to the center of trails and avoid brushing against vegetation at the edges. Don't go into brushy or grassy areas without trails. Be sure to apply insect repellent, preferably one containing DEET, to all exposed skin.

If you have been in an area where ticks are prevalent, check your body and clothing carefully afterward. Hairy areas of the body, especially the head, are very attractive to ticks. Ticks found crawling on the skin or clothing should simply be removed before they can attach themselves. There is no risk here—the tick must embed itself and remain embedded for at least several hours before it can transmit disease. If a tick does attach itself, remove it promptly. Use a pair of tweezers to grasp the tick on either side of the head, as close to the skin as possible, then pull gently but steadily to remove it. Apply antiseptic to the bite site and wash your hands thoroughly. You can ask your doctor to send the tick for testing to see if it's infected, but this is expensive and not completely reliable. Chances are that you'll be fine.

In recent years outbreaks of raccoon rabies have been confirmed in New York and New Jersey. If you see a raccoon that seems sick or injured or is acting strangely, rabies could be the reason. Do not attempt to touch, capture, or help the animal in any way. Report the behavior and the approximate location to the site managers.

Wildlife in the Region

As I was writing this book, my friends made a lot of jokes about the "wildlife" to be found in places like Central Park. As you'll discover, however, there is a surprising abundance of wildlife everywhere in the region. I've emphasized the bird life in part out of personal preference and in part because birds are active, visible, and audible all day and all year.

Humans and dogs aside, the most abundant mammals in the region are probably three members of the squirrel family. Gray squirrels (*Sciurus carolinensis*) are found everywhere covered by this book. They are very visible year-round and all day long as they scamper around the ground and dash through the treetops. Squirrel nests, or drays, are large, untidy masses of leaves fairly high up in trees around the trunk. Look for leafy, rounded bundles, about two feet in diameter, with branches protruding through them. Squirrel noises in the woods sometimes are mistaken for bird sounds. With a little practice, you can soon learn to tell the sounds apart. A loud, rapid *kuk kuk kuk* is a squirrel warning of immediate danger (you, perhaps, or a predator such as a hawk). The same sound, but much slower, tells the squirrel world that the danger has passed. Chattering noises of various sorts are also common.

Occasionally you may notice a black squirrel in New York City parks. When gray squirrel populations become inbred, the recessive gene for excessive darkness (melanism) becomes apparent.

The less common red squirrel (*Tamiasciurus hudsonicus*) is seen sometimes in the forested, higher-elevation areas covered by this book, especially areas with pine trees. Smaller than the gray squirrel, red squirrels are also very vocal, making a lot of harsh calls. They are seen year-round and are most active early in the morning and at dusk.

Eastern chipmunks (*Tamias striatus*) are small, ground-dwelling squirrels; they are reddish-brown with white and black stripes on the head, back, and sides. Chipmunks partially hibernate in winter, coming out during warm spells. They are active all day long, mostly on the ground or low down in trees. Sometimes a chipmunk squeaks in alarm and then vanishes into thin air as you approach it. In fact, it has disappeared into a hidden entrance to its extensive underground burrow.

Other mammals common to the areas covered here include raccoons, opossums, woodchucks, eastern cottontail rabbits, and white-tailed deer. As any suburb-dweller knows, raccoons and opossums are nocturnal, much preferring to raid your garbage cans at night. You probably won't see any live ones (road kills don't count) on a hike, but you might come across signs of their presence. Look for footprints in the soft mud near streams and ponds. Possums have five toes, with a very visible "thumb." Raccoons also have five toes, but they all point straight ahead.

Woodchucks, or groundhogs, are commonly found in grassy areas and open forests. These large, chunky animals are brownish all over, with a big head and short legs. They hibernate in the winter. The rest of the year, they are frequently seen feeding on grass along roads (which is why they are also frequently seen dead). If you come across one on your hike, it will quickly hide in its nearby burrow.

If you'd like to see deer up close, two sites on Long Island are particularly good: Connetquot River State Park Preserve and the South Shore Nature Center. Deer are found in many of the other sites outside the immediate metropolitan area, but usually you will catch just a glimpse of them as they crash away through the underbrush.

The coyote, a type of small wolf, has become increasingly common in this region over the past few decades. These adaptable animals have been sighted even in Riverside Park in Manhattan. Because they are nocturnal, you are unlikely to see one as you hike. If you are fortunate, you might catch a glimpse of one at dusk or very early in the morning.

The open spaces of the New York metropolitan region are there for your enjoyment. Whenever I walk in these areas, my appreciation of the conservation ethic and volunteer spirit that have preserved them grows. I hope that visiting the sites in this book will inspire you to help protect them for yourself and future generations. As the people who have saved these places for you prove, individuals can make a difference.

New York City

Central Park
Manhattan

- 3 miles, on park paths
- 2 hours
- easy

*A leisurely stroll through the oldest
public park in the country.*

Central Park was the first public park built in America. That alone would qualify it for its status as a National Historic Landmark (1965) and a New York City Landmark (1974), but the park is also a true masterpiece of landscape architecture. A competition for the design was held in 1858. The winners over thirty-two other entrants were Calvert Vaux and Frederick Law Olmsted, who submitted a design for a naturalistic "Greensward." Their design included a revolutionary and brilliant feature: sunken transverse drives that allow traffic to cross the park unobtrusively. The land designated for the park was considered a dismal wasteland: rocky, swampy, and home to squatters and such unsavory industries as bone boiling. Olmstead and Vaux began construction in 1858. The construction took sixteen years to complete and cost

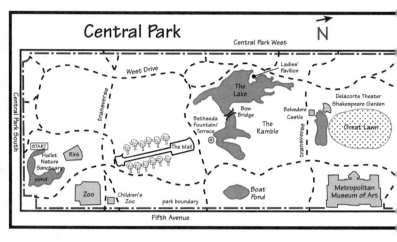

more than $14 million (close to $200 million in today's dollars). In the process, workers moved nearly five million cubic yards of stone and earth and planted more than 500,000 trees, shrubs, and vines. There are thirty bridges and arches in the park and eleven overpasses across the sunken roads. The decision to pave the curving carriage drives and allow automobile traffic on them in 1912 was probably the worst thing ever done to the park.

The 843 acres of Central Park contain fifty-eight miles of pedestrian paths. To my mind, wandering those paths to no particular end is the whole point of Central Park. No matter how often you go, there's always something new to discover. The Central Park Conservancy (see below) publishes an excellent map that shows the paths and details all of the lovingly named walks, gates,

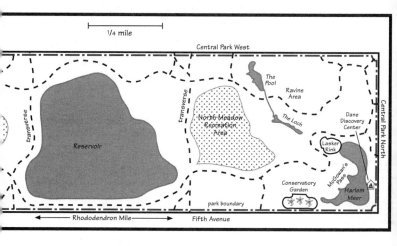

arches, bridges, fountains, monuments, sculptures, and buildings. You can't really get lost here, so there's no need to suggest a particular route to follow. Instead, I'll describe some of the more interesting natural features of the park, more or less from south to north, and let you discover them for yourself.

The Hallett Nature Sanctuary in the southeastern corner of the park includes a large pond that is a reliably good spot for seeing egrets, herons, ducks, red-winged blackbirds, and a variety of other songbirds. All of Central Park is amazingly good for bird-watching. Beyond the ubiquitous pigeons, starlings, and house (English) sparrows, more than 270 species have been spotted here. To the north of the sanctuary is the Wollman Rink. To the east of the rink, at 64th Street on the Fifth Avenue side, is the Wildlife Conservation Center, better known as the

Central Park Zoo, closed (spring '96) for renovation. Walk to the north of the zoo and cross the 65th Street transverse to arrive at the heart of Central Park: the Mall. This formal promenade contains the largest grove of **American elms** (*Ulmus americana*) in the world. The park's arborists maintain these trees very carefully to protect them against the Dutch elm disease that has killed most American elms elsewhere. Additional American elms line the park side of Fifth Avenue from 59th Street all the way to the Metropolitan Museum of Art at 82d Street. All told, there are about 1,800 American elms in the park. Look for tall trees with spreading crowns; the leaves are ovate and distinctly lopsided with serrated edges.

The Mall leads you directly up to the ornate Bethesda Terrace and Fountain. From here, the view overlooks the eighteen-acre Lake to the west; straight ahead is a boating area that is actually an extension of the Lake. The original intent of Central Park's design was to simulate a country outing, with all that implied to the romantic imaginations of the day. Ordinary citizens were meant to refresh themselves spiritually by strolling along the paths, admiring the scenery, and giving way respectfully to the carriages and horses of their betters. The only active recreation was ice-skating on the Lake, an activity that was, to the surprise of Olmsted and Vaux, immediately very popular. When the two later designed Prospect Park in Brooklyn, they made the lake there much larger to accommodate more skaters. Nearly 2,000 flower bulbs have been planted around the charming Ladies' Pavilion on the western shore of the Lake near 75th Street. They are in bloom from mid-March through the end of April.

One of the famous Central Park cast-iron lampposts. This one is in the Conservatory Garden.

To the east of the terrace, just off Fifth Avenue between 73d and 75th Streets, is Conservatory Water, informally known as the model-boat pond. Recently, birders in the park have been following with great interest the progress of a pair of **resident red-tailed hawks**. They have been nesting on a parapet of an apartment building on Fifth Avenue. A nest in 1994 failed, but two chicks were fledged from this nest in 1995.

The two lake segments below Bethesda Terrace are crossed by the delightful Bow Bridge. The bridge is a good spot to look for birds on the water and around the edges. Green herons have been breeding in this area recently.

Crossing Bow Bridge takes you into the Ramble, a **hilly, thirty-three-acre wooded area** filled with thick stands of such trees as oak, locust, willow, black cherry, and mulberry and dense tangles of shrubbery. The Ramble also has a stream and several small ponds; glacial erratics and outcroppings of Manhattan schist make the area somewhat rocky. The conditions are just right for attracting tired, hungry birds as they migrate north or south. This is the best spot in the park for bird-watching, particularly early on a spring morning.

The Ramble eventually brings you north to the 79th Street transverse and Belvedere Castle. This 1872 Gothic gem was designed by Calvert Vaux and is the only building specified in the original park plan. Built on Vista Rock at the second-highest point in the park, the castle has recently been renovated as the Luce Learning Center. Turtle Pond at the base of the hill is another good spot for birds. The outdoor Delacorte Theater, where Shakespeare plays are performed in the summer, is just to the west of the castle. An interesting Shakespeare Garden is near the theater.

From Belvedere Castle you have a good view to the north out over the Great Lawn and the Reservoir. The Great Lawn is the site of frequent outdoor concerts and other events attended by thousands of people at a time. Just north of the Great Lawn the massive Reservoir effectively divides the northern and southern sections of the park. The Reservoir covers 106 acres; it is surrounded by a 1.58-mile running path. For all that the Reservoir is very large, it's not very attractive and you can't get close to the water. The famed Rhododendron Mile, however, runs along the Fifth Avenue side of the Reservoir from 87th Street to 95th Street and is worth a visit when in bloom in early May.

To continue your walk, skirt around the Reservoir to the west. Follow the path north for roughly half a mile and cross the 97th Street transverse. Continue north for a few more minutes, past the recreation area in the North Meadow to the east. On the west, starting near 100th Street, is a lovely, somewhat lonely area called the Ravine. The only **stream valley** in the park, this ninety-acre woodland features ponds, a cascade, rustic bridges, and restored arches. Follow the water until it leads you

A delightful cascade spills down a natural stream in the Ravine section of Central Park. This ninety-acre area is in the northwest portion of the park starting at 100th Street.

out near the Lasker Rink and Pool at the northern end of the park. Walk past to come out on the shores of the Harlem Meer. This restored eleven-acre lake is in the northeast corner of the park. On the north shore near the Lenox Avenue entrance is the Dana Discovery Center for environmental education. Notice the hill of McGowan's Pass and the old Fort Clinton site on the western edge of the lake between the Lasker pool and Fifth Avenue. They loom above the lake, suggesting that this was originally a glacial kettle pond that was extensively modified to make the lake. Walk around the Meer and enjoy the natural scenery here.

For an enjoyable way to end your walk, head south along Fifth Avenue to the formal entrance to the Conservatory Garden at 104th Street. The only **formal garden** setting in the park, this elegant six-acre area features fountains and spectacular seasonal displays of bulbs, perennials, and annuals.

Finding Your Way and Safety in Central Park

Central Park is a giant rectangle running on a north-south axis. The southern edge is at 59th Street (called Central Park South here) and the northern edge is at 110th Street; several entrances lead into the park from these streets. The park is bordered by seven miles of beautiful cut-stone walls with entrances on the east side (Fifth Avenue) at 66th, 72d, 79th, 85th, 97th, and 102d Streets. On the west side (Central Park West), the entrances are at 66th, 72d, 81st, 86th, 96th, and 100th Streets. You can usually tell the compass direction simply by looking at the tall buildings that border the park, but it's sometimes hard to know where you are relative to the entrances. To figure it out, look at the number plates on the cast-iron lampposts throughout the park. The first two digits of the number indicate the nearest cross street. If the last digit is odd, you are on the west side of the park; if it is even, you are on the east side.

Although more than fifteen million people visit Central Park every year, almost all without incident, the park has an undeserved bad reputation for personal security. Highly publicized attacks on female joggers have not helped any. A number of homeless people frequent the park and many spend the night hidden there. In my opinion, these sad people are an indictment of failed social policy, not a danger. If you are concerned about safety, visit the park only during the day and stay in the more heavily used portions in the southern part. Alternatively, look for safety in numbers. Several organizations, including the New York City Audubon Society and the Urban Park Rangers, lead frequent tours and nature walks in the park.

No discussion of Central Park would be complete without mentioning the incredible work of the Central Park Conservancy. A nonprofit organization that works in partnership with the city to help rebuild and maintain Central Park, the conservancy relies on gifts from individuals, corporations, and foundations to raise half of Central Park's annual operating budget. Since its founding in 1980, the conservancy has restored more than half the Park's landscapes and historic structures. The work of the conservancy is a model for concerned citizens everywhere.

Hours, Fees, and Facilities

Central Park is open daily from thirty minutes before sunrise to 1:00 A.M. The zoo, Belvedere Castle, and the Dana Discovery Center have seasonal hours; call first. There are no fees. Restrooms, water fountains, and pay phones are found at or near most of the major park structures and food areas. Dogs must be on leashes; be prepared to clean up after your pet.

Getting There

A number of subway stops are at or near various entrances to Central Park. The A, B, C, D, 1 and 9 trains all stop at Columbus Circle at the southwest corner of the park. The M1, M2, M3, M4, and M18 buses run down Fifth Avenue; the M10 bus runs up Central Park West. Park roads (but not the transverses) are closed to motor traffic on some holidays and on weekends from 7:00 P.M. on Friday to 6:00 A.M. on Monday. On weekdays, the park is closed to motor traffic from 10:00 A.M. to 3:00 P.M. and again from 7:00 P.M. to 10:00 P.M.

For More Information
Central Park Administration
The Arsenal
New York, NY 10021
212-794-6564

Belvedere Castle
212-772-0210

Dairy Visitor Center
212-794-6564

Dana Discovery Center
212-860-1370

Urban Park Rangers
212-772-0210

Central Park Conservancy
The Arsenal
New York, NY 10021
212-315-0385

Riverside Park
Upper West Side, Manhattan

- **1.5 miles, on park paths**
- **2 to 2.5 hours**
- **easy**

A long ribbon of green along the Hudson River.

Manhattan's Riverside Park stretches along the Hudson River for nearly four miles, from its southern end at 72d Street to its northern terminus at 152d Street. Despite its length, this park is basically a narrow green ribbon running along the riverfront—it covers only 323 acres. The park's designers took advantage of the sharply sloping terrain (from 150 feet at its highest point down to sea level at the river) to build walkways on different levels that make the park seem considerably more spacious than it really is.

Riverside Park was planned originally by Frederick Law Olmsted, the architect of Central Park, in 1875. Work on the park didn't begin until 1880, however, and was carried out by Calvert Vaux (Olmsted's associate) and others; the park was completed in 1890. The finished park at that point, however, bore little resemblance to the park today. Olmsted's design included only the broad, tree-lined boulevard of Riverside Drive and the upper terrace area; the park terminated at 125th Street. It was not until the 1930s that Parks Commissioner Robert Moses extended the park to its current terminus and transformed the riverfront from a squalid area of railroad tracks, slaughter-houses, and shanties into the park we enjoy today. The railroad tracks, now used by Metro North and Amtrak, are still there—in a very clever use of space, they have been roofed over and now form a terrace in the park. The Henry Hudson Parkway also runs through Riverside Park, and unfortunately it is not roofed over. Both the parkway and the railroad bisect the park lengthwise; pedestrian access between the upper and lower portions is via elegant tunnels and staircases.

This tour of Riverside Park will be restricted to the original portion between 72d Street and 125th Street. The later addition to the north was designed chiefly for recreation and has little appeal from the aesthetic or natural history standpoint.

Begin the walk at the historic entrance at 72d Street and Riverside Drive. Some of the huge old American linden trees (*Tilia americana*, also called basswood) here date from the original plantings. You can spot these trees by their size (some are well over 100 feet tall) and their long, ovate, serrated leaves. Lindens bloom in the late spring with clusters of yellowish flowers on the end of long, membranous bracts; later, the flowers are replaced by berrylike fruits. In all, Riverside Park contains some **13,000 trees, including many flowering species**. They make the park especially beautiful in the spring.

Follow the asphalt path that leads west and down toward the river; go through the tunnel. You will emerge onto a sweeping dramatic view of the **Hudson River**. It's hard to believe that this mighty river, here nearly a mile wide, begins some 315 miles away at a two-acre pond in the Adirondacks. The pond, fancifully named Lake Tear of the Clouds, is found nearly 4,300 feet up on the south-

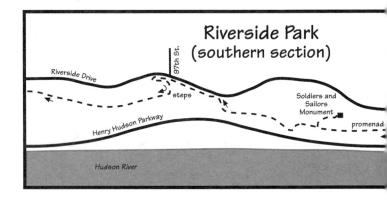

Riverside Park
(southern section)

Riverside Drive

97th St.

steps

Soldiers and
Sailors
Monument

promenad

Henry Hudson Parkway

Hudson River

west slope of Mt. Marcy (which is, at 5,344 feet, the highest mountain in New York State). Flowing entirely within New York State, the Hudson River ends officially at the Battery, the southernmost tip of Manhattan Island, where it enters Upper New York Bay.

Follow the path down to the **riverfront promenade**. Built on landfill, the promenade is very popular with bike riders and joggers. It's also an excellent place to view rafts of migrating ducks in the late autumn. Walk upriver along the promenade toward the boat basin at 79th Street. A tunnel back to the higher parts of the park leads up from the left side of the open, arcaded Rotunda, but as of this writing, the area is undergoing repairs and the tunnel is closed. Instead, continue north for another few minutes and look for another pedestrian tunnel on your right. When you come out, you will be on a level with the railroad tracks. Look up and around—you can see how the terrace of the Lower Promenade above you roofs the tracks. Go up the stairs to your right, which end at a circle forming the southern end of the Lower

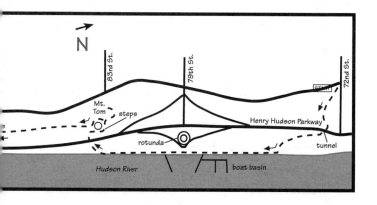

Promenade. This wide, tree-lined mall extends all the way to 92d Street.

Before exploring this part of the park, follow the path leading southwest from the circle, up toward the 83d Street entrance. To the north just inside the entrance is a rocky outcropping of Manhattan schist known as Mt. Tom. Legend has it that Edgar Allan Poe, who in the 1840s lived in a house near 84th Street, used to climb up here to seek inspiration. Try it—the results for me have been uncertain, but it may work better for you.

Retrace your steps to the circle at the southern end of the Lower Promenade and begin strolling northward. This part of Riverside Park has a very European feel to it—you could easily imagine yourself in Paris or Berlin. At the northern end of the promenade are flower beds planted and maintained as a community effort by the local residents. Between 92d Street and 95th Street is a lovely group of Japanese cherry trees that bloom magnificently in May. The Soldiers and Sailors Monument, found on the Upper Promenade at 89th Street, is visible

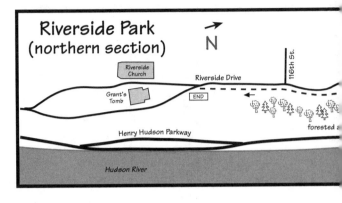

from almost anywhere in this part of the park. The monument, dating from 1902, commemorates those who fought in the Civil War. Its terraces provide sweeping views out over the river.

At the circular terminus of the northern end of the Lower Promenade at 93d Street, you have a choice of going up or down to get past the exit ramp for the Henry Hudson Parkway. Since going down takes you only to some tennis courts, bear to your right (east) and walk uphill toward Riverside Drive. To avoid the dangerous intersection with the ramp, cross to the eastern side of Riverside Drive and walk north two blocks. Cross Riverside Drive again and reenter the park at the 97th Street entrance. Go past the playground and stroll north along the leafy Upper Promenade while admiring the start of the Palisades across the Hudson in New Jersey. (For more information about this unusual geologic structure, see the walk in Palisades Park, page 282). Ten minutes of leisurely walking brings you to a wooded area stretching from 114th Street to 120th Street. This dense

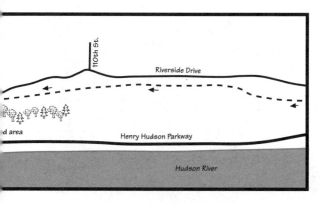

patch of **natural woodland** is what bird-watchers call a migrant trap—a green oasis that attracts tired, hungry birds on their way north in the spring. Look especially for warblers in the early morning.

In this section of the park you are near the crest of a ridge that runs from Inwood Hill Park at the northernmost tip of Manhattan down to 110th Street, where it veers eastward and runs all the way down into Central Park. If you look eastward across 116th Street, you can see Morningside Heights and Columbia University, the true crest of the ridge. On the other side of the crest, the ridge drops down again sharply. (Tiny Morningside Park—only thirty-one acres—another creation of Olmsted and Vaux, is on the far side of the ridge.)

As you walk north through the woods, you'll catch glimpses of the spires of Riverside Church ahead on Riverside Drive between 120th and 122d Streets. Should you be in the area at noon, you will hear the chiming of the seventy-four bells in the church's magnificent carillon. The noise doesn't seem to bother the pair of peregrine

Numerous flowering trees make Riverside Park particularly beautiful in the springtime.

falcons that nest among the spires and feed on the complacent pigeons in the park. If you are very fortunate, you may even see them. This pair has successfully raised a number of chicks over the past few years.

As you reach 119th Street, you'll see the church to your right; straight ahead is the massive, classically inspired structure that is Grant's Tomb. Follow the path to the left as it curves past the tomb. The views of the Hudson from here, about 100 feet up, are breathtaking. (George Washington thought this would be the ideal site for the United States Capitol building.) The original Riverside Park ends here at 125th Street. Take the steps at the end of the walkway down to the street level, or retrace your steps and visit Grant's Tomb and Riverside Church.

Hours, Fees, and Facilities

Riverside Park is free. Restrooms and water fountains are found throughout the park at playgrounds and other recreational facilities; vendors sell food and drink at many of the entrances. The park is open around the clock every day. Dogs are permitted on leashes only. Be prepared to clean up after your pet.

Getting There

By far the most efficient way to get to Riverside Park is via subway. The Broadway/Seventh Avenue local and express trains (numbers 1, 2, 3, and 9) stop at 72d Street and Broadway; walk west two blocks. The local 1 and 9 trains stop at 125th Street and Broadway. The M5 bus runs along Riverside Drive from 135th Street to 72d Street. If you must drive, that rare New York City commodity, free off-street parking, is available at 92d Street from the Henry Hudson Parkway.

For More Information

Riverside Park Administrator
Arsenal West
16 West 61st Street
New York, NY 10023
212-408-0264

Riverside Park Community Fund
475 Riverside Drive
New York, NY 10027
212-870-3070

Fort Tryon Park and the Cloisters

Northern Manhattan

- **1.5 miles, moderate walking on paved park paths**
- **2-2.5 hours**
- **easy**

Beautiful landscaping, sweeping views of the Hudson—and the Cloisters.

The sixty-seven acres that are now Fort Tryon Park were the site of one of the earliest battles of the Revolutionary War. In the summer of 1776, George Washington and his troops fortified this strategic area, which commands the high ground overlooking the Hudson River, and called it the Woodland Battery. On November 16, 1776, a fierce battle erupted between the Continental army and the Hessian troops of the British army. Outnumbered 4,000 to 600, the American troops eventually surrendered. The victorious British took over the battery and renamed it in honor of the colonial governor, Sir William Tryon. New York City remained in British hands until the end of the war, and the name Fort Tryon stuck—even though the general neighborhood is more patriotically called Washington Heights.

In 1917, John D. Rockefeller Jr. acquired the property with the idea of establishing a park. In 1927, he set

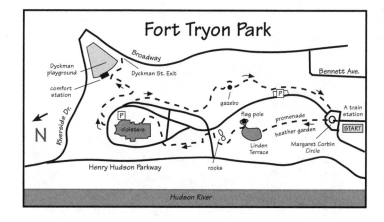

aside four acres at the northern end of the park for the Cloisters, a branch of the Metropolitan Museum of Art that houses a collection of medieval art. He then hired Frederick Law Olmsted Jr., son of the designer of Central Park and Prospect Park, to design the park. Young Olmsted took advantage of the site's elevation and steep topography to reveal **sweeping Hudson River vistas** at many points. Other aspects of Olmsted's design, still largely intact today, include stone architectural elements, unusual plants, and a graceful traffic pattern that keeps the presence of vehicles from intruding on the peace of the park. In all, eight miles of paths follow a series of terraces—complete with parapets, retaining walls, and overlooks—built into the ridge. Winding rock stairs lead from one terrace to the next.

This romantic stone staircase in quiet Fort Tryon Park leads upward to the Cloisters.

The Plants of Fort Tryon

Olmsted's original horticultural plan for Fort Tryon was quite elaborate. Some of the Olmsted plantings, particularly the many **ornamental and specimen trees** scattered throughout the park, are still visible. Over the years, however, many of the original plantings died off—some naturally, some by neglect, and many because such invasive plants as Norway maple and sycamore shaded them out. Recent restoration work has brought back some of the beauty.

Start your walk through Fort Tryon at Margaret Corbin Circle, the main (south) entrance. The London plane trees and the ivy are from the original plantings. The attractive small stone building on the west side of the circle was the gatehouse for the Billings estate, which at one time took up much of what is now the park. Walk through the massive stone gateway straight ahead onto the Promenade, then turn immediately to your left to enter the three-acre **Heather Garden**. This garden was one of the horticultural highlights of the park in its early days. Neglect took its toll, however, and a poorly conceived renovation in the 1950s only worsened matters. By the 1980s, the stunning river vistas from the Heather Garden had disappeared, obscured by diseased elm trees and scrubby invasive growth. The lovely garden you see today is the result of a careful restoration that closely followed Olmsted's original plan. Between 1985 and 1988 Parks Department gardeners planted more than 2,500 heathers, heaths, and brooms, along with 15,000 bulbs, 5,000 perennials, 500 shrubs, and five trees. This time the results were outstanding—the panoramic vista looking some 240 feet down the slope to the Hudson River was restored, while the landscaping again reveals the topography of the ridge. Today Fort Tryon Park boasts one of the largest heather and heath gardens on the East Coast; it is also the largest public garden with unrestricted access in New York City. The garden offers year-round color and texture. The heaths (low-growing shrubs of the genus *Erica*) begin flowering in late January and still have their tiny lavender and white blossoms into May. The heathers (another branch of the *Erica* genus) bloom from summer into autumn with small, delicate pink, lavender, and white flowers. The subtly varied colors of the foliage on the heathers make them very beautiful even when they're not blooming. The bulbs begin blooming as early as February, but the most spectacular display comes in

May, including more than thirty varieties of tulips and daffodils; a thousand lily **bulbs** flower from June to September. The perennial border contains more than a hundred different species that bloom from June to October. Such shrubs as azaleas, roses, and a 600-foot privet hedge provide structure for the garden. A sourwood tree (*Oxydendrum arboreum*) and several franklinia trees (*Franklinia alatamaha*) provide autumn color. Also known as black tupelo or pepperidge, the sourwood has long, pointed, slightly serrated leaves and one-sided clusters of dead flowers or dried fruit hanging from its branches. Sourwoods turn a lovely shade of crimson by the end of August and often retain their colorful leaves well into October. **Franklinia trees** were discovered in Georgia in 1770 by the pioneering botanist John Bartram, but they have not been found in the wild since 1790. All franklinias today are descended from seedlings Bartram raised. This small, slow-growing tree never reaches more than twenty feet in height; it blossoms from late summer through the autumn with gold-centered white flowers some three inches across; the leaves turn brilliant scarlet in late September.

Thoughtful readers may wonder why Olmsted specifically chose heath and heather for this garden instead of, say, day lilies or roses. The answer can be found in the stand of native hackberry trees (*Celtis occidentalis*) that grows at the northwest corner of the garden. (Look for narrow, short-stemmed leaves that are lopsided at the base, slightly serrated, and taper to a long point.) Hackberries, heathers, and heaths all thrive in shallow, rocky, acidic soil underlain by limestone. In fact, where there are hackberries there is certain to be limestone, and that is exactly the case here. The Fort

Tryon ridge is made of Manhattan schist (a type of granite) that overlies and is interlayered with softer Inwood marble—and marble, because it is made of calcium carbonate, is a type of limestone.

After enjoying the Heather Garden and admiring the Hudson views, return to the Promenade and follow it for five minutes or so to the Linden Terrace. This lovely area of benches, parapets, and river views is shaded by big old linden trees. It seems cool even on the muggiest August afternoon and is always full of neighborhood residents enjoying the view and the company. At the northeast corner of the terrace are steps that take you up to another terrace with a flagpole. The flagpole stands at the **highest natural point on Manhattan**: nearly 260 feet above sea level. (The highest *un*natural point in New York City is the 110th floor of the World Trade Center, 1,377 feet above sea level.)

To continue the walk, take the steps back down to the Linden Terrace and look for another set of nearby steps leading down from the terrace and back onto the main Promenade path. Follow the Promenade for a few minutes to a lawn area—you can now see the Cloisters up ahead. The path leads you past the lawn and down toward the ramp for the Henry Hudson Parkway. As you walk along, look on your right for a large, brownish boulder somewhat off the path. This is a chunk of diabase, the same rock that makes up the Palisades across the river, dropped here some ten thousand years ago during the retreat of the last glacier. A little farther on, on the right and close to the path, is a large, gray boulder. This rock is mica schist, the dominant rock in the Manhattan Formation that underlies much of the island. If you look closely at the rock, you'll notice flakes of mica in it. You'll see also some little red and black spots—these are garnets.

The Promenade takes you under the parkway ramp and onto the Cloisters Lawn. Bear to your right and follow the path slightly uphill for ten minutes or so to reach the main entrance of the Cloisters museum (see below). To continue on from the museum, follow the footpath from the parking area around the back of the museum and down the steps under the road. Immediately turn right and follow the path for a minute or two until it intersects with a path leading off to the left. Follow this path down toward the Dyckman Playground and the Dyckman Street exit—about ten minutes. If you prefer to return to the main entrance of the park, stay on the path as it wends its way back. (Just keep the traffic noise from the drive, the auto route through the park, on your right.) This route takes you through pleasant woods and lawns and past some lovely stone work. It brings you back to the main entrance at Margaret Corbin Circle in about twenty minutes.

The Gardens of the Cloisters

The chapter house and various chapels, sections of monastic cloisters, and other architectural elements dating from the twelfth through the fifteenth centuries that make up the Cloisters were brought from Europe and incorporated into the site. Opened in 1938, the Cloisters is primarily an art museum, but it also has three fascinating gardens with outstanding river views. The Cuxa Cloister surrounds a garth, or enclosed yard. The plan of the garden—crossed paths with a fountain in the center—and the flowering plants that fill it are typical of the medieval period. The Trie Cloister contains specimens of all the plants depicted in the Unicorn Tapestries, one of the treasures of the museum. My personal favorite is the Bonnefont Cloister herb garden. Looking at the raised beds, wattle fences, and central wellhead, enclosed within an early-fourteenth-century cloister, you really can imagine yourself back in time. More than 250 herb species are cultivated here. The plants are labeled and grouped in beds according to their uses. It's interesting to note that in medieval times there was little distinction between culinary and medicinal uses.

Hours, Fees, and Facilities

Fort Tryon Park is open daily from dawn to dusk and is free. Restrooms are found at the Cafe (near the parking area on the drive), at the Dyckman Playground at the northern end of the park, and in the Cloisters. Dogs are allowed only on leashes; be prepared to clean up after your pet.

The Cloisters is open Tuesday through Sunday 9:30 A.M. to 4:45 P.M.; it is closed on Mondays. Visitors may pay what they wish for entrance, although they must pay something. The suggested admission is $7.00 for adults and $3.50 for senior citizens and students. Note: The Cloisters is not easily accessible for mobility-impaired visitors. Call in advance for assistance.

Getting There

By all means take the IND Eighth Avenue A subway to the 190th Street station. Follow signs for the Overlook Terrace exit. This is the second-deepest subway station in the city—165 feet. (The deepest—180 feet—is the Broadway IRT station at 191st Street and Saint Nicholas Avenue.) The elevator ride from the platform to the street lasts nearly forty seconds. The station exit brings you directly to Margaret Corbin Circle. The M4 (Fifth and Madison Avenue) bus runs up Fort Washington Avenue and stops at Margaret Corbin Circle; the next and last stop on this bus is at the Cloisters.

If you are driving on local streets, follow Fort Washington Avenue or Cabrini Boulevard to the entrance at Margaret Corbin Circle. From the Henry Hudson Parkway, go north to the Fort Tryon exit—this is the first exit north of the George Washington Bridge. The park drive is open to traffic from 7:00 A.M. to 7:00 P.M. weekdays; it is closed on weekends and evenings, although there is still direct auto access to the Cloisters from the Henry Hudson Parkway. Very unusually for Manhattan, limited free parking is available near the Cafe just past the entrance and at the Cloisters.

For More Information

Fort Tryon Park General Information
212-427-4040

Fort Tryon Park Garden Information
212-795-1388

The Cloisters
Fort Tryon Park
New York, NY 10040
212-923-3700

Inwood Hill Park
Northern Manhattan

- **2 hours**
- **2 miles**
- **moderate**

Untouched woodlands on the very tip of Manhattan Island.

Inwood Hill Park is without a doubt the most natural and unspoiled in the entire New York City system. It may also be the least known to the general public, although it is an open secret among nature lovers. About 140 of the 196 acres of the park comprise the last tract of natural woodland in Manhattan. More than 150 bird species have been tallied here, and it is one of the best places in the entire city—certainly in all of Manhattan—for butterflies. The park also contains some fascinating geologic formations. For all its beauty and interest, Inwood Hill Park's location on the northernmost tip of Manhattan Island makes it a bit out of the way. Even on a sunny spring morning, the only other people you are likely to see are occasional joggers and dog walkers and perhaps a few bird-watchers. Given the run-down quality of the surrounding neighborhood, some people find this solitude a little unnerving. You're unlikely to have a problem, but if it worries you, bring along a friend.

From the mid-1800s until the 1920s, several large estates were built on the heights overlooking the Hudson

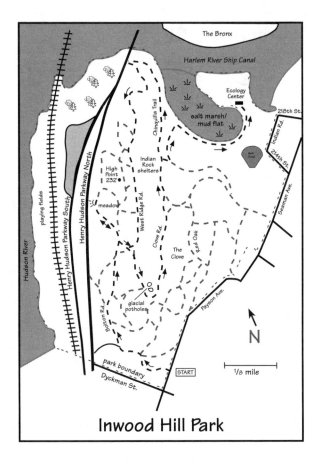

Inwood Hill Park

River. The Lords, of Lord & Taylor department store fame, once had two mansions on the escarpment, but these burned to the ground around the turn of the century. A few traces of old foundations and gardens are still faintly visible here and there. Fortunately, the steepness of the slopes made the area undesirable to real-estate developers. In the 1920s, John D. Rockefeller Jr. purchased the land and gave it to the city for a park. Little was done to the park until the late 1930s, when the Henry Hudson Parkway was constructed through the western edge. Paved paths, ball fields, and playgrounds were added at around this time. Fortunately, the woodlands on their steep hills remained basically untouched. Cast-iron lampposts, in the style of Central Park, were installed in the 1960s but vandals quickly destroyed these intrusions on the natural character, and the lamps never have been replaced. After a lengthy period of benign neglect, the park is now receiving some badly needed attention. Reforestation work is going on to remove invasive, nonnative tree species that have gained a foothold in the park. In an effort to control erosion problems, some of the unpaved paths have been blocked off or moved. An excellent new ecology center has also been opened in what was once an old boathouse on the Spuyten Duyvil Creek.

Today the wooded sections of Inwood Hill Park are a reminder of what once covered all of Manhattan. There are many **massive tulip trees**, some as tall as 80 feet or more. (In 1939 the park's largest tree, a huge tulip tree that was 165 feet high and some 6.5 feet in diameter, died and was cut down. It was nearly 300 years old.) Other large trees found here include hickories and several species of oaks and maples. About ten miles of paved paths wind through the park, and there are many miles more of gravel or dirt paths, some unofficial. The main paved paths have names on the good map available at the ecology center, but there are few if any useful signs. The Henry Hudson Parkway runs north-south up the west side of the park parallel to—and cutting you off from—the Hudson River. You can't really get lost here, though, since the sight of the river and the faint sound of the traffic help keep you oriented. The park reaches its northern terminus where the island does, at Spuyten Duyvil creek, the waterway that divides Manhattan from the Bronx.

To start your stroll through the park, begin at the southernmost end, at the intersection of Payson Avenue and Dyckman Street. If you look up and down Dyckman Street, you'll see it is really a valley that runs approximately southeast-northwest. To the south of Dyckman Street, the ridge of Fort Tryon Park rises sharply, while to the north looms the ridge of Inwood Hill Park. Despite the fault separating them, the ridges of the two parks are part of one geologic formation known as the Fort Washington ridge. This ridge in turn is part of the **Manhattan formation**, a huge mass of metamorphic bedrock made up of mica or hornblende schist. Generically called Manhattan schist, it forms most of the rocky outcroppings in New York City and vicinity. It also forms the bedrock for most of Manhattan south of 110th Street—the ideal geology for building skyscrapers. (The bedrock dips sharply several hundred feet below street level near Washington Square in Greenwich Village and doesn't rise up again until Chambers Street in lower Manhattan. That's why the skyscrapers of the city cluster in midtown and downtown—the part in between can't support buildings that big.)

The valley you are standing in is known to geologists as the Dyckman Street Gap—a textbook example of a **cross fault**. The valley probably was created hundreds of millions of years ago, when unimaginably powerful forces shattered some of the rock in the ridge, causing cracks to appear in it. Over the millennia, water seeping through the cracks caused the rock to shatter further and erode away, creating a gap that bisects the ridge.

After admiring the Dyckman Street Gap, walk north up Payson Avenue and turn left just after the playground to enter the park at its main entrance. Follow the paved path (called Bolton Road on the map) for a few minutes until you come to the intersection of three paths. Follow the path leading up the steps. Stay on the main path for about five more minutes, ignoring all side paths, until the path forks at the entrance to an open meadow. Bear to your left for a lovely viewpoint looking southwest out over the Hudson River. The highest point in the park—232 feet—is nearby.

A view looking west across the Hudson River to the Palisades in New Jersey from Inwood Hill Park.

After admiring the view, backtrack to the meadow entrance. Follow the main path back for just a minute or so and turn left at the fork. Follow the path downhill for a couple of minutes until it meets another main paved path called Ridge Road at a T intersection (again, there's no sign, but Ridge Road runs approximately north-south). Turn right to follow Ridge Road south for about ten minutes. You are now at the point where two ridges, one to the west (left) and one to east (right), converge to pinch off a narrow, steep-sided valley, as if forming the prow of a canoe. Indeed, the valley below you is some-times called Canoe Valley. Why is this valley here? The answer lies in a fundamental point about the geology of the region: differential erosion. Upthrusted folds of the hard, erosion-resistant bedrock form the ridges. The area between the fold was once filled with Inwood marble, a softer rock that is much more susceptible to erosion. Over many millions of years, the marble eroded away at a much faster rate than the bedrock, leaving a valley. (Soft is a relative term in geology. Inwood marble quar-ried at Tuckahoe in nearby Westchester was used to build the majestic—and very sturdy—42nd Street branch of the New York Public Library.)

From this point, Ridge Road curves around the tip of the valley and becomes Clove Road (again, there is no sign). Follow Clove Road north as it descends along the eastern wall of the valley. The wooded area on your right is known as The Clove; it is probably the best area in the park for birdwatching.

After walking about fifteen yards, look to your left for a large, gray rock formation. If you look more closely at this rock, you'll see **glacial potholes** in it. The deep, round depressions in the rock were created between 10,000 and 20,000 years ago, when a stream flowing beneath the ice of the Wisconsin glacier (the last to cover the Northeast) formed an eddy. Grit and pebbles swirling in the eddy carved out the potholes.

Return to the path and follow it for another ten minutes or so. Look up at the steep valley wall on your right. You'll see cliffs with a jumble of gray, distinctly blocky rocks—the Indian Rock Shelters. Centuries ago this area was one of three main **Algonquin Indian settlements** on Manhattan, and the rocks on the cliff were once used as shelters. Henry Hudson had a skirmish with the Indians here in 1609 as he began his exploration of the river, and it is from these same Indians that Peter Stuyvesant "bought" the island for $24 in 1626. The last Indians still to live here were gone by the mid-1700s, but traces of their long occupation survive. In the 1930s archaeologists from the Museum of the American Indian excavated the area and found numerous artifacts, and friends who grew up near the park in the 1950s tell me they could still find arrowheads and pottery shards. In 1992, the City Council of New York named the natural wooded area of the park Shorakapok in honor of the Native Americans. (The word is said to mean "as far as the sitting-down place.")

As you continue past the Indian Rock Shelters, the path flattens out onto the valley floor. Ahead of you is Spuyten Duyvil creek. This waterway gets its odd name from a supposed incident during the Dutch colonial period. A young messenger, sent to warn the Dutch settlers that English ships were in the harbor, could find no way to cross the creek. Vowing to get across in spite of the devil (*en spyt den duyvil*), he decided to swim. He drowned, and the creek has been called Spuyten Duyvil ever since. Sadly, the facts do get in the way of this good story. Because the creek bed is actually another cross fault, in colonial times it was shallow, rocky, and easily crossed on foot at low tide. In the 1920s Spuyten Duyvil was extensively dredged and straightened to make a canal connecting the Harlem River to the Hudson and making it possible to circumnavigate Manhattan. Despite the railroad bridge and the Henry Hudson Bridge connecting Manhattan to the Bronx, wading birds and ducks often can be found along the shore here.

To see the twelve acres of marsh and mud flats that fill a cove of Spuyten Duyvil creek to the east of the Henry Hudson Bridge, and to visit the Inwood Hill Park Urban Ecology Center, look for a path on your right just past the Indian Rock Shelters. Follow the path as it leads past a large boulder called Shorakapok Rock and out to an open playing field. Follow the path to your left for another few minutes until you reach the water. To reach the ecology center, continue to your right along the water's edge for another ten minutes or so.

If you prefer to return through the wooded part of the park, follow the path along the edge of Spuyten Duyvil toward the Henry Hudson Bridge. After a few minutes, you'll see a paved path that runs down from the woods—this is West Ridge Road. Turn left onto this path and follow it as it runs approximately north-south along the top of the broad west ridge of the park; several smaller paths branch off. The views of the Hudson from here are excellent. Follow this path, exploring the side paths if you wish, back to the starting point, a walk of about twenty minutes.

Hours, Fees, and Facilities

The park is free and open all the time. The Inwood Hill Park Urban Ecology Center is open Thursday through Monday from 11 A.M. to 4 P.M. Call 212-304-2365 for information about programs. Restrooms are found at the playground at Dyckman Street and Payson Avenue near the main entrance and at the baseball field near Isham Street. Dogs on leashes only; be prepared to clean up after your pet.

Getting There

The closest subway station is the Dyckman Street stop on the A train. Walk west two blocks to the park. The M100 bus stops at Dyckman Street; walk west two blocks to the park. To drive, take the Riverside Drive exit on the Henry Hudson Parkway and make the first left onto Payson Avenue. Follow Payson one block to the park. Free street parking is generally available in the vicinity; read the signs carefully.

For More Information

Inwood Hill Park Administrator
Arsenal West
16 West 61st Street
New York, NY 10023
212-408-0264

Inwood Hill Park Urban Ecology Center/
Manhattan Urban Park Rangers
212-304-2365

Van Cortlandt Park
Bronx

- 1 mile
- about an hour
- easy

Exploring wetlands in the northwest Bronx.

Van Cortlandt Park covers 1,146 acres in the northwest Bronx. The park is used heavily for recreation, especially on weekends, but it still contains some easily accessible natural history and is surprisingly wild in places. Two popular nature trails go through the park. The Cass Gallagher Trail is a lovely loop of a bit more than a mile. It takes you through the **northwest forest portion** and is certainly worth a visit for its beautiful stands of tulip trees and hemlocks and its dramatic rock outcroppings. Even so, I prefer the John Kieran Nature Trail in the southern portion of the park. This easy trail gives you a good look at the **freshwater wetlands** of the park, lets you explore the bird-watcher's haven of Tibbetts Brook, and incidentally takes in a fair amount of park and local history. John Kieran was a well-known journalist and nature lover who had a lifelong devotion to Van Cortlandt Park. His classic book *A Natural History of New York City*, first published in 1959, remains good reading and a valuable reference.

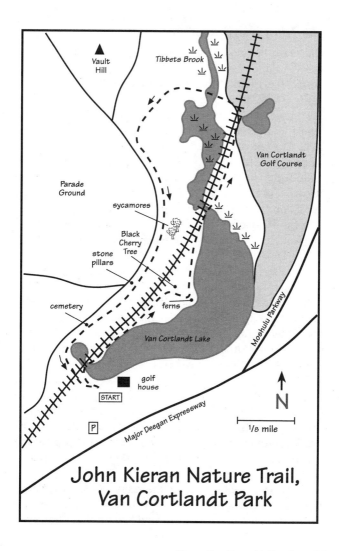

John Kieran Nature Trail, Van Cortlandt Park

The John Kieran Nature Trail

The walk begins at the southern end of thirty-six-acre Van Cortlandt Lake—the largest freshwater body in the Bronx—and winds through the park's **freshwater wetlands**. Look around you a bit before starting. The Van Cortlandt Golf Course has the distinction of being the oldest municipal links in the country, dating back to 1895. The lake itself was formed when Jacobus Van Cortlandt dammed Tibbetts Brook around 1700 to create a millpond. Until the early 1900s, the outflow of the stream continued its natural course south through marshlands to Spuyten Duyvil creek, and from there into the Hudson River. These tidal marshes were filled in; Tibbetts Brook now flows onward through underground conduits.

To start the walk, look for a path starting behind a monument just to the left of the Golf House. Follow the path to the left around the southern tip of the lake. As it turns to the right, you'll notice that you are crossing over the water on an old railroad bridge. This is the former route of the Putnam Division of the New York Central Railroad. This line carried passengers and freight from 1881 until 1958; it remained in use for occasional freight trains until 1981. The rail corridor that once carried commuters to Westchester and Connecticut now serves, minus the rails and ties, as a walking and wildlife corridor instead. Deer sometimes wander into the park along this route, and coyotes and wild turkeys have been seen with some regularity recently.

The trail follows along the edge of Van Cortlandt Lake, but a chain-link fence on your right separates you from the water. After walking for a few minutes, however,

Phragmites, arrow arum, and other freshwater marsh plants are common in the Tibbetts Brook portion of Van Cortlandt Park.

you'll come to a gap in the fence. Turn right to follow the well-worn path into the wooded area here. You'll know you're in the right place when you see a gray birch tree with five trunks. The main trail, marked by branches laid along the ground, takes you past the birch on your right. In just a minute or two you'll come to a big old black cherry tree. Look for long, thin, somewhat leathery leaves; the bark is black and flaky, resembling burnt potato chips. This tree is surprisingly large. Generally, black cherries that grow in former fields or pastures never get very big. Growing in the moist shade of the tree is a colony of New York fern (*Thelypteris noveboracensis*). This fern is fairly easy to identify. The pinnae (the "leaves" that radiate from the stem) on the fronds are delicate and widely spaced; they are broadest in the center of the frond and taper down toward the base.

Continue on the main path for about five more minutes. Look on your right for a short side path that takes you to a huge, twisted old willow on the lake shore. The shallow water of the lake is full here of the arrowhead-shaped leaves of arrow arum (*Peltranda* sp.), also sometimes known as tuckahoe. Skunk cabbage (*Symplocarpus foetidus*) grows in the swampy area to the north of the willow. (These two plants are actually related members of the arum family, which also includes jack-in-the-pulpit and sweet flag. All these plants have acrid or pungent juice and are found in wet, shady places.) In the summer, look for the hairy leaves and clusters of tiny, sky-blue flowers of forget-me-not (*Myosotis* sp.) growing at the water's edge.

Return to the main path and follow it for about ten minutes. Look for a gap in the chain-link fence, go through it, and turn right. Another twenty yards or so takes you onto a bridge. On your right is Van Cortlandt Lake; on your left Tibbetts Brook runs through a marsh. Part of the golf course is in the marshy area, so golfers here sometimes encounter unexpected water hazards. From here you can also see (and hear) the Major Deegan Expressway, one of three major roads that run through the park. The building of this road (completed in 1956) further compromised the peace and beauty of the park, broke it up into unrelated sections, and demolished acres of pristine wetlands. In particular, the wetlands habitat along the beautiful Tibbetts Brook valley was drastically reduced.

Follow the path as it goes farther along the wetland area on your left (the golf course continues on your right). After about five minutes you'll see a short trail leading down to an old concrete block on your left. Pause here for a great view out over the heart of the **marsh**. In the spring or summer, you are quite likely to spot a great blue heron or an egret wading in the shallows near the shore. Red-winged blackbirds and mallards are very common.

As you walk on, in a few minutes the path veers to the left, away from the old rail-bed. Shortly after, a bridge takes you over Tibbetts Brook—look to your right to see the flowing stream. The main path continues, with numerous short side paths leading down to the marsh on your left. Follow the main path for another five minutes or so to the enormous fallen tree that marks a bullfrog pond.

A few more minutes on the main path brings you out of the wooded area and onto the edge of the Parade Ground. To your right rises Vault Hill. This 169-foot hill gets its name from the Van Cortlandt family mausoleum that is still there. During the Revolutionary War, Augustus Van Cortlandt, who had been appointed by the British as city clerk, stashed the city's records in the vault. In 1781, as George Washington was withdrawing his troops from New York for the final battle at Yorktown in Virginia, campfires were left burning on top of the hill, so the British wouldn't realize they had gone. (If you'd like to climb the hill, turn right and follow the paved walkway along the edge of the Parade Ground. As you reach the base of the hill, turn either right or left and look for one of the several unofficial footpaths that lead up the hill. The climb is steep but worthwhile for the view.)

The Parade Ground was once the site of a Native American village. From 1699 until the land was sold to the city as a park in 1888, it was farmland owned by the Van Cortlandt family. Until the end of World War I, the Parade Ground was exactly that: a drill area and polo field for National Guard troops. Today it is a popular recreation area for team sports; the most popular game by far is cricket, played by West Indians. Looking across and to the south of the Parade Ground, you can see the Van Cortlandt mansion. Built in 1748 by Frederick Van Cortlandt, this three-story house is a fine example of vernacular Georgian architecture. The oldest house in the Bronx, the mansion is now a museum. Remnants of the old gardens that once surrounded the house still can be seen.

To continue your walk, turn left and follow the paved walkway along the edge of the Parade Ground. Note the huge old **sycamore trees** along the border—some could easily be well over a hundred years old. There's one with six trunks just opposite the pull-up bars on the fitness path.

After about five minutes, look for a side path on your left leading back into the woods (it will be just before the tennis courts on your right). Standing silently in the woods are thirteen stone pillars made of different kinds of rock from different quarries. They were put here by the New York Central Railroad to test their durability. The stone that won—the Indiana limestone of the two pillars on the far right—was used as the facade of Grand Central Station.

Return to the walkway and turn left. The railed-off old cemetery coming up on your left is considerably less interesting than it looks, especially since there are no tombstones. It dates from the early 1700s and contains the graves of members of prominent settlers of the period, but little else is known about the site. Follow the walkway a bit farther until it turns left onto a dirt path. Follow the path for about ten minutes, past the tip of Van Cortlandt Lake and back to your starting point.

Native Americans in Van Cortlandt Park

Weckquaesgeek Indians (members of the Lenape people) had settled in this part of the Bronx by about 1000 A.D. This agricultural tribe was attracted by the fertile, flat land of the Mosholu valley. (Mosholu, an Algonquian word meaning "smooth stones" or "clear water," was their name for Tibbetts Brook. The name is preserved in local road names such as Mosholu Parkway.) The Weckquaesgeek built an extensive village on the flat land that is now the Parade Ground. In 1639, they sold much of what is now the park to the colonial power of the time, the Dutch West India Company, which in turn sold the land to Adriaen Van der Donck in 1646. Van der Donck seems to have maintained good relations with his Native American neighbors, even though relations between natives and colonists at the time were severely strained and sometimes violent. However, when Van der Donck died in 1655, the Indians attacked the small group of settlers living there and forced them back to the protection of New Amsterdam at the southern tip of Manhattan. In 1693, Frederick Philipse, an English merchant who was the wealthiest man in New York at the time, bought the land from Van der Donck's widow. In 1699, he sold a parcel of the land to his new son-in-law (and a future mayor of New York), Jacobus Van Cortlandt. It was Jacobus Van Cortlandt who made the last purchase of Lenape land, in 1701. By then, the Native American population had been dramatically reduced, mostly by disease. By some estimates, the original Lenape population was between 8,000 and 12,000 before the Europeans arrived. By the early 1700s, there were no more than 3,000. The few remaining Lenape drifted out of the area, intermarrying with other tribes and generally moving westward. Today there are some Lenape descendants living in communities in Oklahoma, Wisconsin, and Ontario, Canada. A few scattered tribal members still live in upstate New York and New Jersey. Little is left to commemorate the Native Americans of the area. A plaque near Indian Field in the eastern portion of the park marks the site where thirty-seven Stockbridge Indians (including some Lenape) were massacred by British and Hessian troops in 1778. The plaque misspells the name of the chief, Abraham Ninham.

Hours, Fees, and Facilities

The park is open daily from dawn to dusk. There are no fees. Van Cortlandt House is open to the public Tuesday through Friday, 11:00 A.M. to 3:00 P.M., and Sunday 1:00 A.M. to 5:00 P.M. Restrooms, water, phones, and a snack bar are at the Golf House. Restrooms are found also at the Urban Forest Ecology Center at the southern end of the Parade Ground. Vendors sell food and drink during the warmer months. Dogs are allowed only on leashes; be prepared to clean up after your pet.

Getting There

If you are driving, try to avoid the congested local traffic on Broadway and Jerome Avenue. Broadway runs along the western edge of the park. Take the Major Deegan Expressway to the Golf Course exit at Van Cortlandt Park and East 233d Street. Follow signs to Van Cortlandt Golf Course. Parking is free in the golf course lot, although it can be crowded on weekend mornings in the warm weather. Free street parking generally is available in the vicinity; read the signs carefully.

The last stop on the Broadway IRT 1 and 9 trains, 242d Street, is just to the west of the Parade Ground near Van Cortlandt House.

The Bx9 bus runs along Broadway on the western edge of the park; get off at 242d Street. The X61 express bus stops at 244th Street and Broadway. Enter the park next to the southern subway staircase and walk east about a quarter of a mile to reach the Golf House. Westchester bus lines numbers 1, 2, and 3 stop at Broadway and 242d Street.

For More Information

Park Administrator, Van Cortlandt Park
Broadway and 246th Street
Bronx, NY 10471
718-430-1890

Urban Park Rangers
718-548-7070

Van Cortlandt House
718-543-3344

Pelham Bay Park
Bronx

- **1.5 miles**
- **1.5 hours**
- **easy**

*Bird-watching and salt marshes in
New York City's largest park.*

Pelham Bay Park is the largest park in New York City. It covers 2,764 acres in the northwest part of the Bronx. Within the park are many popular recreation areas: mile-long Orchard Beach on the Long Island Sound, two golf courses, miniature golf and a driving range, a stable, tennis courts, baseball diamonds, and picnic grounds. If you look beyond all the recreational facilities, however, you'll see that this park has a very diverse range of habitats—the most diverse of any park in the city or nearby. About 660 acres of the park are saltwater marshes; there are thirteen miles of shoreline.

Once the site of Siwanoy Indian hunting and fishing grounds and later the site of fashionable mansions, Pelham Bay became a park in 1888 when New York City bought and consolidated twenty-eight private estates. All the houses, except the historic Bartow-Pell mansion, were torn down. In the 1930s, the park was developed as a major recreation site. Landfill was used to create a huge, mile-long beach with a massive bathhouse at

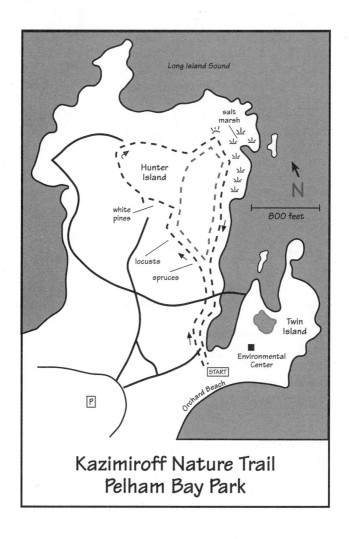

Long Island Sound

salt marsh

Hunter Island

white pines

locusts

spruces

N

800 feet

Twin Island

Environmental Center

START

P

Orchard Beach

Kazimiroff Nature Trail
Pelham Bay Park

Orchard Beach. Extremely popular ever since, Orchard Beach is often called, only half-jokingly, the Riviera of New York City. The beach and surrounding area are always crowded in the warm weather; on a summer weekend, the forty-five-acre parking lot is jammed.

The Thomas Pell Wildlife Sanctuary and the Hunter's Island Sanctuary were created in 1967 as part of an agreement that narrowly avoided having the wetlands of the park being turned into landfill by the city. The fifty-acre Pell sanctuary along the Hutchinson River is all that remains of 5,000 acres of salt marsh. This area is bisected by the Hutchinson River Parkway; it is bounded by the apartment towers of Co-Op City on the east, by railroad tracks on the west, and by the New England Thruway to the north. The paved Split Rock Trail runs along the western border of Goose Creek Marsh and provides some excellent views out over the tidal marsh. This can be a good spot for birding, but frankly, I find the traffic noise very oppressive. If you want to check it out, the trailhead is to the west of the Bartow traffic circle. The round trip is less than a mile.

The Kazimiroff Nature Trail through the Hunter's Island sanctuary is a much more pleasant walk. The trail is named for Dr. Theodore Kazimiroff (1914–1980), a dentist and local historian who was a leader in the fight to defeat the landfill proposal in the 1960s. The trail winds through 189 acres of one of the most beautiful sections of the park. Most of it is paved in asphalt, and it's very easy to follow. There are lots of side trails to explore as well.

Look for the sign for the trailhead at the northern end of Orchard Beach (walk away from the bathhouse), about thirty yards before the Environmental Center

Wooded and remote as the Hunter's Island area seems, you're never reallly very far from civilization in Pelham Bay Park./Martin Kohl.

building. Follow the trail as it leads into the woods of Hunter's Island. In a few minutes you'll come to a collapsed causeway leading across the water to Twin Island. Actually, Twin Island and Hunter's Island are islands no more. When Orchard Beach was expanded in 1934, 2.5 million cubic yards of sand, soil, and rock were used to fill the area between Hunter's Island and Rodman's Neck; in 1947, additional fill connected Twin Island to the tip of Orchard Beach. Currently no safe access to Twin Island exists; Hunter's Island is really now a peninsula. The sheltered lagoon that was formed between the two islands is an outstanding place to see **waterfowl**, particularly ducks. The larger artificial lagoon on the northern side of Hunter's Island is also very good for waterfowl.

In another few minutes, the trail forks at a stand of Norway spruce. These dense evergreens were planted by the Parks Department in 1918 as part of a reforestation effort. They have grown up nicely to be about sixty feet tall.

Follow the trail to the left. The spruces soon give way to large numbers of thin black locust trees—look for the deeply furrowed bark and small, rounded, paired leaves. Black locust is a pioneer tree in forest succession. This tells you that the land here was once an open field—perhaps a pasture or a lawn more than fifty years ago. Your surmise will be proved correct in a few more minutes when you come on the remains of the old Hunter mansion, which was demolished in 1937. Vestiges of the old gardens still can be seen here.

As you continue on, you'll quickly come to a grove of white pines. The dense needles and horizontally layered branches make these trees a favorite roosting place for great horned owls (*Bubo virginianus*). Long-eared, saw-whet, screech, and barred **owls** are also sometimes seen here. They're so well camouflaged that you're unlikely actually to see any, but you should be able to see evidence of their presence, especially in the winter. Look for splashes of "whitewash" excrement on the trunks, branches, and ground around here. Look on the ground for grayish owl pellets. The pellets consist of the regurgitated indigestible parts—mostly the bones and hair—of the animals the owl eats. Pine trees of various sorts have been planted extensively throughout the park. The shelter they offer, combined with the large, open, rodent-filled expanses of Pelham Bay, make the park famous among birders for owls. Another excellent area to see owls here is in the dense evergreens near the Bartow-Pell mansion.

As you continue on, more evidence of the old Hunter mansion comes along. Look here for ailanthus trees and mugwort, a tall, herbaceous plant that grows abundantly in disturbed ground. Some old chocolate brown stone blocks strewn on either side of the trail are all that remain of the estate's front gate. From here, the trail continues on the original winding road that connected Hunter's Island to the mainland.

The trail now leads through a large area of open, mature woodlands. The trees here are mostly oak and hickory, with some towering tulip poplars as well. As the trail curves westward, and then east, you can catch glimpses of Long Island Sound to your left. The trail soon brings you out to a view over **salt marsh** to the Sound. Note the giant, rounded **glacial erratics** here. The really large gray boulder that sticks up out of the water is called Gray Mare; it was sacred to the Siwanoy Indians who once lived here. The flat, gray bedrock visible here is the southernmost extension of the bedrock that underlies most of New England—that's why the shore is rocky here. This rock is very complex and very ancient—perhaps half a billion years old. Glacial scours, or deep grooves, can be seen on the surface. There are some side trails leading down to the rocks that are fun to explore, especially when the tide is low.

The shore area here is an excellent place to watch **hawks and ospreys migrating** south in the fall. The best time of year is mid-September—you could see literally thousands of hawks go by in a single day. If you're lucky, you'll see an osprey snatch a fish from the water.

The large building you see on the shoreline to the north belongs to the New York Athletic Club. The large island just across the water is Glen Island. The island farther to the northeast is David's Island; the buildings on it are part of old Fort Slocum.

The trail now leads you back along the lagoon between Hunter's and Twin Islands. The salt marsh along here is quite interesting (see the description of Marshlands Conservancy for more information about salt marshes). Tall cordgrass lines the water's edge; behind it is a low-growing salt meadow. Look for such salt-marsh plants as glasswort and sea lavender here. The salt marsh is one reason there are so many ducks, geese, cormorants, grebes, and other water birds here. The shallow, tidal waters edging a salt marsh are highly productive of the vegetation and small crustaceans, fish, and other foods these birds need.

Continue to follow the path along the salt marsh and back past the old causeway. You'll be back at your starting point in another five minutes.

Hours, Fees, and Facilities

Pelham Bay Park is open daily from dawn to 1:00 A.M. There are no fees. Restrooms, water, pay phones, and a seasonal snack bar are available at the bathhouse complex on Orchard Beach. Dogs must be on leashes; be prepared to clean up after your pet.

Getting There

Pelham Bay Park is the last stop on the Lexington Avenue IRT 6 train. The station is a very long walk from the main part of the park. In the summer, the Bx5 and Bx12 buses run from the subway station to Orchard Beach. The rest of the year, you'll have to take the Bx29 bus that goes to City Island, get off at the traffic circle on City Island Road, and walk north along the park road about a mile to Orchard Beach.

From the Bruckner Expressway or the New England Thruway, take the exits for Pelham Bay Park/Orchard Beach and follow the signs to the parking area at Orchard Beach. From the Hutchinson River Parkway, take the exit for Orchard Beach/City Island and follow the signs.

For More Information

Van Cortlandt and Pelham Bay Parks Administration
Van Cortlandt Park
Broadway and 246th Street
Bronx, NY 10471
718-430-1890

New York Botanical Garden
Bronx

- **1 to 3 miles**
- **at least 1 hour**
- **easy**

Manicured gardens and beautiful landscaping surround untouched forest in the Bronx.

A National Historic Landmark, the New York Botanical Garden contains 250 acres with dramatic rock outcroppings, wetlands, ponds, a cascading waterfall, and forty acres of unspoiled forest. The Garden was founded in 1891. Today, it is one of the foremost public gardens in America. There are nine specialty gardens, more than a million flowering bulbs, 9,600 blooming annuals, 650 orchid species, 250 day lily cultivars, 200 kinds of ferns, more than forty different kinds of cherry trees, a large number of notable trees, and much more. The 1902 Enid A. Haupt Conservatory, currently undergoing restoration, is a landmark Victorian glasshouse. It's very easy to find your way here; the signs are very clear, and numerous volunteers are on hand to give directions and make recommendations.

I really enjoy visiting here. Unlike most other botanical gardens in the region (see Planting Fields, page 109, and Bayard Cutting Arboretums, page 137), this one was

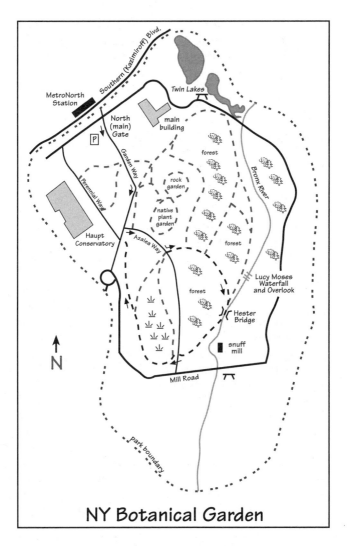

NY Botanical Garden

built for the purpose. The gardens and plantings are laid out for maximum beauty and are maintained perfectly, of course, but there's an underlying seriousness missing from the former estates of the wealthy.

All the gardens, grounds, and greenhouses at the Botanical Garden are well worth a visit, but the **forty-acre forest** at the heart of the grounds is a rare and unusual experience. Amazingly, the forest has never been cut—it contains trees that are more than 300 years old. The Lorillard family of tobacco fame acquired the forest and 600 acres surrounding it in 1792 and held onto it as a private preserve for nearly two hundred years. In 1884, the city of New York bought the land. In 1895, it ceded 250 acres, including the forest, for the establishment of the New York Botanical Garden. Large oaks, hickories, beeches, and maples share the rolling terrain with massive 100-foot hemlocks, some of which have stood here for more than two centuries. The Bronx River, the only river in New York City (the Hudson and East Rivers are tidal estuaries), rushes through a scenic gorge at the heart of the forest. The cool, moist environment along the gorge is the only place in all of New York City and the immediate vicinity with the right conditions for hemlocks. These trees are in trouble, however—they are under siege from air pollution and wooly adelgids. Of the hemlocks standing more than 70 years ago, fewer than half remain today, and there are virtually no young trees or seedlings. The forest's many chestnut trees were killed by the chestnut blight disease that attacked in the early 1900s. The red oaks also have declined in the past few decades. Such faster-growing trees as birch, cherry, and maple are now a large component of the tree species in the forest.

Until 1984, little was done actively to manage the forest. Dead trees were routinely removed for aesthetic and safety reasons, and visitors often wandered off the trails and caused soil erosion and compaction problems. Today, the forest is watched much more carefully. Invasive, nonnative trees such as Norway maples and ailanthus are monitored closely to keep them from taking over. Dead wood is allowed to remain where it falls in order to recycle nutrients into the soil. This, incidentally, is a great boon to birds, especially insect-eaters and such cavity-nesting birds as woodpeckers, flickers, chickadees, and nuthatches. The paths have been improved,

The Bronx River flows naturally through the woods at the New York Botanical Garden, checked only by an old dam built to power the waterwheel at the old snuff mill downstream.

while unofficial trails have been blocked off. You can see the work that has been done to control erosion near the Lucy Moses Overlook above the waterfall. Millions of visitors coming to enjoy this scenic view caused extensive erosion over the years. The wood chips and saplings you see are there to help the forest recover.

The forest is so small that you don't really need a map, much less a route, to see all of it. The easiest way to enter is from the Garden grounds via Azalea Way. From there, just follow the easy paths that wind through the woods. To get to the Bronx River quickly, go straight ahead on the path, ignoring the two turnoffs on your right. From the river, the overlook will be upstream to your left; the Hester Bridge and the Snuff Mill will be downstream to your right. The Snuff Mill is the only thing the Lorillard family built here. The dam channeled water for a water wheel used to grind tobacco into powder. The long, very attractive building of local fieldstone dates back to about 1840. The terrace in the back overlooks the river—a great place to sit and have a snack before starting back.

Look carefully for **wildlife in the forest** and especially along the river. Owls, hawks, egrets, herons, ducks, and warblers are surprisingly easy to see here. Squirrels, rabbits, skunks, chipmunks, and raccoons are common, and you might even spot a river otter along the banks.

After you visit the forest, the manicured grounds of the Garden may seem a little too civilized. Try visiting the nice little **wetland area** on the western side of Azalea Way. A stream runs through this half-mile natural valley; there's a pond, willows, and other wetland vegetation. You also might want to visit the native plant garden, where the flora of the eastern United States and Canada grow in fifteen different habitats. I like the famous 2.5-acre rock garden, which dates back to 1932. There's a picturesque little waterfall (artificial) and thousands of delicate alpine flowers. If you're interested in trees, spend 50¢ on the booklet for the T. H. Everett Tree and Shrub Walk. The route in the booklet takes you past most of the notable trees in the Garden; the notes are very informative. The tree walk takes about an hour and a half.

The New York Botanical Garden is beautiful at any time of year. The spring bulbs and cherries are at their peak in April and May; the numerous azaleas are most gorgeous in May. The roses and rhododendrons are best in June. Look for the day lilies in July and the chrysanthemums in October.

An excellent garden shop and a bookstore with an outstanding selection of natural history titles is in the main building. The research library and herbarium (dried plant collection) are open to the public; call 718-817-8604 for hours. The Garden is a great place to go with kids. Trams take you around the grounds for a small fee, and there are several areas devoted to interesting kids' activities. Beth's Maze and the Children's Corner Tent are guaranteed hits.

Hours, Fees, and Facilities

The grounds at the New York Botanical Garden are open Tuesday through Sunday and Monday holidays year-round. The hours vary seasonally. From April through October the hours are 10:00 A.M. to 6:00 P.M. From November through March the hours are 10:00 A.M. to 4:00 P.M. Admission to the grounds is $3 for adults and $1 for seniors, students, and children. Admission is free all day Wednesday and Saturday from 10:00 A.M. to noon. Restrooms are found in the Main Building and at the Snuff Mill; seasonal cafes serve food in both places. Water fountains are found throughout the Garden. Picnic areas are found at Twin Lakes and near the Snuff Mill. No dogs are allowed.

Getting There

The Garden is very well served by public transportation. To arrive via subway, take the D or 4 train to the Bedford Park Boulevard station. Walk eight blocks east or take the Bx26 bus. The Bx12, Bx19, and Bx41 buses stop near Garden entrances. To arrive via MetroNorth, take the train to the New York Botanical Garden station, which is directly across from the main gate. The ride from Grand Central Station is only twenty minutes. On weekends and holidays from March through November, a minibus shuttle runs between the Metropolitan Museum of Art, the American Museum of Natural History, and the Garden. For details and reservations, call 718-817-8700.

If you are driving, the main gate is on Southern (Kazimiroff) Boulevard. Many expressways run through the Bronx near the Garden. Follow the signs from the Pelham, Saw Mill River, Bronx River, Cross County, Hutchinson River, or Henry Hudson Parkway or call 718-817-8779 for travel directions. Parking in the Garden lot is $4.

For More Information

The New York Botanical Garden
200th Street and Southern Boulevard
Bronx, NY 10458
(718) 817-8700

Prospect Park
Brooklyn

- 3 miles
- 2 hours
- easy

Magnificent landscaping, mature trees, rolling lawns, lakes and ponds—all in the heart of Brooklyn.

Calvert Vaux and Frederick Law Olmsted may be best known for their work in Central Park, but Olmsted always said that Prospect Park in Brooklyn was their true masterpiece. As a Brooklynite I can't help but agree, but even more objective critics think Olmsted was right. The park features any number of brilliant touches, but chief among them are the virtual absence of vehicular traffic, the incorporation of the natural terrain into the design, the vast Long Meadow, and the outstanding use of water, culminating in Prospect Lake at the southern end.

The 526 acres of Prospect Park are designed for strolling on an extensive network of paths. Part of the charm of the park is that wherever you wander is likely to take you to something interesting: an unexpected view, a charmingly rustic bridge, a stream, or a majestic tree. The overall feeling is expansive and relaxing. Rather than provide a defined route, then, I've decided to discuss some of the more interesting aspects of the park's design and natural history in general terms, and let you find them for yourself on your visit.

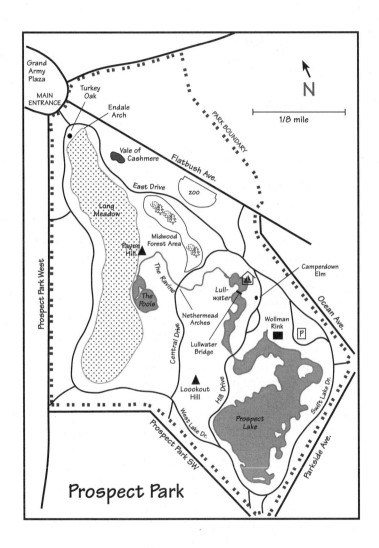

Prospect Park

Enter the park from the northern end at Grand Army Plaza. Take the right fork in the path to go through the tunnel of the Endale Arch, the first structure to be completed in the new park. At the other end is a dramatic vista looking out over the **Long Meadow**. The centerpiece of Prospect Park, the Long Meadow is an undulating, open lawn lined and dotted here and there with **magnificent trees**. The Long Meadow shows naturalistic landscaping at its best. Vaux and Olmsted simply followed the contours of a natural open area, clearing away small trees and underbrush for the lawn area but leaving many of the mature oak trees they found there. Originally, the Long Meadow was nearly a mile long and covered seventy-four acres. (By chauvinistic comparison, the Great Lawn in Central Park covers only a paltry fifteen acres.) In 1959, some popular baseball diamonds were built on the southern third. The vista is still beautiful, however, and the Long Meadow is a wonderful place to stroll. Many of the massive trees here and elsewhere are older than the park. (The numbered tags on some of the trees are part of an ongoing inventory study.) One that's particularly interesting is a huge turkey oak (*Quercus cerris*) inside the main entrance at Grand Army Plaza, just before you pass through the Meadowport Arch. This species is native to western Asia (the name comes from the country, not the bird). A hairy cup almost completely covers the acorns; the bark is deeply fissured.

Geologically, Prospect Park is built on a section of the Harbor Hills moraine (see page 116, Caumsett State Park, for more information). One aspect of the **glacial terrain** that can still be seen easily here is **kettle ponds**.

Several of these depressions dotted the site before park construction began. Some were incorporated into the landscaping, most notably in the Pools and also in the Vale of Cashmere in the northeast corner of the park near the Grand Army Plaza entrance. Steps at the Vale of Cashmere take you forty feet down the side of the kettle to the delightful pond at the bottom. The zoo on the eastern edge of the park is in another kettle depression. The Ravine and Lullwater run along the course of a glacial meltwater stream.

Many of the paths through the Long Meadow converge at the top of Payne Hill on the moraine, about 140 feet above sea level. From this high point several small lakes collectively called the Pools (or sometimes the Swan Boat Ponds) are visible to the west, in the direction

The hidden Vale of Cashmere at Prospect Park has been restored to its original charm, fountain and all.

of the baseball diamonds. To the east the water flows down the Ravine, a narrow, shaded valley meant to evoke an Adirondack stream. The effect was considered very successful in Olmsted's day, when the stream ran clear and fast and pine trees covered the cliffs. Today, erosion and poor maintenance have taken their toll. The stream is silted up and the pines have given way to such invaders as locust and black cherry. This area is currently undergoing extensive restoration (see below). Following the Ravine downhill takes you under the beautiful Nethermead Arches and to the Lullwater, a curving stretch of water that leads into Prospect Lake. The charming iron Lullwater Bridge was designed by the famed architectural firm McKim, Mead & White; it was finished in 1890.

One of the park's most famous trees is a large **Camperdown elm** found behind and slightly to the south of the boathouse on the Lullwater. Camperdown elms are a mutation of the Scotch elm (*Ulmus glabra*). These spreading trees have a wide, full canopy and grow gnarled, drooping branches; the leaves are huge. The trees get their name from their discovery sometime around 1850 on the estate of the earl of Camperdown in Scotland. Prospect Park's tree was probably planted in 1872. It was the subject of a widely publicized rescue operation in 1967 that pruned its limbs and filled in an extensive cavity. The tree today seems perfectly healthy.

Prospect Lake covers sixty acres dug into the flat outwash plain of the moraine. Vaux and Olmsted planned a large lake here based on their experience in Central Park. Ice-skating on the much smaller lake there had immediately become one of the most popular activities

The boathouse at Prospect Park, while still in need of further restoration, retains its elegance.

in the park. Prospect Park was made bigger to accommodate the expected skaters.

In general, Prospect Park is a good birding area—more than 250 species have been recorded here. The best spots for **birding** are near areas with water. Prospect Lake attracts many birds all year, but particularly during the spring and fall migrations. Waterfowl and wading birds, including ducks, grebes, geese, cormorants, and herons, can be seen here. The peninsula on the northern side of the lake is a good lookout point. The Vale of Cashmere, the Pools at the top of Payne Hill, the Ravine and Lullwater, and Lookout Hill (at 170 feet the high point in the park) to the northwest of the lake are all good birding spots. The Midwood, which preserves twenty beleaguered acres of Brooklyn's only forest, is another good spot.

Prospect Park Past and Future

Plans for Prospect Park were drawn up and the land was originally purchased in the late 1850s. The Civil War postponed the start of construction, however, until 1866. The original design was found wanting at that point, and Vaux and Olmsted were brought in. Vaux recommended that land to the east be sold in favor of purchasing additional land to the south and west. This meant sacrificing Mount Prospect, a commanding hill that gave the park its name, but it allowed the designers to avoid having Flatbush Avenue cutting through their park. (Mount Prospect is now a small park with a playground on the eastern side of Flatbush Avenue next to the library. At the top it is 200 feet above sea level.) They also avoided having a large reservoir taking up space on the site. The land they gave up is now home to several important Brooklyn institutions, including the Brooklyn Museum, the main branch of the Brooklyn Library, and the Brooklyn Botanic Garden (see page 72).

There is much of historic, architectural, and artistic interest in Prospect Park, including numerous lovely bridges and arches, an old Quaker cemetery (actor Montgomery Clift is buried here), Battle Pass (where Revolutionary soldiers fought briefly and unsuccessfully against the British troops who took New York City in 1776), and the 1905 Palladian-inspired boathouse on Prospect Lake. The amazing Soldiers' and Sailors' Memorial Arch at Grand Army Plaza was completed in 1892. Over the years the usual memorials and commemorative sculptures have been added, fairly unobtrusively, here and there throughout the park. One major intrusion, in my opinion, is the unfortunate Wollman skating rink on the Lake.

Today Prospect Park receives about six million visitors a year. The park has gone through some lengthy periods of neglect and plain bad management. Sporadic restoration and preservation efforts in the 1970s and 1980s were only partially successful. Problems of erosion, soil compaction, invasive nonnative trees, and deterioration plague the whole park; the forest areas have become severely degraded by invasive exotic species. In particular, the trees that line the border of the park have suffered badly from erosion and neglect. In 1995, the start of a comprehensive long-term plan for revitalizing the park was announced. Work has begun to stop erosion by fencing off some areas, loosening compacted soil by hand, putting in cribbings to stop further erosion, adding topsoil where needed, and removing invasive species to replace them with native plants. The project will cost an estimated $43 million, of which about a third will come from private donations. Would Vaux and Olmsted approve? I think so. Although they specified the planting of the nonnative trees that have since become a problem, they also specified that sections of the original forest be preserved. The restored park will be far less manicured than what they envisioned, but it will be much more ecologically sound and self-sustaining.

Hours, Fees, Facilities

Prospect Park is open from dawn to 1:00 A.M. daily. It is free, although there is an admission charge for the zoo. Restrooms are available at the Picnic House on the Long Meadow. Water fountains are found throughout the park. Dogs are allowed only on leashes; be prepared to clean up after your pet.

Getting There

The most efficient subway route to Prospect Park is via the 2 or 3 trains on the Seventh Avenue IRT to Grand Army Plaza. The B41 bus runs on Flatbush Avenue along the eastern border of the park. By car, follow Flatbush Avenue or Eastern Parkway to Grand Army Plaza. Metered street parking is often available, but read the signs carefully. Limited free parking is available at the Carriage Concourse in the southeastern corner of the park near the Wollman Rink; enter from Ocean Avenue or Parkside Avenue.

For More Information

Prospect Park Administrator
Litchfield Villa
Prospect Park
Brooklyn, NY 11215
718-965-8900

Prospect Park Alliance
95 Prospect Park West
Brooklyn, NY 11215
718-965-8951

Brooklyn Botanic Garden
Brooklyn

- **1.5 miles**
- **2 hours**
- **easy**

*An intimate botanic garden with
some outstanding special collections.*

The Brooklyn Botanic Garden packs an amazing amount of greenery and beautiful landscaping into just fifty-two acres. More than 12,000 plant species from around the world can be seen here. The Cranford Rose Garden, for example, features more than 1,000 kinds of roses. The Garden has a number of fascinating special collections. Outdoors, there's a local flora section, a lilac collection, a small conifer collection, a rock garden, waterlily ponds, and an herb garden arranged as an Elizabethan knot. The magnificent Cherry Esplanade is said to be the finest in America. (Crowds jam the Garden when the cherries bloom in May—try to get there early.) The stunning Japanese hill-and-pond garden, with its delightful pond, is one of the finest in the country.

Additional fascinating plant collections are found indoors in the original Palm House (designed by Mead, McKim & White in 1914) and in the contemporary greenhouses added in 1987. Orchids, an amazing bonsai collection, and a collection of carnivorous plants (very popular

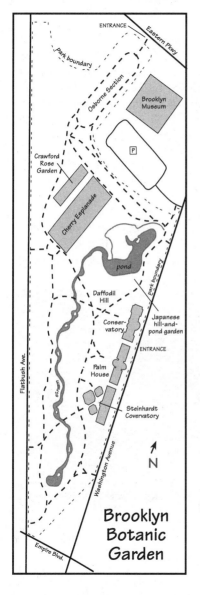

Brooklyn Botanic Garden

with kids) are among the treasures here.

This is a place for strolling and admiring. The paths that lead from one area to the next flow past beautiful old trees, flowering shrubs, annuals, and perennials, and up and down the gently undulating terrain. Benches for rest and contemplation dot the grounds, including some delightfully private nooks. The grounds and gardens are all beautifully kept. It's small enough to see thoroughly in a few hours, so there's no need to suggest a route to follow. Wander where the paths lead and your interests take you.

The grounds of the Garden were part of the original land purchase for Prospect Park in the 1850s. When the park was redesigned in the late 1860s, Flatbush Avenue became the eastern boundary and the land of the Garden was cut off from the park. For several decades nothing was built here. In 1897, the Brooklyn Museum on Eastern Parkway was begun. The adjacent land for the Botanic Garden was a marshy dump when the Garden was founded in 1910. The designers incorporated some aspects of the terrain into the Garden. The pond in the Japanese garden, for example, is actually a **kettle pond** that has been only slightly modified. The typical steep but small hill (knob) that often flanks a kettle pond is seen in Daffodil Hill to the south; it rises to about 120 feet. (To learn more about kettle ponds, see page 96.) The stream that runs from the pond continues westward for most of the length of the garden, more or less on its original course, and is crossed

The Japanese hill-and-pond garden at the Brooklyn Botanic Garden is considered to be one of the finest in the country.

at intervals by small footbridges. Most of the Garden is very natural in its design. The only real exception is the formal Osborne Section at the main entrance, with a central lawn, balustrades, and steps.

There are a number of **notable trees** on the grounds, including many interesting flowering species. A cork tree (*Phellodendron amurense* var.) grows at the southern tip of the garden near Flatbush Avenue. As the name suggests, this tree has thick, corky bark with deep fissures in it; this variety is native to China. Nearby, at the edge of the pond, is a dove tree (*Davidia involucrata*). Also known as the ghost tree or pocket-handkerchief tree, the dove tree is a native of western China. It gets its common name from its large and showy white flowers, which have two pendulous bracts, or "wings." This beautiful specimen is easily sixty feet high. Farther to the east near Washington Avenue is a large silver-leaf linden (*Tilia tomentosa*). This tree is close to ninety feet tall. A bald cypress (*Taxodium distichum*) grows at the eastern end of the Japanese pond. This deciduous conifer, a native of the American Southeast, likes marshy soil. Look for the buttresslike roots and strange protuberances ("knees") near the base. An American linden (*Tilia americana*) grows on Daffodil Hill. Also known as basswood, American lindens can reach heights of 140 feet or more; this one is easily 120 feet tall. Basswoods flower in the late spring. The yellowish-white flowers appear at the end of long stalks with wide bracts—the stalks look like long, thin, pointed leaves. Bees love these flowers. On a quiet day, you can hear their humming from yards away. The garden also has a number of horse chestnuts (*Aesculus* sp.), which bloom beautifully in May with clusters of small red, pink, or white blossoms.

The Brooklyn Botanic Garden is noted for its flowering trees. Here a dogwood blooms in the spring.

All those blossoms, plants, and water mean that the Garden is a good place to spot birds. You can count on seeing egrets and herons around the Japanese pond. Mallards and other ducks float on the pond and down the stream, and all sorts of warblers pass through in the spring.

One of the things I like best about the Brooklyn Botanic Garden is that it's interesting in the late winter, just when I'm starting to think that spring will never come. Witch hazel blooms here in February, and the snowdrops start to come up around then. By the beginning of March the forsythia is starting to bloom, some spring bulbs are appearing, and the dogwoods are getting ready to bud out; by the end of the month, the magnolias are blooming as well.

Hours, Fees, and Facilities

Hours at the Brooklyn Botanic Garden vary seasonally. From April through September, the grounds are open Tuesday through Friday from 8:00 A.M. to 6:00 P.M. and weekends and holidays from 10:00 A.M. to 6:00 P.M. From October through March, the grounds are open Tuesday through Friday, 8:00 A.M. to 4:30 P.M. and weekends and holidays from 10:00 A.M. to 4:30 P.M. The Garden is closed on Mondays except when a public holiday falls on that day; it is closed Thanksgiving, Christmas, and New Year's Day. Entrance is $3 adults, $1.50 seniors and students, and $.50 children six to sixteen. There is a small fee for the Japanese garden on weekends and holidays. Restrooms are available at the administration building. There is a cafe in the Steinhardt Conservatory. No dogs are allowed.

Getting There

The 2, 3, and 4 trains on the Seventh Avenue IRT line stop at Eastern Parkway, literally just in front of the main entrance to the Garden. The B41 bus runs along Flatbush Avenue. Get off at the stop near the Prospect Park Zoo and use the Garden entrance opposite the Lefferts Homestead. Paid parking is available in the lot behind the Brooklyn Museum. The entrance to the lot is on Washington Avenue. Metered street parking is often available, but read the signs carefully.

For More Information

Brooklyn Botanic Garden
1000 Washington Avenue
Brooklyn, NY 11225
718-622-4433

Jamaica Bay National Wildlife Refuge
Queens

- **1.7 miles**
- **1.5 hours; birders will take much longer**
- **easy**

Marshes, birds, and butterflies in the shadow of a jetport.

Early in the morning, gazing out over the islet-dotted waters of Jamaica Bay, it is just possible to imagine yourself back hundreds of years, seeing the region as the Canarsie Indians did. Turn a bit and the illusion is quickly shattered by the looming apartment towers of Far Rockaway and the not-too distant roar of jet engines from nearby Kennedy Airport, but no matter—these reminders of modern life merely reinforce the beauty of the salt and freshwater marshes of Jamaica Bay National Wildlife Refuge. The refuge was established in 1951 by the city of New York; in 1972 the land passed to the National Park Service as part of Gateway National Recreation Area.

A visit to Jamaica Bay begins at the visitor center next to the parking lot. Obtain a free permit from the Park Service ranger at the desk; the permit is good for entry forever after. Although the refuge covers more than 9,100 acres, there are basically only two trails—the West Pond (with some side trails) and the East Pond

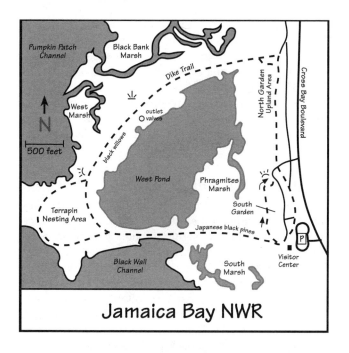

Jamaica Bay NWR

loops. The West Pond Trail is very accessible, with graveled walkways and conveniently located benches. The East Pond Trail, on the other side of Cross Bay Boulevard, is longer, rougher (it's more of a narrow path through beaten-down phragmites than a planned or maintained trail), and wet. In general, the East Pond Trail is of interest only to genuinely dedicated birdwatchers.

Jamaica Bay is a popular spot for such group activities as bird walks, nature walks, and assorted workshops. The park rangers frequently lead walks and conduct workshops, and such organizations as the New York City Audubon Society often have events here. There's something for kids just about every weekend. For a schedule of upcoming events, call the main office at 718-318-4340.

A word of warning: Greenhead flies, which inflict a really annoying bite that itches for days, are abundant here in the late summer. Bring insect repellent and apply it liberally.

The West Pond Trail

The back door of the visitor center leads out to the West Pond Trail. Before you start your walk, check the most recent entries in the sighting book just outside the door—329 bird species have been recorded at Jamaica Bay. On weekends during the migration seasons, the place is jammed with bird-watchers. Next, to get an idea of what you're about to explore, follow the signs a short way to the overlook in the South Garden. You'll get a nice view of the West Pond.

Retrace your steps back to the sighting book, then bear left and follow the signs pointing to the West Pond trail. Soon you emerge from the trees to find a spectacular view on your left. Looking across the bay to the south, you can see the barrier beach of Far Rockaway in the distance. To the southeast is Floyd Bennett Field ("Wrong Way" Corrigan took off from here for his famous flight to Ireland); the residential area directly east is Canarsie. Rafts of bay ducks such as buffleheads and goldeneyes float in the channel, and you'll see dozens of small, low islands, some only a few yards wide.

Continuing along the trail, you pass, on your right, a narrow but dense thicket of Japanese black pine (*Pinus thunbergi*). These nonnative pines were planted several decades ago to provide cover and nesting areas for birds. In the winter, they are particularly attractive to **owls**. Saw-whet and long-eared owls are common winter visitors to the refuge; sharp-eyed visitors may spot them roosting in these pines.

Past the pines, the freshwater West Pond comes into view on your right. But wait a minute—how did this **freshwater pond** get into the middle of the salt marsh that's on your left? Here is revealed the great secret of Jamaica Bay. Despite its natural appearance, large parts of the refuge are man-made. In 1951, as part of a subway construction program, two dikes were built to impound fresh water. In 1953, under the dedicated leadership of Herbert Johnson, the first refuge manager, workers planted, entirely by hand, more than 1.5 million clumps of beach grass to stabilize the sand. The bird-filled, forty-five-acre West Pond is one of those impoundments; the trail you are walking on is the dike.

As you continue along the trail, opportunities for bird-watching are continuous in all directions. Shorebirds, ducks and geese, wading birds, and owls are the specialties here, although during peak migration periods anything can happen. Spectacular numbers of **migrating shorebirds** congregate here in August; huge flocks of snow geese move through in late October and early November. The refuge is managed with migrating birds in mind. The West Pond is lowered artificially in the spring to provide mud flats for shorebirds to feed; in the summer, additional water is pumped in. In winter, parts of the pond are kept ice-free for overwintering water-fowl. The East Pond is lowered artificially in the fall, again to provide feeding grounds for migrating shore-birds. One pond is always kept high for waterfowl.

The plant life along the trail is practically a textbook example of **wetland vegetation**. On the salt-marsh side of the trail, beach grass, two species of *Spartina* (tall cord-grass and low-growing salt hay), and seaside goldenrod are common. A huge phragmites marsh lines the eastern edge of the pond.

Phragmites (pronounced frag-MIGHT-ies) are reeds related to the cattail. The reeds are the tallest grass in the American Northeast, often reaching ten feet or more, with feathery tops; they grow in dense stands that spread by underground runners. (The word phragmites is both singular and plural, but there is really no such thing as just one phragmites.) Because phragmites are more tolerant of salt than cattails, they are found often in tidal areas. In areas that have been disturbed by such human activities as dredging, phragmites tend to take over and crowd out other vegetation that is more useful to wildlife.

Among the wildflowers and shrubs on both sides of the trail are wrinkled rose, autumn olive, Virginia creep-er, little blue stem grass, camphorweed, and common mullein. The most common shrub, however, is the aro-matic northern bayberry (*Myrica pennsylvanica*). This twiggy plant thrives in the sandy soil and produces clus-ters of small berries in the fall. There's also poison ivy—be careful. All these plants, poison ivy included, are valuable food sources for songbirds and small rodents.

As the trail rounds the southern tip of the West Pond and begins to bear northward, the seven-acre **tern nesting area** comes into view on the left. Sadly, this protected area is now home only to common terns; the skimmers, least terns, roseate terns, and piping plovers that formerly nested there were eliminated by rodent predation and human interference by 1960.

Moving on, you'll come to a bench, the ninth you've seen so far. This spot offers an unimpeded 360-degree view of the refuge area. Turn slowly in a circle and you will understand why it is so desperately important to preserve our open spaces: the edges of this spectacular area are hemmed in with roads, an airport, bridges, apartment complexes, garbage dumps, and all the other structures of life typical of the late twentieth century.

Looking out over Jamaica Bay toward Far Rockaway. This is a good place to see rafts of migrating ducks in the fall.

Continuing along the trail, you come to a grove of black willows, planted as a windbreak to buffer the northwest winds that howl off the bay in winter. When the pond is lowered, you can see the outlet valves here. This is perhaps the best part of the trail to see the wading birds and shorebirds; it's good for ducks, too.

On the saltwater side all along this portion of the trail are **mud flats** that are exposed at low tide. This is a good spot to see such shorebirds as sandpipers and plovers probing the mud for tiny crabs, insects, worms, and other food.

The trail has been gradually curving east, back toward Cross Bay Boulevard. Soon after the phragmites marsh again comes into sight on your left, the trail leaves the pond and turns right to enter a half-mile stretch of upland habitat. This section of mixed woodland was planted with such forage plants as autumn olive and coralberry in the late 1950s as a way of attracting birds. It worked—the area is good for spotting songbirds, especially spring warblers. Such butterfly-attracting plants as butterfly bush (*Buddleia davidi*) and orange milkweed (*Asclepias tuberosa*) are also found along the trail. Numerous **butterfly species**, including monarchs, black swallowtails, orange sulfurs, American coppers, pearl crescents, red admirals, and American painted ladies are common here. The plant life isn't quite thick enough, however, to muffle the traffic noise from Cross Bay Boulevard, which runs parallel to this last segment of the trail, which ends back at the visitor center.

Hours, Fees, and Facilities

The refuge trails are open daily from sunrise to sunset. The visitor center and parking lots are open every day except Thanksgiving, Christmas, and New Year's Day from 8:30 A.M. to 5:00 P.M. Parking and admission are free. The visitor center is staffed by National Park Service rangers and volunteers. It has restrooms, water, pay phones, and a small bookstore; there is a small picnic area. No pets are allowed.

Getting There

Take the Belt Parkway to exit 17 (Cross Bay Boulevard) south. Continue south on Cross Bay Boulevard for 3.0 miles and cross over the North Channel Bridge. Continue for another 1.5 miles; the entrance to the parking lot is on the right.

Jamaica Bay is very easy to reach via subway. Take the IND A (express) or C train to Broad Channel station; walk west (toward the Key Food grocery store) .25 mile to Cross Bay Boulevard; turn right (north) and walk 0.5 mile to the visitor center. Alternatively, take the Seventh Avenue IRT 2 train to the New Lots Avenue station, then take the Q21A bus from the stop in front of the station to the refuge; the ride is approximately twenty minutes.

For More Information

Chief Ranger
Jamaica Bay Wildlife Refuge
Gateway National Recreation Area
Floyd Bennett Field
Brooklyn, NY 11234
718-318-4340

Clay Pit Ponds State Park Preserve
Staten Island

- **1 mile**
- **about an hour**
- **easy**

Ponds, meadows, sand barrens, bogs, woodlands, and marshes—all in one place.

Most New Yorkers think of Staten Island, the city's smallest borough, as nothing but strip malls and execrable residential architecture—a place to be passed through on the way elsewhere, if visited at all. A visit to Clay Pit Ponds State Park Preserve, however, shows another side of Staten Island, one that recalls its rural past as a place of small farms and early industry. The preserve consists of a 260-acre natural area near the southwest shore of the island. It was established in 1977 as a result of community efforts to preserve its unique ecological and historic interest; today, it is New York City's only state park preserve. About ninety acres of the park are designated as state **freshwater wetlands**; seventy more acres are designated as a state unique natural area. Most of these designated areas are in the northern half of the park (north of Clay Pit Road) and are closed to visitors. Even so, there's still plenty to see.

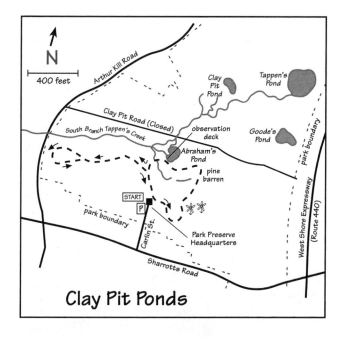

Clay Pit Ponds is geologically quite interesting. Sand and clays deposited during the Cretaceous period, some 70 million years ago, are overlain by much more recent glacial deposits that are only 12,000 years old. The **mixed underlying geology** creates a variety of different soil types, and this in turn provides the park with an interesting mixture of habitats. Ponds, meadows, sand barrens, bogs, woodlands, and swamps are all found within the preserve's borders. The park is particularly noted for the **amphibians and reptiles** found in it. Among the crawly creatures you could glimpse here are northern black racer snakes, box turtles, Fowler's toads, green frogs, spring peepers, red-backed salamanders, and fence lizards. More than 170 bird species have been spotted here, and forty species—including ospreys and indigo buntings—are known to breed in the park. The mixed habitat also leads to a wide range of plant life. Trees found here range from the weedy gray birch to the stately white oak.

There are two interesting but short walking trails at Clay Pit Ponds. The walk described here combines them, but even so it is still no more than a very easy mile, making this a particularly good place to bring children. Numerous bridges and boardwalks take you over the wet areas, and most of the walk is through one of the designated unique areas.

Start your walk on the Abraham's Pond Trail. Look for the round blue plastic markers and the sign just to the

One of the numerous boardwalks that lead through the varied terrain at Clay Pit Ponds.

right of the picnic area behind park headquarters. After passing through a garden area with a beehive and weather station, follow the trail as it goes into the brush. In a few minutes you'll come to steps leading down to a bridge over a stream. Note the sandy soil and abundance of cat brier here. Also called greenbrier or smilax, cat brier is a green-stemmed, woody vine with tendrils, sharp thorns, and large leaves. In the late fall and winter it bears clusters of blue-black berries. The dense, thorny tangles of cat brier provide year-round shelter for birds and mammals, and the berries are an important food for them.

As you cross the bridge, note the numerous ailanthus trees growing on both sides of the ravine. This weedy, very hardy tree, also called tree of heaven, is an invasive species imported to the United States in the 1750s. Look for thin branches with anywhere from ten to forty alternate leaves; the leaves give off an unpleasant odor when crushed. The bark is gray-brown with narrow, light-colored grooves. The ailanthus is the most rapidly growing woody plant found in the Northeast. It can grow twelve inches a year in even the poorest of soils, is immune to air pollution, and is almost impossible to eradicate.

Follow the trail past the bridge for a few minutes as it leads through more cat brier. Look here for sassafras saplings (*Sassafras albidum*) rising up through the thicket. This plant is easy to identify because its leaves have three different shapes. Some leaves are oval, others are mitten shaped with a distinct thumb, and still others have three lobes. In the winter, you can spot a sassafras by the large buds at the ends of bright green twigs. Sassafras bears blue-black berries that are a valuable wildlife food.

The trail soon comes out into a large, open field covered with **wildflowers**. This area was once a pasture (perhaps for the mules used in the clay-mining operation?) and is now a meadow filled with wildflowers, blackberries, and thistles. This is a good place to look for butterflies and white-throated sparrows. Follow the trail as it skirts the meadow over a small bridge and then takes you to a long boardwalk. Just past the boardwalk, the trail forks. Bear right and walk along a sandy trail to a large, open area. This is a little patch of **pine barrens**— dry and sandy, with stunted trees. The abundant undergrowth of cat brier and blueberries is an ideal habitat for the fence lizard. At one time fence lizards may have been native to the area, since they are also found in the pine barrens of New Jersey, but the ones found here today are probably descendants of those deliberately released on Staten Island in the 1940s to create a new population. The fence lizard (*Sceloporus undulatus hyacinthinus*) is about five to six inches long. It is a brownish color with spiny scales and dark, wavy cross-bands; males have blue patches on their undersides. It gets its name from its habit of scampering along fence rails (or fallen logs) as it searches for insects. If you sit quietly in this part of the park on a sunny summer day, you may spot one.

From here, the path leads downhill past an enormous, gnarled old beech tree to Abraham's Pond. As you walk, note how the sandy trail gives way to harder, rockier soil. You'll see plants that look a bit like pine seedlings growing on the slope leading down to the pond. In fact, these are horsetail, the only living survivor of a long line of primitive plants. Gritty particles of silica are found in grooves on the outer surfaces of the plant, which makes it an excellent natural scrub brush.

The sandy soil of a small pine barrens area has eroded away from the roots of a huge beech tree at Clay Pit Ponds. Just a few yards away the terrain is entirely different.

The path leads you to a wooden observation platform overlooking Abraham's Pond. This pond and another large pond in the restricted section of the preserve are former **clay pits**. Starting in the early 1800s, these deposits of white kaolin clay were mined for use in brick making, paints, and dyes. By the 1920s, however, demand for kaolin had dropped off and the clay pits were abandoned. Natural springs and rainfall soon filled the pits with water; vegetation and wildlife quickly followed. Today, nearly a hundred years later, the pond is edged with cattails and phragmites; the surface is covered with yellow waterlilies in the summer. Red-winged blackbirds nest among the cattails and muskrats open paths through the reeds. In the summer, look for painted turtles basking on rocks and logs.

From the observation platform, the path leads on to a bridge over a slow-moving stream (it may be dry in the summer). Just after the bridge is a T intersection. Turn right and follow the yellow markers for the Ellis Swamp Trail. In a few minutes another bridge takes you over a natural spring lined with cinnamon ferns and mosses; note how the spring drains into a swampy area. As you walk on, you'll come soon to a small, open, sandy area. Continue along the trail until you come to a set of steps leading off to the right. Follow them to a bridge that takes you over another swampy area full of ferns, red maple, and phragmites. As you continue to follow the path, bridges and boardwalks take you over the wet parts and protect the fragile mosses, ferns, and other vegetation from trampling. In about ten minutes, you will climb a small, wooded hill. The trail curves to the left and takes you back down the hill. From there, it rejoins the main path and you will retrace your steps nearly back to Abraham's Pond. When you notice both yellow and blue trail markers on the trees, bear left (a sign also points the way) to arrive back at the park headquarters in five more minutes. In the yard behind headquarters, look for a labeled wildflower garden on your right.

Hours, Fees, and Facilities

Clay Pit Ponds State Park Preserve is open every day from dawn to dusk, although park headquarters is staffed only from 9:00 A.M. to 5:00 P.M. weekdays. There is no fee. Restrooms and water are available at park headquarters; a picnic area is behind the headquarters building. No dogs are allowed.

Getting There

If driving from New York (via the Verrazano Bridge or Staten Island ferry), take Rte. 440 (the West Shore Expressway) south to exit 3 for Bloomingdale Road. Make a left onto Bloomingdale Road and then a right onto Sharrotts Road. Follow Sharrotts Road 0.4 mile. At the sign for Clay Pit Ponds, make a right onto Carlin Street and follow it for 0.1 mile to the entrance gate at the end. If you are driving from New Jersey, take Rte. 440 north to exit 3 for Woodrow Road. Follow the service road and bear left under the overpass onto Sharrotts Road. Follow directions as above. The park gate is closed before 9:00 A.M. and after 5:00 P.M., so park on Carlin Street if you arrive early or will be staying late.

The park is also accessible via mass transit. The S113 bus from the ferry terminal stops at Arthur Kill Road at the intersection with Sharrotts Road. Cross Arthur Kill Road and walk east on Sharrotts Road for 0.25 mile, then turn left onto Carlin Street and follow it 0.1 mile to the park entrance.

For More Information

Clay Pit Ponds State Park Preserve
83 Nielsen Avenue
Staten Island, NY 10309
718-967-1976

High Rock Park Conservation Center
Todt Hill, Staten Island

- 4 miles
- 2.5 hours
- moderate

A pleasant walk through the woods to the highest coastal point from Maine to Florida.

A range of rolling hills, part of the Harbor Hills terminal moraine left behind by the retreat of the Wisconsin glacier some 10,000 years ago, runs through the center of Staten Island. The range includes Todt Hill, at 410 feet above sea level the highest point on Staten Island and in all of New York City. In fact, it's the **highest point** on the entire Atlantic coastline south of Acadia National Park in Maine. In the face of relentless development pressures on Staten Island, a good portion of the hills has been conserved as part of the contiguous series of preserves that make up the Staten Island Greenbelt (see below).

Ninety-acre High Rock Park was once a Girl Scout camp (there's still an adjoining Boy Scout camp). Since 1964, it has been part of the New York City park system. A number of trails go through the surprisingly varied terrain here. For a good short walk, try the mile-long Swamp Trail, which circumnavigates an interesting freshwater wetland. The walk described here is a longer,

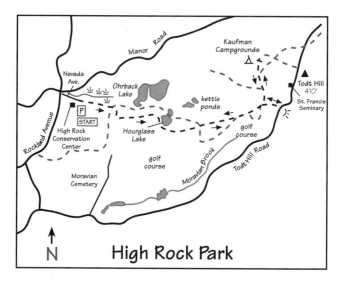

High Rock Park

more difficult hike that goes almost, but not quite, to the top of Todt Hill.

The walk begins near the vehicle entrance to the park off Nevada Avenue. Look for the rectangular yellow paint blazes near the red benches by the sign for the Swamp Trail. Follow the blazes and signs onto the Swamp Trail and bear to the right (keep the swampy area on your left). After a few minutes, turn right at the small bridge and walk toward the chain-link fence that separates the park from the adjacent Moravian Cemetery. Turn left and follow the trail through the woods as it parallels the fence. Another trail, a portion of the blue-blazed Staten Island Greenbelt, weaves across the yellow trail here and there. Stick with the yellow blazes and follow them for another ten minutes or so as they lead into and out of the woods again.

In a few more minutes you'll arrive at Hourglass Pond, the highest of a series of ponds that spill down the upland ridge. This pond is well on its way to filling in and becoming a marsh, due to slope erosion and the buildup of plant matter at the bottom. You can see that a meadow of sedges and cattails is growing up between the open water and the trees. Waterlilies and bladderwort cover the water. These floating plants are common in shallow water.

Follow the trail around Hourglass Pond to the right. Continue for another twenty minutes or so as the trail climbs gently up and down (mostly up) through a mixed upland forest of oak and beech, with some tulip trees and hickories here and there. You'll pass two **kettle ponds** down the slope on your left. If you want to explore, short but steep side trails lead down to the ponds, which are quite interesting. As the Wisconsin ice sheet retreated, massive chunks of it broke off and simply stayed put until they melted away. In some cases, smaller blocks of ice left on the terminal moraine were buried in outwash sediments or till. The blocks eventually melted away, leaving behind steep-sided pits, or kettles, that eventually filled with water. A moraine generally has numerous kettle ponds of varying sizes, separated by small hills of till, a characteristic terrain that geologists call knob-and-kettle. You can see the effect best here in the winter after a light snowfall has outlined the terrain. Note that the trees at the edges of the ponds are primarily red maple, swamp white oak, sweet gum, and tupelo (sour-gum), which are well adapted to a wetter environment.

In another few minutes you'll see some houses straight ahead and come to a trail intersection marked by wooden posts. Turn right here and follow the gravelly trail until it ends a few minutes later at a latticed observation deck overlooking the golf course of the Richmond County Country Club. The view faces south—on a clear day you can see the shore and the Atlantic Ocean. The overlook is at the confluence of three very different ways to use the land: residential, preserve, and active recreation. It's a good place to think about how to balance conflicting needs and the role of conservation. It's also a great place to eat lunch. Technically, you're not at the top of Todt Hill here—the actual high point is near the parking lot of St. Francis Seminary just south of the intersection of Todt Hill Road and Ocean Terrace—but it's pretty close.

To continue the walk for another half-mile or so, backtrack to the intersection and keep going straight ahead on

Three land uses intersect at this corner of High Rock Park. In the foreground is a manicured golf course; to the left are the woods and trails of the park; in the center is the park's viewing platform, which abuts an area of private homes.

the yellow trail. In about ten minutes you'll come to a very large wooden shelter that belongs to a nearby summer day camp. The yellow trail continues on for a bit from here, leading eventually into a residential area. Turn around here and backtrack to the wooden posts. Turn left to return the way you came via the yellow trail.

If you'd like to explore Ohrbach Lake on the way back, turn left onto the blue trail at Hourglass Pond. In a few minutes you'll see a red metal disk on a tree. Go past the blaze and turn right to get down to the lake. This kettle pond is fairly deep with a rapid drop-off from the shore, so there isn't that much vegetation growing on or around the water. A few small marshes have formed in places where the slopes have eroded.

To return, backtrack to the yellow trail. You'll be back at the trailhead in ten more minutes.

The Staten Island Greenbelt and Bluebelt

Because of its surprising **diversity of habitats**—there are seven distinctly different vegetative zones—Staten Island historically supported one of the most diverse floras in the entire Northeast. Sadly, most of Staten Island, once a rural backwater of forest, meadows, and quiet farms, has been swallowed by sprawling residential development. As a result of concerted community action, a significant remnant of natural lands in the center of the island has been preserved, more or less intact, as the Staten Island Greenbelt. All told, the greenbelt covers approximately 2,500 contiguous acres and strings together twelve individual parks, connecting them by narrow corridors that are sometimes adjacent to private property. Two major trails run through the area. The

Blue Trail is about 8.5 miles long and runs approximately east-west. The White Trail is about 4 miles long and runs approximately north-south. The two trails intersect at Bucks Hollow in Latourette Park. These are interesting trails through some attractive areas. The spring wildflowers can be very enjoyable, and this is a great place to see colorful autumn foliage. For a map and descriptive brochure about the greenbelt and the bluebelt, contact greenbelt headquarters at High Rock Park.

The Staten Island Bluebelt runs along the unglaciated southern edge of the island and preserves some valuable wetlands. One of them is the William T. Davis National Wildlife Refuge (NWR), the first NWR in New York City, established in 1933. To my mind, the chief virtue of this site is its overlooks of the Fresh Kills Landfill, the largest landfill in the world. This massive dump receives some 17,000 tons of refuse daily. It releases up to 2 million gallons of liquid refuse a day into the channel, nearby creeks, and ground water, following the courses of the wetlands it has smothered. Amazingly, despite the garbage from Fresh Kills and oil spills in the Arthur Kill channel, herons and other birds live and breed on the shore and on the bird sanctuary at Prall's Island.

The bluebelt isn't yet as well organized as the greenbelt, so you can't really walk it from end to end. Many of the wetlands it preserves are in smallish recreation parks that are worth a visit but don't really have nature trails of any significant length. If you're interested in geology, Wolfe's Pond Park, Conference House Park, and Blue Heron Park all have what are known as **perched ponds**. The outwash plain here consists of sandy soil overlain by clayey soil washed down from the moraine. Ponds form where depressions in the sandy underlayer are sealed by a coating of clay that keeps the water from draining away. The ponds in these parks are all actually above the water table.

Hours, Fees, and Facilities

High Rock Park is open daily from 9:00 A.M. to dusk. There are no fees. Free maps, restrooms, and water are available at the visitor center, 0.3 mile past the entrance. Dogs are allowed only on leashes; be prepared to clean up after your pet.

Getting There

From the Staten Island Expressway (I-278) exit at Manor Hill Road/Bradley southbound. Follow Manor Hill Road for 0.8 mile to a traffic triangle. Bear left at the triangle to stay on Manor Hill Road—which here becomes a smaller road—for another 2.1 miles. (Don't get onto Brielle Avenue by mistake.) Turn left onto Rockland Avenue and follow it for 0.3 mile to Nevada Avenue. It's easy to miss the turnoff—look for the High Rock Park sign on the right.

From the Staten Island Ferry terminal at St. George, take the S74 bus to the corner of Richmond Road and Rockland Avenue. Walk north on Rockland Avenue (watch for traffic) for three blocks to Nevada Avenue and turn left. Follow Nevada Avenue uphill for 0.4 mile to the park entrance. The S54 and S57 buses also stop here.

For More Information

High Rock Park Conservation Center/
Greenbelt Administrator
200 Nevada Avenue
Staten Island, NY 10306
718-667-2165

Long Island

Sands Point Preserve
Port Washington

- **2 to 3 miles**
- **2 hours**
- **easy**

A walk along bluffs and beach on the Gold Coast.

In the 1890s, the north shore of Long Island, once a quiet place of sleepy farms and fishing villages, became the playground of the very wealthy. In the next fifty years, between 600 and 700 mansions were built along a thirty-mile stretch of the north shore reaching from Great Neck to Eatons Neck. This is the land of *The Great Gatsby*, filled with the people who were different from you and me and dubbed, for good reason, the Gold Coast. Today, most of the old mansions are gone, burned down or demolished when the land was sold off for housing developments in the 1950s and 1960s. Of the 200 to 300 mansions still standing, about half are privately owned. Almost all of the rest are now schools, colleges, country clubs, religious retreat houses, and the like. A handful of estates, however, were given as gifts to New York State and survive as parks (see also the walks in Caumsett

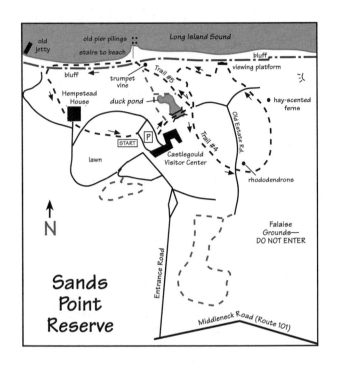

State Park, page 116, and Planting Fields Arboretum, page 109).

Sands Point Preserve has not one but two Gold Coast mansions on its 209 acres. The estate was first owned by Howard Gould, son of railroad tycoon Jay Gould. He built Castlegould, the elaborate stable and servants' quarters that is now the visitor center, between 1902 and 1904. His Tudor-style mansion, now known as Hempstead House, was built in 1910. The Sands Point property was purchased by mining millionaire Daniel

Guggenheim in 1917. His son, Harry F. Guggenheim, built his Normandy-style mansion, Falaise (French for cliff), on ninety acres of the land in 1923. During World War II, the unused portion of the land was acquired by the Navy, which developed electronic systems for the military here until 1966. In 1971, 128 acres were deeded to Nassau County for environmental use. The Falaise estate was given to the county the same year under the terms of Harry Guggenheim's will. Today, most people seem to visit the Sands Point Preserve to tour the mansions and enjoy the exhibits and events held at Castlegould. The preserve has several nature trails, however, that include some very interesting habitat and almost a mile of **untouched beach** along Long Island Sound.

There are five self-guiding nature trails at Sands Point, all beginning near Castlegould. For a longer walk that includes a nice stretch of beach, a combination of Trails 4 and 5 works well. Look for the sign pointing to Trails 3, 4, and 5 at the museum end of the parking lot. Follow the asphalt path into the wooded area and ignore the turnoff onto Trail 3 that comes up soon on your left. In another moment the path becomes a bridge across the tip of a 1.5-acre, man-made freshwater pond. The only freshwater pond on the preserve, it is surrounded by dense underbrush and covered with a luxuriant layer of duckweed—a great spot for bird-watching, particularly in the spring when the vegetation is filled with warblers. Just past the pond is the beginning of the purple-blazed Trail 4, a mile-long loop through young woodlands and meadows. Turn right to follow the loop in a counterclockwise direction. The path here is dirt or sand; it's flat and very easy to follow. In a few minutes you'll descend

Castlegould, once a stable (really), is now the visitor center at Sands Point Preserve.

into a little valley and pass under a stone bridge that carries an old estate road. On the other side is a stand of **rosebay rhododendrons** (*Rhododendron maximum*), a native broad-leaf evergreen once found widely in dry, sandy areas of Long Island. In the past fifty years or so, most of these shrubs have been destroyed by development or removed by nursery growers, so this is one of the few natural stands still to be seen. It blooms with lovely white or yellow blossoms in May.

In another ten minutes or so, you'll come to a sign on your right that says No Walking Beyond this Point and Authorized Personnel Only. (The side trail leads off to the ninety-acre restricted section of the preserve that includes Falaise. Access is via the museum tour bus only.) Look around here for lacy fronds of hay-scented fern (*Dennstaedtia punctilobula*). The fronds are about a foot or more high; cuplike spore cases grow on the margins of the pinnules. Hay-scented fern grows well in sandy soil and forest openings such as the one here.

In another five minutes, the trail brings you to the edge of a **bluff overlooking Long Island Sound**. Do not attempt to follow the steeply eroded trail that leads down from here. The trail continues along the bluff (ignore the unmarked side trails) and soon leads you to a wooden platform looking out over Long Island Sound. From the overlook on a clear day you can see Hempstead Harbor far to your right in the south. The land diagonally across from you to the southeast is Glen Cove. On the left across the Sound is lower Westchester County; across the Sound to the right (northeast) is Connecticut.

To continue, follow the trail as it leads into a tunnel-like path through a dense area of shrubs. Look among the honeysuckle, sumac, wild grapes, and multiflora roses here for American ampelopsis. This vine is easily confused with the wild grape because it too has toothed leaves and tendrils and produces clusters of blue berries. Wild grape, however, has larger leaves with indentations on both sides of the stem, deeper teeth, and pointier tips. The grapes hang down in bunches, while ampelopsis berries are in upright clusters. Both plants are important to wildlife and birds for the shelter and food they provide, but humans can eat only the grapes.

Continue to follow the path for another ten minutes or so, until it ends almost where it started, by the bridge over the pond. From here, you can return to the parking lot or enter onto the blue-blazed, 1.5-mile Trail 5 to walk along the shoreline. Turn left onto the broad asphalt path of Trail 5 and follow it for a quarter of a mile to the Sound. Just before the path arrives at the beach, look on your right for a large trumpet vine (*Campsis radicans*). The nectar-filled tubular flowers of this creeper are very attractive to **hummingbirds**. If you're here in the summer when the vine is in bloom, you might see a ruby-throated hummingbird feeding among the blossoms.

A wooden staircase leads down to the pebbly, narrow beach strewn with boulders that have eroded out from the cliffs. The rubble just ahead of you is the remains of a concrete sea wall erected decades ago in a vain attempt to slow erosion. Pilings from an old pier are visible in the water near here. Look for cormorants (double-crested in the summer, great in the winter) perched on the pilings with their wings outstretched. Unlike most seabirds, cormorants do not have oil glands to waterproof their feathers. After diving for fish, they must hang their wings out to dry.

From here, you can explore the beach for nearly half a mile in each direction. On the bluffs east (right) of the pilings, the glacial till contains a lot of clay; a colony of bank swallows has dug nest burrows here near the top. If you're fortunate, you may spot an osprey soaring over the beach or perching in the trees along the bluff. Do not attempt to climb up the cliffs!

To return, backtrack from the wooden stairs or continue west along the beach for about fifteen minutes. About fifty yards before the stone jetty that marks the end of the property, look on your left for wooden steps leading up over the old sea wall and into the woods. The steps lead you to a narrow asphalt path that leads almost immediately to a larger asphalt road. Take the narrow asphalt path on your left. It leads quickly to shallow concrete steps and then a narrow concrete walkway that skirts the edge of a small meadow. In about five minutes you'll arrive at Hempstead House. The mansion now is used only for special events, so you can't go in, but it's fun to wander around the grounds and enjoy the water view. From the porte-cochere of Hempstead House you can see Castlegould (with an unfortunate blue town water tower looming over it) across a broad expanse of tree-dotted lawn. Follow the asphalt roadway or stroll across the lawn to return to the parking lot.

Hours, Fees, and Facilities

The grounds at Sands Point Preserve are open every day (except some holidays) from 10:00 A.M. to 5:00 P.M. Falaise and Hempstead House are open seasonally for guided tours—call for information. Admission to the preserve is free; small admission fees are charged for house tours. Free trail maps, restrooms, water, and pay phones are available at the visitor center. No pets are allowed.

Getting There

Take the Long Island Expressway to exit 36 (Port Washington/Searingtown Road). Turn left (north) at the light and continue north on Rte. 101, here called Searingtown Road (later on it is also called Middleneck Road but it is still Rte. 101). Stay on 101 for 11.7 miles, following the occasional brown signs for Sands Point Museums. The entrance to the preserve is on the right. Follow the entrance road 0.4 mile to the parking area.

For More Information

Sands Point Preserve
95 Middleneck Road
Port Washington, NY 11050
516-571-7900

Planting Fields Arboretum State Historic Park

Oyster Bay

- **1 to 3 miles**
- **2 to 3 hours**
- **easy**

Enjoyable walking among stately trees, rolling lawns, and magnificent gardens.

With more than 400 acres of cultivated gardens, rolling lawns, and natural woodlands, Planting Fields Arboretum is a delight to visit. Extensive pathways wind in and out of the lawns and wooded areas, making this a great place for a long walk at any time of year. The sweeping lawns are sprinkled with majestic beech and linden trees, along with oak, cedar, fir, elm, tulip, and magnolia. Massed plantings of bulbs flower along the drives in the spring. Mature groupings of rhododendrons, azaleas, and hollies bloom spectacularly in May—there are more than 600 species and hybrids in the collection. In January, February, and March, the camellia collection is in full bloom in its own greenhouse—a visit then is guaranteed to make even the grayest winter day seem a lot brighter.

Planting Fields Arboretum was once a private estate of the Coe family (see below). The old estate roads are now the main walkways through the grounds, so the walking is extremely easy. In fact, this is one of the very

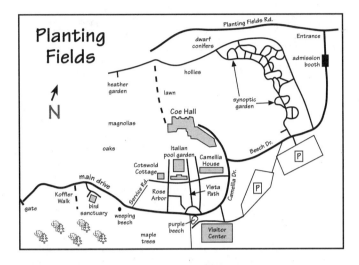

few sites in this book that is truly accessible to someone in a wheelchair. Numerous very clear signs point you toward the various gardens and walks.

For a walk that covers the highlights of the arboretum, start at the visitor center. Stroll through the extensive greenhouses here to see collections of cacti and succulents, hibiscus, begonias, orchids, bromeliads, houseplants, ferns, and seasonal exhibits.

After enjoying the main greenhouse, look for a giant purple beech tree behind the visitor center. The tree is at the intersection of Main Drive and Camellia Drive. If you want to stretch your legs, turn left and follow Main Drive for about 0.7 mile to its end at the Carshalton Gates. These magnificent wrought-iron gates are 133 feet wide. They were made in England in 1712 and once guarded the entrance to Carshalton Park. They were

installed here in 1926. Numerous trees and other plantings, most carefully labeled, are along or near the drive.
Just as you start, you'll see European lindens on your
left. Next you'll come to the maple collection on your
left; opposite it on your right are native azaleas. As you
continue, a yew field is on the left, opposite a service
road. Still on your left, just past the service road, look for
a magnificent European weeping beech; magnolias line
the road on your right here. A little farther on, a side
road on the left leads to a bamboo collection and the
small but charming Carl Wedell bird sanctuary area. The
next side trail on your left is the short (0.1 mile) Claire
Koffler Memorial Trail, a pleasant stroll into the woods.
As you continue downhill along Main Drive, rhododendrons and azaleas line the road on your left and beeches
line it on the right.

The southwestern corner of Planting Fields will be
on your left; some side paths lead off into it from Main
Drive. This area includes about ninety acres of **mixed
hardwood forest**, crisscrossed by some five miles of
nature trails and bridle paths. The trails don't really have
any blazes or signs, and I don't think they're that interesting anyway. You can't really get too lost in here, but if
you'd like to wander around, ask for a trail map at the
visitor center.

To return, you'll have to backtrack. After passing the
service road again (now on your left), go past the azaleas
and turn onto the first path on your left, which leads to
the rose arbor (dating from 1910); side paths lead to a
group of carefully manicured gardens containing roses,
tree peonies, perennials, and lilacs. The charming little
Cotswold-style cottage near the rose garden was once a
playhouse for the Coe children. Now it's a potting shed.

Once a playhouse for the Coe children, this charming cottage in the rose garden at Planting Fields Arboretum is now a potting shed.

To get the full effect of Coe Hall and the gardens surrounding the house, however, follow the path to the right at the center circle of the rose arbor. This leads to the Vista Path; turn left. Ahead of you is Coe Hall; to your right are azaleas. The Vista Path leads you to the mansion and the Italian Pool Garden, which dates from 1915. This is landscaping in the formal European tradition, with the hand of man evident throughout. To get to the Camellia House, turn right at the rose garden intersection.

The major lawn areas of the arboretum are to the north of Coe Hall. There aren't any paths here—just stroll around, admiring the **specimen trees**. There's another purple beech here, moved in 1915 from Mrs.

Coe's childhood home in Massachusetts. It was, according to the arboretum, the second-largest tree ever moved. (I have no idea what the largest was.) Make your way across the lawn toward the holly collection. The paths through here lead out onto a service road that borders the northern edge of the lawn. Turn right onto the service road and follow it for a few minutes. On your left will be a path leading to an interesting dwarf conifer garden. On your right will be a path taking you into the Synoptic Garden.

Covering five acres, the **Synoptic Garden** is a unique planting of more than 400 species of flowering shrubs and small trees that are particularly well suited to the soil and climate of Long Island. It's the only garden of its kind in the United States. The plants are arranged in eleven groupings alphabetically by genus—you will be entering at the end of the alphabet among the zenobias. As you follow the winding paths through the garden, eventually you'll come out in the A section among the abelias. From here, make a left onto Beech Drive. When the path forks, turn left to reach the parking lots again within five minutes.

Planting Fields and Coe Hall

The name Planting Fields is a legacy from the Matinecock Indians who occupied this land. They planted crops in clearings in the woods. In 1653, ownership of the land passed to colonial settlers, and from that time until the late nineteenth century, Oyster Bay was a quiet farming and fishing community. The sandy loam was particularly well suited for growing asparagus. By 1900, the farmers and watermen were giving way to wealthy

New Yorkers, who bought up the land for vast residential estates. The land that is now the arboretum was first assembled into an estate in 1904 by James and Helen Byrne, who built a house and many of the extant outbuildings. In 1913, William Robertson Coe bought the estate from the Byrnes and began an extensive planting program that turned the estate into a horticultural showplace. The original house burned down in 1918, and Coe decided to replace it with the magnificent, sixty-five-room Tudor Revival mansion now known as Coe Hall. Visitors today can see outstanding craftsmanship and an interesting mixture of decorative objects, furniture, and paintings in the restored period rooms. In 1949, Planting Fields was deeded to the people of New York State; William Robertson Coe remained in residence until his death in 1955. Since that time many different gardens, including the Synoptic Garden, have been developed and facilities for education and entertainment have been added.

Hours, Fees, and Facilities

Planting Fields is open every day except Christmas. The grounds are open from 9:00 A.M. to 5:00 P.M. The main greenhouse is open from 10:00 A.M. to 4:30 P.M.; the camellia house is open from 10:00 A.M. to 4:00 P.M. Coe Hall is open for guided tours April through September, Monday through Friday. Admission to the arboretum is $3. Water, vending machines, pay phones, and restrooms are available at the visitor center near the main greenhouse. No pets are allowed.

Planting Fields runs an active education program of short courses in horticulture, crafts, and natural history for adults and children. There's also a sizable horticultural library and an herbarium with more than 10,000 pressed specimens. A nonprofit organization called Friends of the Arts offers a wide range of concerts on the lawns and in the Hay Barn.

Getting There

Take the Long Island Expressway to exit 39 (Glen Cove Road). Go north on Glen Cove Road for 2.0 miles to NY Rte. 25A (Hempstead Highway). Turn right (east) onto 25A and follow it 3.4 miles to Wolver Hollow Road (look for a brown sign for the arboretum here). Turn left and follow Wolver Hollow Road for 1.5 miles to Chicken Valley Road (there's another sign here). Turn left and follow Chicken Valley Road for 1.0 mile to Planting Fields Road. Turn right and follow Planting Fields Road 0.9 mile to the main entrance on your right.

For More Information

Planting Fields Arboretum
Box 58
Oyster Bay, NY 11771
516-922-9201

Coe Hall Tours
516-922-0479

Friends of the Arts
Box 702
Locust Valley, NY 11560
516-922-0061

Caumsett State Park
Lloyd's Neck

- **4 to 5 miles**
- **about 3 hours**
- **easy but long**

A very private walk to a secluded beach.

Caumsett State Park is located on Lloyd's Neck, a scenic peninsula that juts out into Long Island Sound. The name comes from a Matinecock Indian word meaning "place by a sharp rock." The 1,500 acres of the park are on land that was once the estate of Marshall Field III, scion of the department store family and publisher of the Chicago *Sun-Times* newspaper. In the 1920s, Field built his country estate here on Long Island's fashionable Gold Coast. The estate became a state park in 1961. Today the sixty-five-room mansion houses the Queens College Center for Environmental Teaching and Research; it is not open to the public. The old polo-pony barn is now the Caumsett Equestrian Center. The park is very popular with the horsy set. There are miles of bridle paths, and polo is still played here on weekends.

Those of us who rely on our own legs enjoy Caumsett too. This is a very spacious, very quiet, very private park with a variety of habitats, including a long stretch of deserted shoreline, a salt marsh, a big freshwater pond, and lots of woods. Field built miles of roads

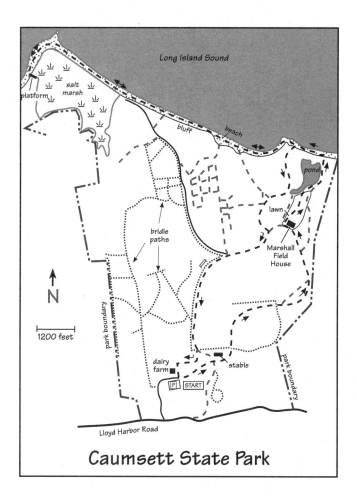

Long Island Sound

salt marsh

platform

bluff

beach

pond

lawn

bridle paths

Marshall Field House

N

1200 feet

park boundary

dairy farm

stable

park boundary

P | START

Lloyd Harbor Road

Caumsett State Park

through his property for riding and motoring. No motorized vehicles are allowed in the park, however, so walkers and bike riders have the roads to themselves. In addition, the park is surprisingly flat—the bluffs along the shore are the highest point, and they reach only about 120 feet. It all makes for easy, very enjoyable walking—which is good, because the most interesting parts of the park are at least two miles from the entrance.

All walks at Caumsett start at the entrance booth near the parking lot. You can pick up a good free map of the park here. Just past the entrance on the right is a complex of barns and outbuildings. Once a showcase dairy farm, these buildings now house park administration offices. The only restrooms in the park are also here, so don't hesitate. From the dairy farm you can see a very large and elegant brick building with an elaborate turret straight ahead. Follow the paved path leading toward the building. In about five minutes, you'll be close enough to it to realize that this is not the mansion—it's the stable. Walk straight ahead past the stable. Look for a paved road with a sign that forbids entry to vehicles and another that says "Service Drive." Follow this road for the next 1.5 miles to get to the mansion. Along the way, the road curves through very pleasant areas of mixed woodlands and open meadows.

The road leads directly to the mansion. (There's a water fountain on the left side.) Circle around behind the building to a large terrace with a stone balustrade and enjoy the view out over a huge lawn that slopes down to the Sound. A big **freshwater pond** is at the foot of the lawn. To get down to the beach, make your own way down the lawn, aiming for the pond. This is a great place to look for basking turtles and migratory birds.

A foot trail circles the pond to the right (east) and leads to a broader dirt path that skirts through shady woods at the edge of the pond. After about ten minutes, the path brings you abruptly out onto the **beach**. Turn left (west) to walk along the pebbly beach. In a few minutes you'll pass a red brick structure with a milepost near it. You can turn in here to leave the beach and head back (see below), or you can keep walking for about another mile until you reach a salt marsh. As you walk, look at the **bluffs along the narrow beach**. They're made of sand, pebbles, and soft clay, and the drop from the top to the beach is nearly vertical. This is an ideal environment for bank swallows (*Riparia riparia*). These small, brown-backed birds dig colonies of nest burrows directly into the cliffs; if you look carefully toward the top of

Glacial bluffs look out over Long Island Sound at Caumsett State Park. The rocky, narrow beach is typical of Long Island's north shore.

the bluffs, you can see the entrance holes. The burrows are sometimes three feet deep.

If you continue walking westward along the beach, you will come to a parking area for surf fishers (parking and fishing by permit only). The parking area is at the edge of a **salt marsh**. If you want to explore here (there are a lot of interesting birds), follow the narrow, mucky path that skirts the marsh for nearly a mile and ends at a small, sandy cove. Backtrack to return. Be warned: Like all salt marshes, this one has biting insects in ferocious profusion. You'll stay drier if you walk at low tide.

To return, backtrack to the red brick structure you passed earlier. Look here for a broad, curving dirt path leading away from the beach into the woods. In about five minutes, you'll pass the freshwater pond on your left. Ignore the smaller path that leads off to the left. Continue to follow the main dirt path, ignoring the bridle trails that occasionally lead off on your right. There are some nice vistas out over meadows dotted with huge old oaks along this portion of the trail. In a few more minutes the dirt road becomes paved again and climbs upward for a steep but mercifully short way before joining the Main Drive. Turn right and follow the road a short distance to the next intersection. At the Y, bear right. Just a little farther on is a milepost and a resting bench. Continue on the paved road for another ten minutes or so. The stable will come into view again on your right. In another five minutes, turn right onto a dirt path that leads toward the dairy farm complex. Five more minutes brings you to the parking lot.

Long Island Geology

As the Wisconsin ice sheet that covered the Northeast from 20,000 to 12,000 years ago moved south, it pushed a huge pile of boulders, rocks, gravel, and sand called glacial till ahead of it, just as a bulldozer pushes dirt. That glacier reached its southernmost point exactly where Long Island is today. As it began to retreat, it left the till behind as a band of low hills called a **terminal moraine**. In fact, there are two east-west trending terminal moraines on Long Island. The Ronkonkoma Moraine, which runs inland from Montauk Point on the eastern tip of Long Island's south fork to Lake Success on the border between Queens and Nassau County, was formed when the glacier retreated between 12,000 and 15,000 years ago. The glacier then advanced again, but didn't reach quite as far south this time. Instead, it deposited a second moraine, called the Harbor Hills Moraine, that runs from Fisher's Island off the northeastern tip of the north fork to form the bluffs of the north shore as far west as Lake Success. From there, the Harbor Hills Moraine trends southwestward, passing through Queens and Brooklyn and nearly blocking the entrance to New York Harbor. Fortunately, the moraine here was cut through by a natural channel that we now call the Verrazano Narrows. The moraine continues along the southern and eastern shores of Staten Island and extends into New Jersey at Perth Amboy. It trends northwestward across New Jersey and finally peters out near Belvidere, close to the Pennsylvania border. The path of the moraine can be traced by the place names along it: Forest Hills, Ridgewood, Crown Heights, Bay Ridge, and Summit are just some examples.

Streams of meltwater flow out from a terminal moraine as the glacier melts. The heavier boulders, rocks, and gravel stay behind as the water carries the lighter, smaller particles outward. As the water moves away, it loses velocity and drops the particles, forming an **outwash plain** that extends in front of the glacier. In this case, the outwash plain forms the south shore of Long Island, a flat, smooth terrain that contrasts markedly with the hills of the north shore.

As you might expect, a moraine is easily eroded. You can see this at Caumsett State Park (and also at Sunken Meadow State Park, Sands Point Preserve, and elsewhere on the north shore) by looking at the bluffs that rise up from the narrow beaches. The beaches themselves are very gravelly and strewn with large rocks that have eroded out from the bluffs. You can see that the bluffs, which are a hundred feet thick in places, are made of sand, gravel, and rocks, mixed here and there with clay.

Lloyd's Neck is just one of a number of peninsulas that stick out from the north shore into Long Island Sound. The peninsulas, the sheltered bays they enclose, and the Sound itself are remnants of ancient, pre-glacial geology. Long before the onset of the last glacial era—more than 50,000 years ago—what is now Long Island Sound was the valley of a large, east-flowing river. Smaller north-flowing rivers emptied into the river from what is now Long Island, carving valleys of their own. During the last ice age, glaciers locked up the water as ice, lowered the sea level, and buried the land with glacial till. As the glaciers receded, the sea level rose, but not enough to drown the old river valleys—now mostly filled in with till—completely. The end result is the deeply indented shoreline we see today.

Hours, Fees, and Facilities

Caumsett State Park is open daily from 8:00 A.M. to 4:30 P.M. There is an entrance fee of $3 per vehicle from Memorial Day weekend through Labor Day weekend; it is free the rest of the year. Restrooms are found only at the dairy farm complex near the entrance. Water and pay phones are found at the dairy farm and at the mansion. No motorized vehicles are allowed in the park. No pets are allowed—except horses. If you want to bring your horse here call the Caumsett Equestrian Center at 516-673-5533.

Getting There

Take the Long Island Expressway to exit 49N (Huntington/Rte. 110). Go north on Rte. 110 (here called New York Avenue) for 7.1 miles to NY Rte. 25A, here called Main Street in Huntington Village. Turn left (west) onto 25A and follow it for 0.2 mile (two blocks) to West Neck Road. Turn right onto West Neck Road and follow it for 4.7 miles until it turns into Lloyd Harbor Road. Continue on Lloyd Harbor Road for 0.6 mile to the park entrance on the left (the sign is on the right). Follow the entrance road 0.2 mile to the parking lot.

For More Information

Caumsett State Park
West Neck Road
Lloyds Neck, NY 11743
516-423-1770

Caleb Smith State Park Preserve
Smithtown

- **2.25 miles**
- **2 hours**
- **easy**

*Wetlands, woodlands, and monarch migration
along the Nissequogue River.*

Nestled in the middle of suburban development, the 543 acres of Caleb Smith State Park Preserve are surprisingly untouched. The freshwater wetlands, ponds, streams, fields, and upland woods here are a refuge for more than 150 bird species and 20 mammals. A freshwater section of the Nissequogue River flows through the southeastern portion of the park.

The land of the park was purchased in 1663 from the Nesaquake Indians by Richard Smith, the first of a long line of Smiths to live here. The land stayed in the Smith family until 1888, when the Brooklyn Gun Club purchased it as a hunting and fishing preserve for members only. The club later renamed itself the Wyandanch Club after Wyandanch, the seventeenth-century sachem (leader) of the Native American tribes on Long Island. The land remained in the hands of the Wyandanch Club until 1963, when New York State purchased it as part of an overall effort to preserve open space. The land was leased back to the club for a final ten years; in 1974 it

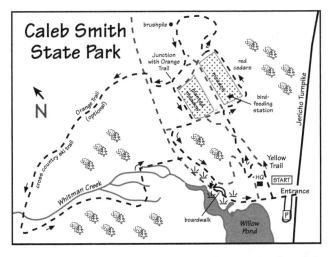

became Nissequogue River State Park. In 1983, the park was renamed for Caleb Smith, the original builder and resident of the building that is now the nature museum. The preserve designation was added in 1989 to ensure that the land is kept permanently as an environmental area with limited public access.

The preserve, unfortunately, is bisected by the Jericho Turnpike. The Nissequogue River and several ponds are on the southern side, with access through a locked gate. A cross-country ski trail runs through this portion of the preserve. Fly-fishing is allowed by permit on the river, and several trails lead to the stream sites. The foot trails described here, however, are on the northern side of the turnpike. All are marked clearly with plastic tags.

To start your walk, obtain a permit for the nominal fee of $1 at the office in the nature museum. The entrance to the yellow-blazed self-guided nature trail is behind the museum—walk through the gap in the split-rail fence and past the herb garden. (A shorter half-mile, accessible nature trail begins to the right of the driveway.) Turn right and follow the trail as it takes you past a wildflower meadow and then into a wooded area. In about five minutes you'll emerge onto an open field on your left; the woods continue on your right. Look for a bird-feeding station in the field at the end of a side trail to your left. The flat object on top of a long pole is a solar panel that provides power to run a small water fountain (for the birds, not you). There are also some feeders and a bird blind. Although the feeders are filled only in the colder months, the water is available year-round. Actually, in very cold weather when all the natural water is frozen, the water here is as valuable as food for the birds.

Continue on the path as it skirts the field. Eastern red cedars (*Juniperus virginiana*) line the path on your right as you skirt around the edge of the field. This tree is also called the pencil cedar because it was long the wood of choice for making pencils (cheaper and more abundant California incense cedar is used today). The needles of this tree are distinctive: on the most mature trees, the needles are small, scalelike, and have three sides with a triangular cross section. On younger trees, including many that are fairly substantial, some needles are scalelike while others are short, sharp, and prickly. Look for red berries in the fall.

The meadow is full of tall grasses and wildflowers. Because there is a lot of milkweed growing here, there are also a lot—sometimes dozens or more—of monarch butterflies (*Danaus plexippus*), especially when they are migrating south in late August, September, and October (see below for more on monarchs).

Continue on the path as it enters an area of open woods. In about five minutes the path goes past a large brush pile deliberately made to shelter small mammals such as rabbits and chipmunks. The path soon becomes a dirt road. Continue on for five minutes or so until you come to signpost 13 by a tangled thicket of cat brier and Japanese honeysuckle. From there, you can turn left to return to the nature museum in about fifteen minutes, or you can take the 1.25-mile, orange-blazed hiking loop for a woodland stroll that is enjoyable but has no outstanding natural features. In the winter, this loop is a cross-country ski trail. It is well marked and easy to follow. The loop brings you back to the nature trail at signpost 15. To return to the nature museum from there, see below.

If you choose to stay on the nature trail, turn left and follow the path as it leads past another field. To attract wildlife and birds, this field is planted every year with a mixture of seeds, including millet, oats, sunflowers, corn, and buckwheat. The oats are very attractive to bob-white quail (*Colinus virginianus*), a ground-nesting bird that has become scarce on Long Island due to a shortage of suitable nesting sites. You may catch a glimpse of one here. More likely is that you'll hear its call, a clearly whistled *Bob-white!* or *Poor, Bob-whoit!*

At signpost 15, the path reenters a patch of fairly dense woods. As you walk along, the ground becomes wetter and such swamp plants as red maple, spicebush, and skunk cabbage are visible. This patch of **freshwater marsh** is caused by a layer of clay below the surface. Rainwater and seepage from nearby springs collect on top and slowly drain off into Willow Pond. **Vernal ponds** form here in the spring. These temporary ponds are vital to many amphibians, including tree frogs and salamanders.

A female mallard, followed by her brood of ducklings, sails peacefully on Willow Pond.

Because the ponds are temporary, they have no fish or turtles in them, so the eggs these amphibians lay in the water are safe from predators. Look for a boardwalk on your right a little way past signpost 15—this takes you over the wet area and to a fishing platform on Whitman Creek where it enters Willow Pond. The **pond** was formed around 1795 when the stream was dammed to make a millpond. The mill had long ceased operation by the time the Wyandanch Club bought the property. The club built a new dam that raised the pond level and made it bigger. The pond is fed by Whitman Creek, which now drains out through a culvert under Jericho Turnpike, and by underground springs rising up from the aquifer below. The cool water from the aquifer keeps the pond temperature cool enough for trout even in the summer.

Turn left off the boardwalk and continue on the

paved road along the pond to return to the nature museum in a few more minutes.

Monarch Migration

The monarch is a common, large, orange and black butterfly. Its coloration is so distinctive that it is often the only butterfly people can identify with any certainty. Adult monarchs feed only on nectar from the flat-topped clusters of the milkweed's pinkish flowers. The larvae (caterpillars) feed only on the leaves, ingesting the bitter, milky sap that gives milkweed its name. The toxic chemicals in the sap make the larvae and, later, the adult butterfly, taste terrible. The brilliant orange color of the monarch advertises this fact to such potential predators as birds. Another butterfly, the viceroy (*Limenitis archippus*), mimics the coloration of the monarch. Even though the viceroy isn't toxic, the colors fool predators into leaving it alone. Scientists call this Bates mimicry, after Henry Walter Bates (1825–1892), the pioneering English naturalist who first described it. You can tell the difference between the two without tasting them by looking at how they fly. Monarchs sail along with their wings held in an upright V. Viceroys often glide along on flat wings.

In one of nature's most amazing spectacles, **monarchs migrate** south every autumn along the Atlantic coast. They gather in millions at communal roosts in the Mexican mountains to spend the winter. The roosts in Mexico are under severe pressure from logging activities in the area. Unless the logging is stopped, the monarch soon could become extinct. Very early in the spring, they mate and begin moving north again. None will return. These butterflies will lay their eggs while they are still far to the south and die soon afterward. It is their off-spring that will arrive on Long Island in May or June.

Hours, Fees, and Facilities

Caleb Smith State Park Preserve is open from 8:00 A.M. to 4:30 P.M. Tuesday through Sunday from April 1 to September 30; at other times it is open Wednesday through Sunday. There is a $1 permit fee for trail use. Restrooms, water, and pay phones are available at the nature museum. No pets are allowed.

Getting There

Take the Sagtikos Turnpike to the Sunken Meadow State Parkway and get off at exit SM3 east. At the light, turn right (east) onto Jericho Turnpike (NY Rte. 25). Follow Jericho Turnpike for 3.2 miles to the inconspicuous entrance on the left—it's 0.5 mile past Old Willets Road. If you take the Long Island Expressway, get off at exit 52N (Commack Road) and follow it north until it intersects with Jericho Turnpike, then follow directions as above. Be very careful driving on Jericho Turnpike—the quadruple yellow lines dividing the highway near the park entrance are there for a reason.

This park is one of the few on Long Island that is accessible by public transportation. Take the Long Island Railroad to Smithtown station. Suffolk County bus S58 goes to the preserve entrance.

For More Information

Caleb Smith State Park Preserve
Box 963, Jericho Turnpike
Smithtown, NY 11787
516-265-1054

Sunken Meadow State Park

Kings Park

- **2 miles**
- **1 to 1.5 hours**
- **easy**

A walk along the glacial bluffs above Long Island Sound.

Most people go to Sunken Meadow State Park for its nearly three miles of **beach** along Long Island Sound—this is one of very few public swimming beaches on the north shore of Long Island. The three-quarter-mile-long boardwalk is a popular spot for strollers and exercisers all year long. But this 1,200-acre park has topography that also includes high glacial bluffs, tidal flats, and the mouth of the Nissequogue River. To see the varied terrain here, this walk will go along the bluffs in one direction and return via the shore. The bluffs section is on the northern portion of the Long Island Greenbelt Trail, part of a longer trail that stretches thirty-four miles from Sunken Meadow on the north shore of Long Island to Heckscher State Park on the south shore. Opened in 1978, this National Recreational Trail connects 12,000 acres of state, county, and town parks. The trail is part of an extensive network created and maintained by the Long Island Greenbelt Trail Conference, a nonprofit, all-volunteer organization. The shore section starts at the

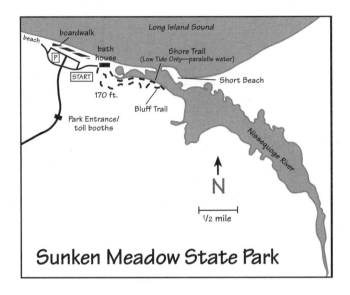

Sunken Meadow State Park

Map labels: Long Island Sound, boardwalk, beach, bath house, P, START, Shore Trail (Low Tide Only—parallels water), Short Beach, 170 ft., Bluff Trail, Park Entrance/ toll booths, Nissequogue River, N, 1/2 mile

mouth of the Nissequogue River and takes you along an **estuary with tidal flats**.

An estuary is the wide, lower course of a river where its current is met and influenced by tides—in this case, by the tides of the Long Island Sound. The rising and falling tides expose mud flats where the Nissequogue River empties into the Sound. This is a particularly good place to visit in the autumn, when numerous waterfowl stop to rest and feed on the flats and along the river before heading farther south along the Atlantic flyway.

The trail begins in the southwestern corner of parking lot 3. Look for a footbridge here near the trailer used as headquarters for cross-country skiers. The bridge takes you over Sunken Meadow Creek, here a rather broad and quite beautiful stream that is actually a side branch of the Nissequogue. After crossing the bridge, turn left and walk through the picnic area. Look for the white blazes of the Greenbelt Trail on the asphalt path. After about seventy yards the path forks; bear right and follow the asphalt path for another twenty yards or so. When the asphalt ends near some benches, bear left onto a dirt path. Follow it up a short, somewhat steep hill, then bear right at the fork. Go through the gap in the chain-link fence here and walk straight ahead, ignoring the smaller trails that branch off. In a few minutes you'll come to a T intersection. Turn left and follow the blazes through a grove of pitch pines and oaks to come out onto a beautiful view over Long Island Sound. The **bluffs** here are 150 feet or more above sea level—on a clear day you can easily see across the Sound to Connecticut. The trail becomes very sandy as it leads to your right (east) along the bluff. Because the terrain is fragile here, stay on the main trail to avoid contributing to erosion problems. In addition, some of the side trails end abruptly—and dangerously—at the edge of the bluff. Follow the trail along the bluff (it winds into the woods in places) for another twenty minutes or so. You'll come to a tree with four blazes on it. Walk straight past the tree and follow the blazes down to some wooden steps. These take you into the parking lot of the marina at adjacent King's Park in the town of Smithtown. The marina is built at the mouth of the Nissequogue River. Looking out, you can see a beach running parallel to the shore; the river runs into the sound through the narrow inlet.

If the tide is low, return via the beach; if it's high, return the way you came. Walk down to the western end

Looking out over Long Island Sound from atop the bluff at Sunken Meadow State Park. It's low tide—note the exposed mud flats.

of the parking lot and look for a double blaze on a boulder there. Walk past it on the left and follow a rocky, pebbly section of the estuary beach for about 200 yards. The footing then gets much easier as you walk along the edge of a firmer salt-marsh area that fringes the estuary. (In the summer, this part of the walk may be too full of mosquitoes and greenhead flies to be any fun. If that's the case, backtrack along the bluffs to return.) At low tide, you'll see many seabirds, including sandpipers, semipalmated plovers, and sanderlings, probing the exposed mud of the **tidal flats** in search of the small creatures at the bottom of the food chain, including worms, insects, small crabs, and the like. In about fifteen minutes the trail brings you to a lovely little sandy cove.

From there, it leads back in a few more minutes to the footbridge that starts the walk.

How Sunken Meadow Park Got Its Name

A little-known fact is that this park is officially called Governor Alfred E. Smith/Sunken Meadow State Park. Smith (1873–1944) was the progressive governor of New York for four terms between 1919 and 1928. In 1928, he ran unsuccessfully for president and lost by a landslide to Herbert Hoover. Governor Smith's name was given to the park after his death to honor his role in the 1920s in acquiring the land from a former estate. The Sunken Meadow part of the name comes from the large, grassy meadow found between the narrow beach and the bluffs. The meadow is actually slightly lower than the beach level—hence the name. The glacial bluffs on the north shore of Long Island usually rise straight up behind a narrow beach (see the walk at Caumsett State Park to learn why), so this sort of formation is unusual. In fact, I haven't been able to find any explanation for it. Access to the beach was originally across a boardwalk on stilts across the meadow and creek. Most of the meadow is now covered by roadways, parking lots, golf courses, picnic areas, and other "improvements," and there is little natural vegetation left.

Hours, Fees, and Facilities

Sunken Meadow State Park is open daily from sunrise to sunset. From late May to mid-September there is an admission fee of $4 per car. Restrooms, water, and pay phones are available year-round at the refreshment stand at parking lot 3. No pets are allowed.

Getting There

From the Long Island Expressway take exit 53 north onto Sunken Meadow State Parkway. Follow the parkway for 7.5 miles to its northern terminus at the park. After the tollbooths, follow the signs to parking lot 3, another 1.7 miles.

From the Southern State Parkway, take exit 41 north onto the Sagtikos/Sunken Meadow Parkway. Follow the parkway for 11.5 miles and then follow directions as above.

For More Information

Sunken Meadow State Park
Sunken Meadow State Parkway
Kings Park, NY 11754
516-269-4333

Bayard Cutting Arboretum
Oakdale

- **1 to 2 miles**
- **2 to 3 hours**
- **easy**

Serene botanizing along the banks of the Connetquot River.

Beautifully sited along the Connetquot River on Long Island's south shore, the Bayard Cutting Arboretum is an oasis of beauty and quiet. The landscaping incorporates an important **pinetum** (conifer collection) and extensive plantings of dwarf evergreens, rhododendrons, azaleas, hollies, and oaks. Wildflowers and daffodils are featured in many native woodland settings. The overall effect is surprisingly natural—an outstanding example of informal planting in the English tradition. The arboretum is interesting even in winter because of the numerous evergreens, but I think it is at its best from April through the middle of June. The spring wildflowers, spring bulbs, flowering shrubs, dogwoods, lilacs, azaleas, and rhododendrons are all in bloom then, and the bird-watching is good too. In all, there are five different well-marked walks meandering through the 690 acres of the arboretum. Individually, each walk is short; in total, they cover only two miles. The paths are all broad, flat, well maintained, and very easy to follow. There are many convenient benches, all placed carefully

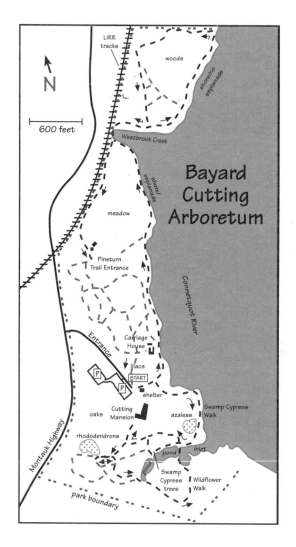

N

600 feet

LIRR tracks

woods

shoreline esplanade

Westbrook Creek

shore/ esplanade

Bayard Cutting Arboretum

meadow

Pineturn Trail Entrance

Connetquot River

Entrance

Carriage House

lilacs

START

P

P

shelter

Montauk Highway

oaks

Cutting Mansion

azaleas

Swamp Cypress Walk

rhododendrons

pond

inlet

pond

Swamp Cypress trees

Wildflower Walk

park boundary

to overlook pleasant views. Specimen labels are attached to most of the trees. You can see the grounds here quite thoroughly in one pleasant afternoon.

William Bayard Cutting (1850–1912) was a very wealthy lawyer, philanthropist, and political reformer much involved with improved housing for the poor of New York City. His own modest summer cottage, called Westbrook, is the rambling, sixty-eight-room Tudor-style mansion that is now park headquarters. It was built in 1886–87 and remained in the Cutting family until 1954, when the house and land were given in trust to the Long Island State Park Commission.

The paths in the arboretum all start near the mansion. I always enjoy Walk 4, also called the Birdwatcher's Walk. It starts near the small rustic shelter just to the left of the mansion and leads almost at once down to an esplanade along the eastern bank of the Connetquot River, here an estuary that leads into the Great South Bay. From there, the walk takes you almost the entire length of the property to a small area of native woods. The bird-watching here along the river is quite good in the spring and again in the autumn. Gulls and water-fowl, including ducks, swans, and Canada geese, can be seen floating on the river. In the spring, warblers dart among the trees and shrubs.

Follow the path along the esplanade for about twenty minutes; a lovely meadow will appear through a screen of trees on your left. The path soon leads you over a small, short bridge over Westbrook Creek, where it enters the Connetquot through a culvert under the Long Island Railroad tracks. On the other side of the bridge is the one part of the arboretum that does not consist of manicured lawns and carefully tended specimen plants. Instead, you enter an area of native woods left in a natural state—well, natural for an arboretum—as a bird sanctuary. A loop trail leads around the area. The path takes you along the river, here unconstrained by embankments, and then into the woods to return. Walking the loop takes about thirty minutes—longer if you stop to bird-watch. On a quick swing through here once on a nice day in late October, I easily spotted sixteen species, including a kingfisher and a hermit thrush. The trail loops back through the woods, which are the usual somewhat scrubby woods found in the shallow, sandy soil typical of this region—red maple, black oak, white oak, alder, and birch. Actually, scrubby is a little unfair; it's just that after seeing the rest of the grounds, real nature seems terribly untidy.

When you arrive back at the bridge, cross over and carry on straight ahead to walk along the western edge of the meadow. In about ten minutes you'll pass some attractive maintenance buildings (part of a showcase dairy farm maintained by the Cuttings). Just after the buildings the white gravel paths of the Pinetum Walk, also called Walk 1, come up on your right—look for a huge holly tree. This walk meanders among the specimen conifers and hollies; convenient benches make it a good place to take a rest. The sixteen-acre **Pinetum** was severely damaged by Hurricane Gloria in 1985. Hundreds of trees in the arboretum were lost or damaged, including 18 of the 22 that were on the list of Long Island's largest trees. Only 40 of the original 120 major specimens in the Pinetum are still there. Fortunately, because additional plantings were made in the 1940s, and

The manicured grounds of Bayard Cutting Arboretum include many conveniently placed benches. This scene is in the Pinetum.

because replanting began in 1988, the current collection of fir, spruce, pine, cypress, hemlock, yew, and other lesser-known conifers is still impressive. This is a good place to practice your conifer-identification skills (see below).

The paths in the Pinetum eventually lead you through a lilac collection and toward the parking lot. Look near here for one of the largest trees in the arboretum: a weeping European beech (*Fagus sylvatica pendulus*). Planted between 1890 and 1900, this tree is more than ninety feet tall. The hanging branches cover a huge area.

From the Pinetum, look for the rustic shelter again, just past the parking lot on the road to the mansion. To follow any of the remaining three trails—the Swamp Cypress Walk, the Rhododendron Walk, and the Wildflower Walk—start here. Follow the path just past the shelter for a short distance and then turn right onto the

Swamp Cypress Walk, also called Walk 5. The path will go past the lawn behind the mansion on your right. In about ten minutes, you'll come to a side path that takes you into a native azalea garden. Stop to visit—you'll come out where you entered. Continue on the Swamp Cypress Walk for another ten minutes as it leads past an inlet from the river and then a pond with a rustic bridge. The Swamp Cypress Walk ends here. Look for **swamp cypress** (*Taxodium distichum*) trees along the edge of the pond. This deciduous conifer has double-ranked needles and reddish-brown bark with long, shallow cracks. At the base of the trunk are enlarged, fluted roots that buttress the tree. Knobby protuberances known as knees take in air for the roots. Also called the bald cypress, this tree is native from Mississippi to Florida; it prefers swamps and riverbanks and is surprisingly hardy, as these specimens show.

From here, turn right to get onto the Rhododendron Walk. Ignore the first left and follow the path at the second left for about five minutes to get to the Rhododendron Garden (best seen from mid-May to mid-June). After viewing the plantings, backtrack abut fifty yards to get onto the Wildflower Walk. Turn right on to this longer loop, which takes about twenty minutes to walk and leads you among ponds, streamlets, and rustic bridges. The spring wildflowers are at their best in April; most of the summer wildflowers bloom toward the end of July. Follow the Wildflower Walk to the right as it brings you out again to the Swamp Cypress Walk. Turn right and then left almost at once for a path that leads you back to the mansion in a just a few minutes.

Conifer Identification

A conifer is any tree that bears woody cones. Most but not all conifers are evergreens—that is, they keep their leaves year-round. Conifers usually can be identified by their leaves. (And also by their cones, but there isn't room to go into that here.) Conifer leaves are generally needle-like (as in a generic Christmas tree), but some are scale-like. Assuming the tree has needles, take a good look at them. If there are a lot of needles (ten or more) in the bunch, the tree is a larch. The larch is the only conifer that is deciduous—it drops its needles in winter. If the needles are in bunches of five, three, or two, you're looking at a pine of some sort. If the needles form a cylinder around the branch, the tree is a spruce. If the needles are double ranked (like hair parted in the middle), the tree is probably a fir, although it is likely to be an eastern hemlock if you're in the region covered by this book. Scale-like leaves are found on junipers and red cedar, arborvitae (a widely used ornamental also called white cedar), and Atlantic white cedar.

Hours, Fees, and Facilities

Bayard Cutting Arboretum in open Wednesday through Sunday and on legal holidays from 10:00 A.M. to 5:00 P.M. (4:00 P.M. in the winter). There are no fees. Restrooms, water, and a seasonal snackbar are available at the mansion. No food, beverages, picnicking, or pets are allowed on the grounds.

Getting There

Take the Southern State Parkway to its end, where it becomes the Hecksher Parkway. Get off at exit 45E (Rte. 27A, also called Montauk Highway). Turn right (east) onto Montauk Highway and follow it for 0.4 mile to the well-marked entrance on the right.

For More Information

Bayard Cutting Arboretum
Montauk Highway
Oakdale, NY 11769
516-581-1002

Connetquot River State Park Preserve

Oakdale/Bohemia

- **2 miles**
- **1.5 hours (bird-watchers may take longer)**
- **easy**

Pure water and untouched woodlands in the state's first park preserve.

The only truly wild place still remaining on crowded Long Island, this beautiful preserve is a rare gem. The Connetquot River flows clear and free for six miles through its 3,400 wooded acres on the way to the Great South Bay; the water here is fresh and remarkably clean. The river's name comes from the Algonquian-speaking Secatogue Indians who once lived here. It is said to mean "at the long river." This is the Long Island of four hundred years ago: piney woods, pure water, deer, birds, and silence.

The land here is amazingly untouched even though English settlers were in the region by the mid-1600s. Sometime before 1760, James Nicolls, holder of a large land patent, had dammed the river and built a gristmill. The mill still stands—it was listed on the National Register of Historic Places in 1972—but the surrounding land never was cleared or developed. Because it was still

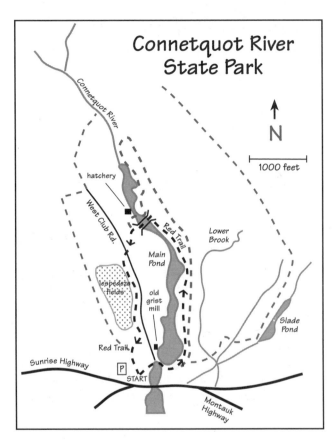

Connetquot River State Park

Connetquot River

hatchery

West Club Rd.

Red Trail

Main Pond

lespedeza fields

old grist mill

Red Trail

Lower Brook

Slade Pond

Sunrise Highway

P

START

Montauk Highway

N

1000 feet

wild, the region became very popular with sportsmen. There was often no room for them at Snedecors Inn, which had been built near the gristmill in 1820 for travelers on Old South Country Road (today's Montauk Highway). A group of 100 wealthy sportsmen solved their accommodation problem in 1866 by forming the South Side Sportsmens Club and buying the land. They built themselves a large, shingled clubhouse and maintained the land as a private wildlife preserve. In 1963, the club (now called the Connetquot River Club) sold the land to New York State. The club promptly leased it back again for ten years, so it was not until 1973 that the preserve was opened to the public on a limited basis. In 1978, legislation was passed in New York establishing state park preserves where no development was allowed; Connetquot River was the first site designated under the new law.

A number of enjoyable trails wind through Connetquot River State Park, including a four-mile stretch of the Long Island Greenbelt Trail. The walk described here takes you up one bank of the Connetquot and down the other, with a stop at the fish hatchery on the way.

Start your walk by picking up your permit (see below) at the administration office. Go past the office to the old gristmill at the southern tip of the imaginatively named Main Pond. **The pond is a great place for birdwatching** year-round. It's especially good for ducks and other waterfowl in the early spring and late autumn; a number of ducks also overwinter on the pond. Birds that are locally rare on Long Island find a haven at Connetquot. Among them are brown creepers, American woodcocks, wild turkeys, ruffed grouse, great horned owls, red crossbills, and Acadian flycatchers. A number of warblers breed in the preserve but rarely if anywhere else on Long Island, including Canada warblers, northern parulas, and chestnut-sided warblers. Prairie and palm warblers are abundant.

Walk past the mill to a wide, sandy road and look for a red arrow nailed to a tree. Follow the arrows as the road bears quickly to the left to follow the eastern shore of Main Pond. The **wooded terrain** here is typical of the glacial outwash plain that makes up the south shore of Long Island: flat—the elevation here is only eight feet— and sandy. The dominant trees are pitch pine and white oak in the dry parts and red maple in the wetter sections. The pitch pine is easily recognizable by the sharply pointed needles that grow not only from the twigs but also directly out from the trunk. The needles are about five inches long and grow in clumps of three. The rough bark of a pitch pine has a characteristic "alligator skin" pattern. The acid soil here is also ideal for a type of heather called trailing arbutus, also known as ground laurel or mayflower (*Epigaea replens*). This low, trailing evergreen has leathery, alternate leaves and bears fragrant clusters of pink flowers. Look for it in open areas in sandy soil.

After a few minutes the path takes you over a small bridge. Shortly after this the red trail forks. Bear to the left to stay close to the water. As you walk along, you'll start to notice numbered fishing sites along the banks. The Connetquot is stocked every year with brook, brown, and rainbow trout (you'll come to the hatchery in a little while). The numerous fishing sites on both sides of the river are a great way to get close to the water without damaging the banks or fragile stream vegetation.

Continue to follow the red-blazed trail. The arrows are fairly few and far between, but the path is easy to see—just keep the river on your left and you can't get lost. There are some interesting if somewhat swampy side trails to the east that you can explore. In another fifteen minutes or so you'll arrive at the charming, turn-of-the-century fish hatchery.

The river is particularly beautiful around here. The trails and bridges by the hatchery are an excellent place to look for all sorts of wildlife. The black-crowned night heron (*Nycticorax nycticorax*), a large, heavy-bodied wader with a short, thick neck; a dark back; and surprisingly short legs, can often be seen here, roosting on tree branches during the day and feeding in the shallows at dusk. Great blue herons, egrets, and other wading birds are seen frequently here; so are ducks. You might also spot painted turtles and spotted turtles basking on a sunny rock. If you haven't yet seen a deer, you

Deer are plentiful and very tame at Connetquot River State Park Preserve. This unconcerned little doe was only about ten feet away.

are very likely to see one near the hatchery. The **deer** in Connetquot haven't been hunted for more than twenty years—they are remarkably tame and often will allow you to approach within ten feet. Do not, however, attempt to feed or touch them. You might even see a red fox.

Cross the river, either on the bridge that is downstream from the hatchery or over the boardwalk that is upstream. On the other side is a parking lot (for hatchery staff and handicapped fishers), a picnic area, and restrooms. A short but interesting interpretive trail starts at the parking area and goes around the hatchery.

To start the return walk, look for two wooden benches near the bridge. Follow the wood-chip trail that leads away from the river. After about twenty yards, the trail turns sharply left (south). To return to your starting point, you can then follow either the yellow trail or the old fire lane called West Club Road. The two routes parallel each other closely; West Club Road is paved. (The white blazes on West Club Road indicate the Long Island Greenbelt Trail.) In about fifteen minutes, you'll come to a large, open field on your right; you'll go past two more fields soon after. Many years ago, these fields were cleared by the Sportsmens Club and planted with lespedeza, a type of legume, to provide food and cover for deer. It works—one November afternoon I saw a buck in each field.

In another ten minutes you'll come to a corral with horses and see some of the outbuildings near the main entrance. A few more minutes' walk brings you back to your car.

Hours, Fees, and Facilities

Access to Connetquot River State Park Preserve is limited and you must make arrangements in advance for a permit. To obtain a permit, write to the preserve (see below). Be sure your letter includes your name and address, the purpose of your visit (e.g., hiking or birding), and how many people will accompany you. If you don't have time to make arrangements by mail, call the preserve. The very helpful staff there will arrange for you to pick up a day permit when you arrive. There is a nominal $1 fee per person, payable when you arrive.

From April 1 to Labor Day, the preserve is open Tuesday through Sunday from 8:30 A.M. to sunset. The rest of the year the preserve is open Wednesday through Sunday, same hours. Restrooms and water are available at the main entrance and at the parking area near the fish hatchery. No pets are allowed.

Getting There

Take the Southern State Parkway east to exit 44E (Sunrise Highway, also called Rte. 27). Drive east on Sunrise Highway for 1.5 miles until you reach the stoplight at Pond Road. Shortly before the light, you'll see the preserve entrance on the northern side of the divided highway. Make a U-turn at the light, backtrack .02 mile, and turn right at the entrance.

For More Information

Connetquot River State Park Preserve
Box 505
Oakdale, NY 11769
516-581-1005

South Shore Nature Center
East Islip

- **2 miles**
- **2 hours**
- **easy**

A range of habitats on the south shore of Long Island.

For about thirty-five miles between Babylon to the west and Bellport to the east, the south shore of Long Island is bordered by the Great South Bay, a shallow, salty lagoon between the shore and Fire Island. The South Shore Nature Center preserves, in the midst of ever-expanding residential housing, 206 acres of upland woods, fresh-water swamp, and salt marsh that are a precious reminder of the distinct habitats typical of the region. The preserve also shelters a small and very tame deer population. You're almost certain to see some.

Sometimes called Islip Meadows in older books and maps, the South Shore Nature Center was established in 1977. It is owned jointly by the Town of Islip, Suffolk County, and The Nature Conservancy. The town operates the nature center facility and leases the county and Nature Conservancy lands under cooperative agreements for unified management of the land.

Begin the walk on the upland trail. Look for the brown trailhead sign across the parking lot from the nature center. (None of the trails in the preserve is blazed, but all are very clear and easy to follow. If you get confused, just

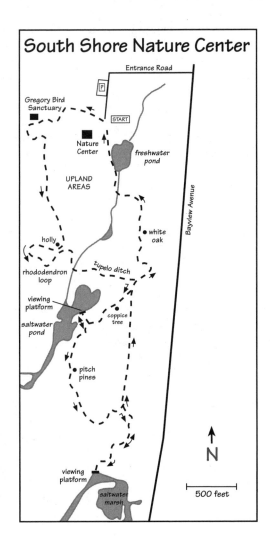

South Shore Nature Center

Entrance Road

P

START

Gregory Bird
Sanctuary

Nature
Center

freshwater
pond

UPLAND
AREAS

Bayview Avenue

white
oak

holly

tupelo ditch

rhododendron
loop

viewing
platform

coppice
tree

saltwater
pond

pitch
pines

viewing
platform

saltwater
marsh

N

500 feet

South Shore N.C.   153

look for brown signs pointing you back to the nature center.) The trails through the woodlands and wetlands of the South Shore Nature Center illustrate just how much of a difference even a **small change of elevation** can make in nature. The upland section of the preserve is only about two feet higher than the saltwater marsh, but those two feet mean a very different ecology. The dry, sandy soil supports a forest of oak, hickory, pitch pine, and red maple that is very typical of the region. Follow the path for about five minutes. At signpost 3, the trail forks off to the right for a short loop called the Gregory Bird Sanctuary. As you walk along this portion of the trail, you can see why preserves of this sort are so important—a recent condo development comes right up to the preserve border. When the loop returns you to the main trail after a few minutes, turn right. In a few more minutes, the trail will take you onto a short boardwalk over a depressed, swampy area. As you leave the upland area, you drop down about two feet in elevation. The ground water is now just a foot or so below the surface. The hickory and oak trees, which prefer a dryer soil, give way to red maple and tupelo (also called sour-gum) trees; cinnamon ferns and pepperbush fill the understory. In another five minutes or so, you'll come to a very large old American holly tree. Once found only in the southern states, American holly gradually has moved northward, helped along by landscape architects. This tree tolerates salt spray and shading by larger trees, so it has done well in coastal areas. Just after the holly tree turn right to follow the short Rhododendron Loop. This portion of the path takes you past some rosebay rhododendron (*Rhododendron maximum*), a native shrub on Long Island. Rosebay rhododendrons prefer acid soil and heavy shade, so they do well in the understory of wooded areas. The stand doesn't look quite natural to me—I think it was planted here for landscaping.

The loop returns you to the main trail after about five minutes. Turn right onto the boardwalk leading to the Freshwater Trail. You'll soon come to a bench area on the boardwalk. Follow the boardwalk as it leads into a dense stand of phragmites, also called common reeds. Phragmites often crowd out cattails and other reedlike plants. They are often a telltale sign that the area has been disturbed in some way. In a few more minutes, you'll see that this is indeed the case here. The boardwalk parallels a drainage ditch, probably dug for mosquito control in the 1930s. Interestingly, the drainage ditch is lined by a **row of tupelo trees**, all about the same height. Here's another example of how an apparently minor difference in elevation can affect what grows where. All the tupelo seedlings probably sprouted simultaneously when the ditch was dug and a slightly raised bank was created on one side. The seedlings found the elevated soil just right—not too dry and not too wet—and took hold.

In another five minutes, turn right onto the boardwalk for the Saltwater Trail. Look on your right for a five-trunked red maple tree. At one time, the original tree was destroyed by fire or lumbering. The tree sent up sprouts around the dead stump, which eventually rotted away, and formed the multiple trunks you see here. Botanists call this a coppice tree. After another few minutes, you'll come to an intersection in the boardwalk. Continue on straight ahead for another twenty yards to a viewing platform overlooking a saltwater pond. The numerous nesting boxes you see on the posts in the pond are meant for tree swallows—a form of airborne mosquito control. These small, agile birds have green backs, brown wings, and pure-white underparts. A single tree swallow (*Tachycineta bicolor*) can eat thousands of mosquitoes in a single day. In the spring and summer you can see them catch insects as they swoop gracefully over the water; in colder weather when few insects are on the wing, tree swallows eat bayberries. Tree swallows congregate in flocks of thousands along the Atlantic coast as they prepare to migrate south for the winter. If you visit here in the early autumn, you may notice smaller flocks of tree swallows starting to form. Later in the autumn, larger flocks may gather here to rest and feed before heading south.

After enjoying the sights of the saltwater pond, backtrack to the intersection and turn right. Look for bayberry and pepperbush growing among the phragmites

The saltwater pond at South Shore Nature Center. Note the dense stands of phragmites lining the shore. The bird houses on posts are to attract tree swallows.

along the boardwalk. Pepperbush blooms in the late summer with sweet-smelling spikes of white flowers. The flowers give way to slender stalks of small, round, green seed capsules; when these dry, they resemble peppercorns.

After a few minutes, the boardwalk comes to an end as you again enter a slightly elevated area. This "island" is higher and drier than the surrounding marsh. The pitch pine (*Pinus rigida*) thrives here on the dry, sandy soil. You can always tell a pitch pine by its alligator-skin bark and sharp, pointy needles in bundles of three. The needles, which are generally less than five inches long, sometimes grow directly from the trunk.

After following the path through this elevated area for another five minutes, you'll be back on the boardwalk through phragmites for five minutes more. When the boardwalk ends, turn right onto the side trail. In five minutes the trail ends at a viewing platform looking out over a salt marsh. Tall phragmites crowd up to the edge of the platform. If you look over them, you can see a wide expanse of *Spartina patens*, also known as salt-meadow grass or salt hay. Perfectly adapted to the changing water levels and salt concentrations of a tidal marsh, salt hay was once harvested by New England and Long Island farmers as cattle fodder. A narrow trail that leads through the phragmites down to the grass tells you the deer here enjoy salt hay too.

Backtrack to the brown nature-center sign at other end of the boardwalk. Turn right; after ten yards, you're back on another boardwalk for a short stretch of phragmites. When the boardwalk ends, you're at a slightly higher elevation again. As you walk along, notice how the vegetation changes quickly to red maples and tupelos. In about ten minutes you'll arrive back at the boardwalk for the Freshwater Trail. Bear right and stay on the dirt path as it leads you back through the upland woods. In a few minutes you'll come to a large white oak on your right, by signpost 20. One of two easily distinguished **oak trees** common at the South Shore Nature Center, the white oak (*Quercus alba*) has deeply lobed leaves that are about four inches long; the lobes are somewhat similar in size and shape. White oaks produce edible acorns that are somewhat sweeter than those of the black oak. These acorns were a staple food for the Native Americans of Long Island. After gathering the acorns in the autumn, they would grind them into flour, soak the flour in water to remove the bitter tannins, and then use the flour to make a sort of griddlecake. The black oak (*Quercus velutina*) can be a bit tricky to identify by its leaves, because it usually bears leaves of several different forms. In general, look for leaves that are thick, leathery, and about four inches long; they usually widen toward the tip and have seven lobes. The lobes on some leaves may be very shallow, while other leaves will have deeper, more obvious lobes. In general, white oaks will be found in higher, drier areas than black oaks.

Another few minutes brings you to a short boardwalk over a swampy area. It ends at the lovely freshwater pond right next to the nature center.

The nature center itself is small but has some exceptionally interesting exhibits. An excellent saltwater aquarium holds fish found in the Great South Bay. The pipefish—long, very thin relatives of the sea horse—are particularly interesting. The nature center also has a large, glass-sided, fully functional **beehive** that gives you an outstanding look at the amazing activity inside an apiary. The bees come and go through a tunnel leading to an outside window. We actually were able to see the queen, attended by worker bees, laying her eggs.

Hours, Fees, and Facilities

The South Shore Nature Center is open daily from 9:00 A.M. to 5:00 P.M. between April and October. From November 1 until March 31, the center is closed on weekends. Entrance is free. Restrooms and water are available at the nature center. No pets are allowed.

Getting There

From the Long Island Expressway, take exit 56 south to Rte. 111 (called Wheeler Road here). Follow Rte. 111 for 5.9 miles to Rte. 27A (Montauk Highway, here called Main Street). Turn left onto 27A and follow it for 0.8 mile to Bayview Avenue. Make a right onto Bayview and follow it for 0.8 mile to the entrance on the right. Turn in and follow the road 0.2 mile to the parking lot. From the Southern State Parkway, take exit 43S to Rte. 111 (here called Islip Avenue). Follow Rte. 111 south for 1.8 miles to Rte. 27A. Follow directions as above.

For More Information

South Shore Nature Center
Bayview Avenue
East Islip, NY 11730
516-224-5436

Fire Island National Seashore
Fire Island

- **2.5 miles**
- **2 hours**
- **easy**

*Sand dunes and solitude on one of the world's
most beautiful ocean beaches.*

Fire Island is a thin barrier beach that divides the
Atlantic Ocean from the Great South Bay. The island
stretches for thirty-two miles east and west along Long
Island's south shore, from Moriches Inlet in the east to
Democrat Point in the west, but is on average only a
quarter of a mile wide. Fire Island may be known best
for its seventeen popular, sometimes raffish, summer
beach communities, but the bulk of the island is actually
taken up by Robert Moses State Park and Fire Island
National Seashore (FINS). Robert Moses State Park covers 875 acres at the westernmost portion of Fire Island. It
is managed primarily as a recreation park and beach and
is the only part of Fire Island that allows motorized vehicles. (See below for how this park came to be.) Fire Island
National Seashore was established in 1964 to preserve
the only developed barrier island in the United States
without roads. In 1980, 1,400 acres, including an uninter-
rupted seven-mile stretch west of Smith Point, were

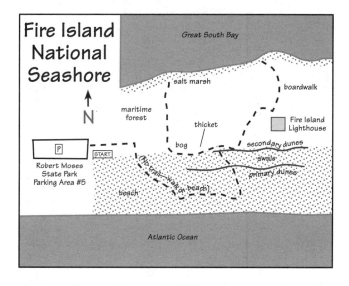

Fire Island
National
Seashore

↑
N

Great South Bay

salt marsh

boardwalk

maritime
forest

thicket

Fire Island
Lighthouse

P

START

bog

secondary dunes

swale

Robert Moses
State Park
Parking Area #5

(No trail—walk on beach)

primary dunes

beach

Atlantic Ocean

designated as a National Wilderness Area—the only such area in New York State. In all, the national seashore covers twenty-two miles.

To enjoy the Fire Island National Seashore within the travel parameters of this book, park at the eastern end of lot 5 in Robert Moses State Park. A large sign points you to the 0.6-mile path to the lighthouse. From there, a boardwalk leads down through the dunes to the beach. You can walk westward along the beach for about two miles before arriving at civilization again at the community of Kismet. The beaches are open to all, of course, and you can keep walking for miles longer.

The beach here is glorious. If you go during the off-season, or even early on a summer weekday, you're likely to have it pretty much to yourself. At low tide you'll see plenty of shorebirds feeding along the shore. Shorebird identification can be a little tricky—bring your field guide if you're interested. If you don't want to get specific, just call them all peeps. You'll also see a lot of gulls. Gull identification can be very tricky, with as many as seven different plumage variations for some species. The two most common are herring gulls and great black-backed gulls. These birds breed in a huge, raucous colony on nearby Captree Island—it's worth a visit if you're here in May.

To enjoy the beach, follow these rules. Don't walk on the dunes; don't swim (no lifeguards); avoid deer ticks by staying out of brushy areas; and watch out for poison ivy. There is a clothing-optional beach near the lighthouse.

Reminder: Sand dunes are fragile—don't climb on them.

Beach Ecology

The **ecology of a barrier beach** is a fascinating mixture of habitats in a very compressed area. An excellent way to see the nine different ecosystems on Fire Island in cross section is to start on the ocean beach and then go onto the 0.75-mile boardwalk nature trail that starts behind the lighthouse.

The ocean beach is the first ecosystem in the cross section. The beach can be defined as the sandy portion exposed between low tide and high tide; it ends above the wrack line, or the point where debris from the highest tides is deposited. From the surf to the dunes there is very little vegetation due to the constant erosion. The boardwalk begins at the dunes behind the beach. These wind-blown piles of sand are held together by such plants as beach grass, saltwort, poison ivy, dusty miller, sea oats, and seaside goldenrod. Dune plants seem to thrive on salt spray and sand movement or even occasional burial.

Unusual for a barrier beach, Fire Island has a second set of dunes behind the beach or primary dunes. These secondary dunes are actually former primary dunes that have been pushed back behind new primary dunes. In between is a valley called a **swale**, and plants that live in the swale or on the sides of the dunes must be very tolerant of temperature extremes, wind, and salt spray. The swale is hottest in summer, when the sides of the enclosing dunes form a sort of lens that reflects sunlight into it. The swale is also very dry, since any rain that falls drains away quickly in the sandy soil. Plants in the swale are adapted to the desertlike conditions. They usually grow outward along the ground, in mats with shallow roots,

Beach grass and dusty miller thrive on the shifting sands of the dunes at Fire Island National Seashore.

and have thick, leathery leaves. Look here for seaside goldenrod, beach heather, bearberry, salt spray rose, and poison ivy. On the leeward side of the primary dune, where there is some shelter from the wind, such woody plants as beach plum and bayberry grow. If the vegetation of a primary dune is disturbed by humans or animals walking over it repeatedly, the beach grass dies and wind starts to scour away the sand, creating a blowout, or gap. If the blowout is large enough, sand spills down the lee side of the dune into the swale, smothering the vegetation. Regrowth is a very slow process—don't walk on the dunes!

At this point the ocean boardwalk meets the nature trail boardwalk at marker 15. Turn left and continue on the nature boardwalk. (Turn right to visit the lighthouse.)

On top of and behind some secondary dunes is yet another ecosystem, the **maritime forest**. There really isn't any forest here, but you'll be able to see one in the distance (slightly out of sequence) a little farther on. For now, look for the thicket habitat found in the lee of the secondary dunes. Characterized by shrubby growth, the thicket is a transitional zone between dunes and marshlands. Vegetation here includes American holly, highbush blueberry, shadblow, Virginia creeper, poison ivy, and chokeberry. This is a very good habitat for migrant songbirds in the spring and especially the autumn. You might also spot a rabbit or even a red fox here.

Markers 13 and 14 on the nature boardwalk indicate boggy areas. These small, damp depressions are filled with rainwater and, surprisingly, ground water. A "lens" of fresh water lies underneath Fire Island, extending in places as much as 131 feet below sea level. In low places, the ground water comes to the surface. The plants here include cattails, cinnamon ferns, cranberries, and tupelo trees—an amazing contrast to the dry swale literally just a few yards away.

As you continue on the boardwalk toward the bay, you can see maritime forest on the dunes in the distance to the west. Because the secondary dune line acts as a barrier to the everpresent salt spray, such trees as American holly, shadblow, pitch pine, black cherry, sassafras, and post oak can grow in the dunes' shelter. The trees on the top of the secondary dune are low-growing, twisted, and stunted; those in the shelter of the dune are larger. Even so, any twigs that poke up above the dune are sheared off by the salt spray. The pruning effect of the spray gives the trees wide, flat canopies. Sunken Forest at Sailors Haven, a few miles to the east, is a well-known maritime forest. Made up mostly of American holly, the sheltered 125-acre forest has survived numerous severe storms for far more than two hundred years.

As you walk along the boardwalk toward the bay, the next ecosystem will be a **salt marsh**. The marsh isn't that large here, but you can still see typical plants: phragmites, cordgrass (*Spartina alterniflora*), salt hay grass (*Spartina patens*), cattails, glasswort, and others. There are many deer on this part of Fire Island; you may see them feeding here on the salt hay.

The boardwalk ends at the Great South Bay. The shallow, sheltered waters of the bay are less salty than the ocean, but there are still two tides a day. Vast beds of ribbonlike eelgrass near the shore shelter and provide food for clams, crabs, and young fish, as well as sea horses and their relatives, pipefish. Huge flocks of waterfowl can be seen floating on the bay, resting and feeding, during the spring and winter migrations.

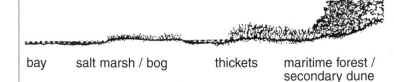

bay   salt marsh / bog   thickets   maritime forest / secondary dune

Barrier Beach Dynamics

Fire Island is a **barrier beach**—a thin, sandy island that lies along a mainland coast and protects it from storms. To the dismay of those who build beach houses on them, barrier islands move as their sand is carried away by waves and redeposited elsewhere. For a classic example of barrier beach dynamics, look at the Fire Island Lighthouse. When the lighthouse was built in 1858, it was on the western tip of the island. Today, it is nearly five miles from Democrat Point at the tip. Every day, more than 10,000 waves pound the beach of Fire Island, shoveling sand into currents that carry 500,000 cubic yards westward every year—what is known technically as **littoral drift**. Most of the sand is transported during the winter and during the highly energetic hurricanes and nor'easters that periodically lash the island. To get a handle on the volume of sand, imagine 25,000 people a day pulling red Radio Flyer wagons full of sand to Democrat Point and dumping them. In a year, they would add about 200 feet to the beach. Today the western tip of Fire Island overlaps the eastern end of another famous barrier island, Jones Beach. The channel between the two is kept open only by constant dredging.

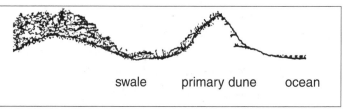

swale   primary dune   ocean

A cross-section of Fire Island shows the nine different ecosystems found on this narrow barrier beach.

In addition to moving westward by sand accretion, Fire Island also is creeping slowly northward toward Long Island. The ancestral island was once several miles farther out on the continental shelf. In a sense, the island is rolling over on itself as sand from the ocean side is gathered by wind and waves, blown or washed across the island or moved by currents and tides through inlets, and then deposited on the bay side.

Robert Moses State Park

In 1923 Robert Moses, then New York State parks commissioner, visited the small state park on Fire Island. His maps showed that the park occupied the western tip of the island, where a telegraph tower stood on an abandoned Coast Guard station. As he stood at the station, however, he realized that the natural forces of littoral drift had created pristine new ocean beach stretching for nearly four more miles. The original 200-acre park now covered an additional 600 acres. Moses envisioned a wonderful new park here, connected to Long Island by a causeway. It wasn't until the mid-1960s, however, that the causeway was built and the park was developed as a recreation area with bathhouses, refreshment stands, boardwalks, and parking lots for 5,000 cars.

Hours, Fees, and Facilities

Fire Island National Seashore is open all the time. Hours at the lighthouse visitor center vary seasonally; call for information. Robert Moses State Park is open daily from dawn to dusk. There are no fees at FINS; from Memorial Day to Labor Day, the entrance fee at Robert Moses is $4;

it is free the rest of the year. Restrooms, water, pay phones, and food are available at parking lot 5 in Robert Moses. Restrooms are available at the lighthouse, but the water there is not potable. No pets are allowed.

Getting There

From the Long Island Expressway, take exit 53 to the Sagtikos Parkway southbound; this road turns into the Robert Moses Causeway after crossing the Southern State Parkway. From the Southern State Parkway, take exit 41 directly onto the Robert Moses Causeway southbound. Follow the causeway for 4.2 miles until you arrive at the entrance to Robert Moses State Park. At the traffic circle, follow the signs for parking lot 5, another 0.5 mile. Walk toward the lighthouse from the lot. There is, at this writing, a disgraceful lack of public transportation to this site.

For More Information

Fire Island National Seashore
120 Laurel Street
Patchogue, NY 11772
516-289-4810

Fire Island Lighthouse
516-661-4876

Robert Moses State Park
Long Island State Park Region
Box 247
Babylon, NY 11701
516-669-0449

Westchester and Putnam Counties

Teatown Lake Reservation
Ossining

- **Lakeside Trail, 1.6 miles, about 1.5 hours, easy**
- **Hidden Valley Trail, 1.6 miles, about 1.5 to 2 hours, moderate**

An oasis of wildness amid suburban sprawl.

Located in the heart of Westchester County, Teatown Lake Reservation is a private, not-for-profit nature preserve and education center. The 190 acres surrounding Teatown Lake are the original portion of the reservation. This land was donated by the Gerard Swope family in 1963. Since then, the reservation has grown to 470 acres (not all of them contiguous) even as the surrounding area has become more densely covered with residential housing. An elegant Tudor-style former carriage barn at the main entrance has been converted for use as an education center and offices; there's also a very good nature shop.

Teatown Lake Reservation covers an interesting range of habitats. The lake is surrounded by mixed hardwood forests, hemlock and laurel groves, grassy mead-

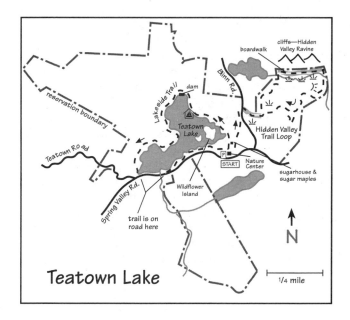

Teatown Lake

1/4 mile

N

ows, and wetlands. The rolling terrain offers some nice views from hilltops as well as some fairly dramatic ravines. The variety of habitats makes this a particularly good spot for bird-watching, especially in the spring. The checklist put out by volunteers lists 184 species.

For a very enjoyable stroll, try the walk around Teatown Lake. Because the lake is surrounded by deciduous trees, this walk is particularly enjoyable in the autumn. If you prefer bird-watching, try it in the spring. If you enjoy a walk that is a little more challenging, try exploring the rock cliffs on the Hidden Valley hike.

Lakeside Trail

The popular Lakeside Trail goes all the way around thirty-three-acre Teatown Lake. It is a pleasant walk with some lovely views. On a nice day, don't be surprised to find an artist or two working on a landscape along the shore. The walk begins from the parking lot near the nature center. The trail entrance is just to the left of a large notice board. The trail is very clear, flat, and well maintained; it is somewhat unnecessarily blazed in blue. From the trailhead, bear right to circumambulate the pond in a counterclockwise direction. The path leads downhill toward the lake. On your left you'll notice a small island with a small wooden structure on it; a bridge leads to the island. This is Wildflower Island, home to a cultivated garden of native wildflowers. The island is accessible from April through October only by guided tour (call for information).

The shoreline comes into view on your left in just a minute or two. After another ten minutes or so, you'll come to a rustic bench by a small beach area. There's a picnic shelter here and a boathouse where members can keep canoes. Look for masses of beautiful white waterlilies blossoming here in the summer. Follow the sign for the Lakeside Trail and bear to your left to continue—the path that leads off at the first right takes you onto the Hilltop Trail. The woods road at the second right is a short detour called Old Wagon Road; it brings you back out on the Lakeside Trail some 500 feet farther on. In a few more minutes you'll come to a T intersection with another trail. Turn left and walk across the dam that forms the northern end of Teatown Lake. (Ignore the trail on your right near the spillway.) Continue on the Lakeside Trail. Note the old stone walls and some ruined old foundations in the woods on your right. These are the remains of an old farm. The woods around you were cut down once to make open fields; the lake was dammed in the early 1900s to make a stock pond and for ice in the winter.

Continue to follow the path for another few minutes. At a gap in a stone wall, the trail forks. The blue-blazed trail leads off to the left and skirts quite close to the shore. In about fifteen minutes, you'll reach the southwestern tip of the lake and be very near the intersection of Teatown Road and Spring Valley Road. These are paved through-roads for the residential area surrounding the reservation. As of this writing, to continue the walk you will have to make a left onto Spring Valley Road and follow it for about 700 feet along the edge of the lake. (When sufficient funds have been raised, a boardwalk to complete the trail will be built.) The road is pretty quiet, but it is curvy—stay on the shoulder and keep an eye out for traffic. Arrows on your left indicate where the trail turns off the road and back into the woods again. Continue to follow the trail for another fifteen to twenty minutes. It is slightly rough here—you have to climb over a few rocks—but still easy. When you see Wildflower Island on your left, the parking lot where you began will be just ahead and to your right.

How did Teatown Lake get its name? Legend has it that after the Boston Tea Party of 1773, a tea merchant left New York City and set up here, selling tea to the local residents despite the boycott. A group of patriotic housewives cornered him and forced him to give up his tea, which they then destroyed. Did this really happen? Probably not, but it does make a good story. I think it is far more likely that Teatown is a corruption of an earlier

Dutch name, just as nearby Tarrytown is a mangled English version of Terwen Dorp, or Wheat Town.

Hidden Valley Trail

The Hidden Valley Trail takes you through a range of terrain, from open fields to wetlands to hemlock gorge. This trail also passes through some extensive mature forests of hardwoods and hemlocks. There are some small vernal ponds in the wetlands area where wood ducks breed. To start this trail from the parking lot, turn right and follow the path past the nature center. You will come almost immediately to a cluster of small outbuildings, including a functional sugar house. As you would expect, a number of sugar maple (*Acer saccharum*) trees grow nearby. Look for tall trees with gray bark that has distinctive vertical fluting. The leaves have five lobes and are about as long as they are wide. In the late winter, when the days are warming but the nights are cold, the sap runs in the sugar maples as they awaken from winter dormancy. With a sugar content that can range as high as 4 percent, the sap is quite sweet. The sugar house is where the buckets of sap were taken to be boiled down into syrup. (Maple syrup is still made at Teatown on a demonstration basis. Call for more information.)

Continue past the buildings. Look for red trail markers that lead you parallel to Blinn Road for a few minutes. You'll then have to cross Blinn Road to pick up the main part of the trail. This is a quiet street, but there is still traffic, so be careful here. Make a left onto the road and follow it for about twenty yards. Look in the woods on your right for the trailhead by a wooden fence and culvert with a stream. Enter the woods and follow the red-blazed

The sugar house at Teatown Lake Reservation is still used to boil sugar maple sap down to syrup.

trail to the right through a rocky area. Walk through a gap in an old stone fence and onto a boardwalk over a marshy area. Look along here for the sensitive fern (*Onoclea sensibilis*), a tall fern that generally reaches from 1 to 2.5 feet in height. In the summer, the fronds of this fern have green pinnae (the subdivisions of the blade, which is the leafy part of the frond) that are nearly opposite each other. In the fall and winter, distinctive rusty brown stalks with small, beadlike sori (spore cases) stand up. The short boardwalk takes you into a lovely open field full of wildflowers and butterflies. Look for the Hidden Valley sign after the boardwalk and follow the arrow to the left. The path becomes narrow and grassy. In a few minutes, a pine grove will come up on your right. In the winter, this is a good place to look for roosting owls; great horned owls, barred owls, and eastern screech owls are also not uncommon here. As the path continues, it turns to the right and brings you into Hidden Valley, **a hemlock-lined ravine with some dramatic rocky cliffs**. At this point the trail goes down over boulders for a short, sharp drop into the ravine. This is slightly difficult to negotiate, but there's a handrail to help you along. Follow the trail along the base of the cliff. A brook runs along the bottom of the ravine, creating a wetland area on your right. In about fifteen minutes, a boardwalk takes you over a marshy area. The trail turns to the right and starts to climb very steeply up out of the ravine; the brook rushes down the hillside at the side of the trail. Shortly after reaching the top of this short, steep section, you'll come to a nice viewpoint looking out to the east (although it's pretty much blocked by vegetation in the summer). Continue on the trail as it leads through a dense area of mountain laurels. When you emerge from here after about five minutes, the trail opens out. On your right is a swampy area of vernal ponds; on your left are dramatic rock outcroppings.

Continue on the trail for another fifteen minutes or so. Look for the red trail markers where the path bears left; follow it downhill for another fifteen minutes. Eventually you'll find yourself back at the grassy meadow you crossed at the start of this walk. Look for a huge old tree called the Mowers' Maple at this end of the meadow. When this field was cleared more than a century ago to become a pasture, the farmer left the maple to provide shade for animals grazing in the field and humans mowing the field for hay. Look near here for a sign pointing you back to Blinn Road. From the boardwalk, retrace your steps to return to the parking lot.

Hours, Fees, and Facilities

The trails at Teatown Lake Reservation are open daily from dawn to dusk. The nature center is open 9:00 A.M. to 5:00 P.M. Tuesday through Saturday and 1:00 P.M. to 5:00 P.M. on Sunday; it is closed Mondays and holidays. There are no fees, but a contribution of $2 per person is suggested. Restrooms, water, and pay phones are available at the nature center. Dogs are allowed on leashes only.

Getting There

From the Taconic State Parkway, exit at Rte. 134/Ossining. Go west on Rte. 134 to the second right (it comes up very quickly), which is Spring Valley Road. Follow Spring Valley Road for 1.0 mile to the reservation. Several smaller roads come off Spring Valley Road. Since this is a suburban residential area, street signs are few and far between. To stay on Spring Valley Road, bear left at all forks.

From Rte. 9A at the intersection with Rte. 134, turn east and follow Rte. 134 for 2.5 miles to Spring Valley Road. Turn left and follow directions as above.

For More Information

Teatown Lake Reservation
Spring Valley Road
Ossining, NY 10562
914-762-2912

Rockefeller State Park Preserve

Tarrytown

- **Swan Lake Trail, 1.3 miles, 1 hour, easy**
- **Pocantico River Trail, 2.6 miles, 3 hours, moderate**

A walk through beautiful woods on winding carriage roads.

The extensive network of trails that wind through Rockefeller State Park Preserve was developed originally by the Rockefeller family as carriage trails designed to capture all the beauty of the surrounding landscape. And beautiful it is. This quiet park covers 831 rolling, wooded acres; the small but lovely Pocantico River runs through it. The preserve, along with a generous endowment, was given to New York State by the Rockefeller family in 1983. You still can drive your horse-drawn carriage in the preserve. If you don't have one, you can watch others on some weekends in the spring, summer, and fall.

There are twenty miles of carriage paths at Rockefeller State Park Preserve. Many of the trails intersect, so it's easy to figure out a loop that's a good length for you. Some of the trails have a moderate grade, but most are flat; all are broad (to accommodate the carriages), very well maintained, and easy to follow. A short (0.9 mile) section of the Old Croton Aqueduct Trail runs north-

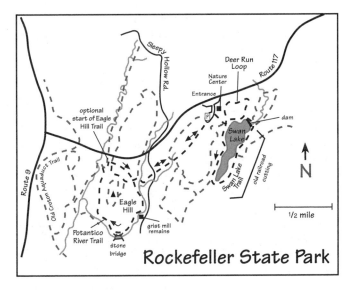

Rockefeller State Park

south through the westernmost part of the preserve (see below). As of this writing, the colored plastic disks that mark the trails are being replaced. You can pick up a very good free map at the nature center even when it's closed, so you shouldn't really notice the absence of markers.

Swan Lake Trail

The 1.3-mile walk around twenty-four-acre Swan Lake defines the word "stroll." It's flat, easy, and beautiful, and there's something about it that made me slow my normal walking pace down by about 20 percent. The lake was formerly a wetland that was dammed in the 1930s. Start your walk behind the beautiful new nature center and office buildings (opened in 1994). A short path leads in just a minute or two down past an information kiosk to the main path encircling the lake. It doesn't really matter which way you go—the lake is lined by lovely woods and wildflowers; ducks float peacefully on the water and birds, including many woodpeckers and warblers, flit through the trees. The dam is at the northern end of the lake. An old railroad cutting from the Putnam branch of the old New York Central runs along the eastern side. The tracks and ties were removed in the 1930s, but you can still see the cuts in the rocks. Pinkster flower (*Rhododendron nudiflorum*) flowers along here in May. This native shrub bears fragrant pink blossoms in profusion. A number of other wildflowers bloom around the lake in the spring, including hepatica (liverwort), rue anemone, and trout lily.

If you are strolling around Swan Lake early or late in the day, detour to Deer Run, a short (0.4 mile) loop path that starts near the information kiosk. You're almost guaranteed to see deer, especially in the early morning or at dusk.

The Pocantico River Trail

This walk begins on the Old Sleepy Hollow Road Trail at the western end of the parking area—look for the metal gate to the right of the nature center building. The path is an old colonial roadbed that continues for 0.4 mile through brush, wetlands, and woods. More than 170 bird species have been spotted in the preserve, and this path is a good place to look for them. Indigo buntings have been breeding near the parking lot, and a pair of great horned owls can sometimes be seen roosting in the distant willow trees on your right.

In about ten minutes you'll come to a turnoff for the Overlook Trail on your right. Ignore it and keep going straight ahead into the woods. In another few minutes you'll come to a gate and have to cross Old Sleepy Hollow Road. This is a real, though very quiet, road with blind curves. Be careful. The trail continues on the other side of the road and then soon crosses the Pocantico on a small bridge. Just past the bridge, there's a T intersection. Turn left here and follow the trail as it parallels the Pocantico. After about ten minutes you'll see that the river drops sharply. Look around on the banks here for the remains of the Karle gristmill that stood here in the late 1700s.

After another ten minutes or so you'll see a large field on your right. Look here for deer and wild turkeys. In another minute you'll come to a lovely stone bridge over the river on your left. If the bridge looks vaguely familiar to you, it's because George Page, longtime host of the PBS television show *Nature,* lives nearby. His segments of the show occasionally are filmed here. The bridge leads to private property—don't cross it. This is also Washington Irving (1783–1859) country. If you're well read, the bridge may remind you of how Ichabod Crane galloped across a bridge over the Pocantico in his flight from the headless horseman in "The Legend of Sleepy Hollow."

Continue to follow the trail along the river for another fifteen minutes or so. When you come to a Y intersection, turn right to stay on the Pocantico River Trail. Eagle Hill, a very **dramatic escarpment** studded with outcroppings of the bedrock Fordham gneiss, looms up on your right. Stay on the trail as it continues along the base of

A stone bridge over the Pocantico River at Rockefeller State Park Preserve. This bridge leads to private property.

the hill for another ten minutes or so. Don't turn off onto the dirt road that enters on your left. When the overpass for Rte. 117 comes into sight, turn right onto the Thirteen Bridges Trail. Stay on this trail for just a hundred yards or so.

If you're feeling energetic and would like to get a panoramic view from the top of Eagle Hill, take the trail that comes up on your right. It's a steep, 0.9-mile walk to the top, but you can see the Hudson and Kykuit (a former Rockefeller estate recently opened to the public), and more from the top. To return, backtrack to the main trail.

Thirteen Bridges Trail veers quickly off to the left. Go straight ahead to stay on the Pocantico River Trail. In another ten minutes or so you'll arrive at the Y intersection with the Old Sleepy Hollow Road Trail. Turn left and then quickly right to retrace your steps to the parking area.

The Old Croton Aqueduct Trail

In the 1830s, it became apparent that the water supply in New York City was hopelessly inadequate. A radical solution was proposed: an aqueduct that would bring large amounts of pure water from the Croton River in the wilds of Westchester County, north of the city. A massive undertaking that was one of the engineering marvels of its day, the Croton Aqueduct opened in 1842. It was a gravity-fed system that ran forty-one miles through masonry aqueducts, ending up at two reservoirs in Manhattan. One was in the Murray Hill area; today, it is Bryant Park behind the main branch of the New York Public Library. The other was in Central Park; it is now the Great Lawn. New York City grew so quickly that the original system was inadequate by the 1880s. A new, bigger dam was built on the Croton River, and construction began on the new aqueduct in 1885. The Old Croton Aqueduct gradually was shut down and dismantled; the last trickle of water went through in 1955. The **route of the aqueduct** still exists, however, as a thirty-three-mile walking corridor stretching from northern Westchester to Van Cortlandt Park in the Bronx. Most of the route of the Old Croton Aqueduct Trail is now through developed areas or areas that are somewhat run-down; most of the more rural parts are close to major through-roads. Some parts, such as the portion in the preserve, are still quite rural and pleasant, but even here you will hear traffic noise from Rte. 9. For an informative booklet about the Old Croton Aqueduct Trail, write to the Taconic Division of the New York State Office of Parks, Recreation, and Historic Preservation. For maps and detailed information about walking the trail, see *The New York Walk Book.*

Hours, Fees, and Facilities

The preserve is open daily from 9:00 A.M. to dusk. There are no fees, but you do need a permit to drive your carriage. Restrooms, water, and pay phones are available at the charming nature center building. Dogs are allowed only on leashes.

Getting There

Rockefeller State Park Preserve can be approached in three different ways. If you take the New York State Thruway (I-87), get off at exit 9 and go north on Rte. 9 for 4.0 miles to Rte. 117. Turn right (east) on Rte. 117 and follow it for 1.3 miles. The well-marked entrance to the preserve is on the right. From the Saw Mill River Parkway or the Taconic State Parkway, take the exit for Rte. 117 westbound. Because the preserve can be entered only from the eastbound side of this divided highway, follow Rte. 117 for 3.3 miles until it intersects with Rte. 9, reverse direction, and follow Rte. 117 back for 1.3 miles to the entrance.

For More Information

Rockefeller State Park Preserve
Box 338
Tarrytown, NY 10591
914-631-1470

Croton Point Park
Croton-on-Hudson, Westchester County

- **about 2 miles**
- **about 2 hours**
- **easy**

A walk past a former garbage dump transformed into a haven for wildlife.

When considering sites to include in this book, I selected those that are managed entirely or mostly as natural areas. Croton Point Park is the exception. Even though this site is managed primarily for recreation, it is well worth a visit to enjoy the views out over the Tappan Zee and to see what Westchester County has done with a polluting eyesore of a dump. Once a shameful desecration of the Hudson's shores, the dump today is a model of ecological restoration.

Croton Point Park is built on a rocky, diamond-shaped peninsula that juts out from the eastern bank of the Hudson River right next to the large Croton-Harmon railroad station. Croton Point was formed millennia ago as glacial streams deposited a delta made of layers of sand and gravel into what was then glacial Lake Hudson. After the retreat of the Wisconsin glacier some 12,000 years ago, Lake Hudson became a river; the glacial streams consolidated here to become the Croton River.

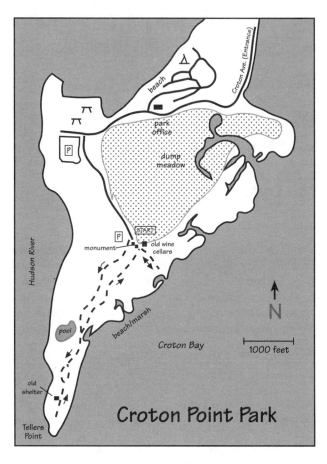

In the late 1830s, work had begun to dam the Croton River and provide pure water to New York City via an impressive forty-one-mile aqueduct (see page 183). By the 1880s, the system was inadequate. A new, larger dam was built below the first. A huge reservoir, large enough to cover the old dam, is still an integral part of the city's water system. With the Croton River much reduced, and with the peninsula cut off from the mainland by the New York Central railroad tracks, it was perhaps inevitable that a large, marshy tidal cove on the south side of Croton Point would become a municipal landfill. Starting in 1926, this is indeed what happened. Simultaneously, the area was used as a county park, which meant that you had to go past what was jocularly called "Dump Mountain" to get to the beach and recreation areas. Despite this, people actually swam in the Hudson here and the area remained a good one for fishing, although people were warned not to eat any fish they caught.

The landfill finally was closed in 1986 after a garbage-to-electricity incinerator was opened in nearby Peekskill. By that point, 10.4 million cubic yards of garbage were on the 200-acre site—enough to fill nearly five World Trade Center towers. To keep toxic wastes from leaching out of the landfill and into the river, the dump had to be sealed and capped. Westchester County, under pressure from the many conservation groups that are watchdogs over the Hudson River valley, decided to take the capping an extra step and convert the former dump into a **wildlife-attracting meadow**. Starting in 1992, the park was closed to the public. Layers of plastic, fabric, and soil were placed over the garbage. A network of 113 wells was installed to collect the 1 million cubic feet of methane gas given off every day by the decomposing garbage. (The gas will be used eventually to generate electricity to power lights and other equipment at the park.) The top of the soil-covered mound was then seeded with more than 1,000 pounds of wildflower mix; the sides of the mound received 1,000 pounds of a scrubbier mix of wild broccoli, dwarf corn, wheat, rye, and such other grassy plants as alfalfa, red clover, and tufted vetch. In June of 1995, the park was reopened. Instead of a festering mountain of garbage, visitors to the park now see a large, vegetation-covered mound. Insects, butterflies, birds, and other wildlife quickly found the area and began to enjoy its food and shelter. Look for monarch butterflies, red-winged blackbirds, phoebes and other flycatchers, ospreys, crows, and gulls. As the meadow matures, other birds of the open fields will find their way here. Look for bluebirds, killdeer, many sparrow species (especially white-throated, chipping, and song), kestrels, meadowlarks, and mourning doves in years to come.

The former garbage dump at Croton Point Park has been converted to a wildlife-attracting meadow.

The former dump at Croton Point Park comes into view as you drive into the park past the entrance booth. To get a good view of it, look to your left as you continue 0.7 mile on the park road past the park office to the main parking area. If you wish, park here (the entire area is built on landfill) for a closer look at the garbage mound. On the river side of the parking lot is a beach area good for fishing, birding, and scenery. You can also swim from another nearby beach. To get to the dump, walk across the park road and go onto the gravel walkway that circles the base. You can easily see the protruding white pipes of the gas wells here and there on the mound. They must be working, because there is no odor.

Croton Point Park is worth visiting just to see this amazing transformation, but the park has other attractions as well. To see them, begin by driving on another half-mile to a small parking area on the right, near the RV camping area. Leave your car here and take an enjoyable stroll to Tellers Point at the very tip of the Croton Point peninsula. Continue on foot on the main park road. Right by the sign saying Authorized Vehicles Only, look for a monument commemorating a peace treaty signed in 1645 between the Mohegan Indians and the Dutch settlers. Continue on the paved road, walking past the RV camping area. You can catch glimpses of the river on both sides of you from here. After about ten minutes, you'll see a swimming pool complex on your left. You'll soon enter an open area of scattered cabins around a large field. This is Camp Echo, a family camping area that is deserted except in the summer. Walk straight ahead through the camp area on the paved road for about five minutes. At the far end, the road becomes dirt. Follow it for a few more minutes to its end at a dilapidated brick camping shelter. Look for a short, steep, heavily eroded dirt path directly opposite the shelter. Go down the path carefully, avoiding the poison ivy. You'll emerge onto a rocky, triangular beach with a fabulous, **unimpeded view of the Tappan Zee**. The name for this section of the river comes from the Tappans, a Lenape Native American group that lived here, and the Dutch word for sea. The river broadens out so much here because the underlying rock consists of soft shale, sandstone, and arkose (a type of sedimentary rock that is mostly feldspar) dating back to the Triassic period, 225 million to 190 million years ago. This easily eroded rock has been worn away by the water to make a broad "sea" that stretches some eighteen miles between Dobbs Ferry in the south and Stony Point in the north. On average, this part of the river is three miles wide.

Looking south, you get a good view of the Tappan Zee Bridge leading to Rockland County. Directly across the river is the northern section of the Palisades; the high mountain to the right is Hook Mountain. Looking out at the river from here, you might spot an osprey snatching a fish from the water. You might even see a bald eagle. In the fall, this is a good location for spotting migrating hawks. From November through March, look for loons, grebes, geese, and rafts of ducks floating on the water.

To return, scramble back up the path to the camping shelter and retrace your steps through Camp Echo back to the paved road. Look for a road sign that points vehicles to the exit. At the sign, turn right onto a graveled road that leads down toward the water. Follow this open, sunny road as it leads along past phragmites, meadows, and scrubby woods at the river's edge on your right. In about ten minutes you will arrive at a brick house that is a private residence. Turn right here and follow the dirt road down through the marsh (look for a side path on the left that takes you to some old wine cellars dating back to the late 1800s). Another five minutes' walk brings you to a sandy beach on the edge of South Cove. Explore the beach and some of the side paths here. Although this spot can be pretty buggy in the summer, it's a good place for birding. You should spot yellow-rumped warblers easily here in the spring.

After enjoying the beach area, return by retracing your steps to the brick house. Notice how the dump mound looms over the house. Continue straight ahead, with the dump on your right, for just a few minutes to arrive back at your car.

Hours, Fees, and Facilities

Croton Point Park is open daily from dawn to dusk. The entrance/parking fee is $6; $2.50 for Westchester County residents with park passes. Seniors pay $.75 Monday through Friday. Restrooms, pay phones, picnic areas, a seasonal refreshment stand, and a bathhouse are found near the main parking area. Tent camping, RV parking, and cabins are available for a fee; reservations are required. Pets are allowed only on leashes.

Getting There

From the Saw Mill River Parkway, take exit 25 for Hawthorn and Rte. 9A. Turn left (north) onto Rte. 9A and follow it for 10.0 miles to the Croton Point Avenue exit. Turn left and follow Croton Point Avenue for 0.1 mile to a narrow, one-lane bridge leading over the MetroNorth tracks. You enter the park almost immediately on the other side of the bridge.

Although all MetroNorth trains stop at the Croton-Harmon station, it would be dangerous to attempt to walk to the park. The Westchester County BEE-LINE bus system stops at the park.

For More Information
Croton Point Park
Croton Point Avenue
Croton-on-Hudson, NY 10520
914-271-3293

Brinton Brook Sanctuary
Croton

- **about 2 miles**
- **about 1.5 hours**
- **easy**

Farm roads and trails through a peaceful wildlife sanctuary.

In the early 1900s, Willard and Laura Brinton purchased 112 acres of old farmland and woods in what was then rural Westchester. In 1957, after the death of her husband, Laura Brinton deeded the land to the National Audubon Society as a permanent wildlife refuge. After Mrs. Brinton died in 1975, another 17 acres were added to the refuge by Mr. Brinton's niece, Ruth Brinton Perera. In all, then, Brinton Brook Sanctuary, now managed for the National Audubon Society by the local Saw Mill River Audubon Society, contains 129 acres and a variety of habitats, including a pond, meadows, swamps, woodlands, and rocky slopes. The land was a working farm from around 1865 to around 1900; many traces of the old farm still remain.

Four marked trails covering a total of three miles wind through Brinton Brook Sanctuary. The half-mile Laurel Rock Trail in the southeastern portion of the sanctuary is fairly rugged, although it's quite pretty when the mountain laurel is blooming in the spring. For this walk we'll stick to portions of the other three trails. This is a

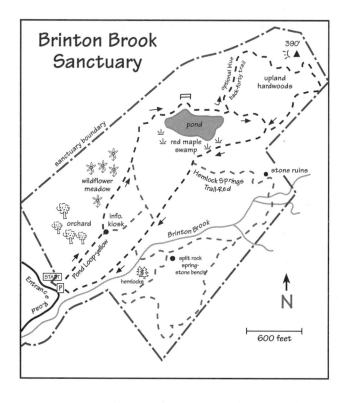

Brinton Brook Sanctuary

390'

optional blue back-forty trail

upland hardwoods

pond

red maple swamp

sanctuary boundary

stone ruins

wildflower meadow

Hemlock Springs Trail-Red

info. kiosk

orchard

Brinton Brook

Pond Loop-yellow

START

Entrance Peo-R

split rock spring-stone bench

hemlocks

N

600 feet

very private place—I have yet to see another car in the lot or meet anyone else on the trail (on the other hand, one major advantage of being a writer is that I get to go to these places on weekdays). The Saw Mill River Audubon Society does conduct group activities here, including birding walks and an annual butterfly count in July. Parking is limited, so if you're planning to come on a spring weekend or if you'd like to bring a group, call ahead.

From the parking lot, look on your left for a trailhead blocked by a metal cable strung low between posts. Step over the cable onto the Pond Loop Trail, blazed in yellow. (The trail markers at Brinton Brook are a mixture of paint blazes and plastic disks. They're sometimes a bit faded, but the trails are very obvious.) Follow the trail as it goes through a grassy meadow. You'll come quickly to a kiosk with a large map of the sanctuary and some other information. You can pick up a free trail map here. Follow the trail onward through another beautiful field (look for metal posts with plain wooden number signs on them) and the remnants of an old apple orchard. This area was probably a pasture when the land was a farm. Today, it is a **meadow filled with wildflowers**, including such numerous composite flowers as butterfly weed, ironweed, yarrow, boneset, and joe-pye weed. These flat-topped, nectar-filled flowers make this a good spot to look for butterflies in the summer. To keep the fields open, the Saw Mill River Audubon Society mows them every few years. If they didn't, such sun-loving weedy trees as flame sumac, honey locust, chokecherry, white birch, and eastern white pine gradually would start to take over. Over a period of decades, larger hardwoods such as hickories and oaks would also start to grow here. Eventually they would shade out the scrubbier growth and the land would start to look much more as it did before it was cleared for farming. This, in fact, is exactly what has happened elsewhere in the sanctuary, as we'll soon see.

Continuing along the path for another few minutes, a swampy area filled with red maple (*Acer rubrum*) trees will appear on your right. Also called swamp maple, red maple is a sure sign of a cool, moist area with a high water table. You'll soon see a lovely, five-acre pond. Like most ponds in Westchester, this one was created artificially. As you skirt along the edge, you'll pass over a stone-and-earth dam just before you reach the intersection with the blue-blazed Back Forty Trail. The dam probably was built by the original farmer as a stock pond for the animals in the pasture; he may also have harvested ice from it in the winter. A bench has been placed very thoughtfully along the pond's northern edge in an ideal spot for birding in the spring. Herons and other wading birds feed in the shallows on the abundant fish and frogs. Flycatchers and warblers are also common in the woods and underbrush surrounding the pond, and you might spot an indigo bunting.

The Pond Loop forms a T intersection with the Back Forty Trail just past the dam. Make a left onto the blue-blazed Back Forty Trail and follow it as it takes you on a half-mile loop through a hilly area of **upland hardwoods**. Black birch, hickory, and oak are the dominant tree species here. The trail reaches an elevation of 390 feet near where it adjoins a Con Edison power line right of way. You can see the Hudson and the Bear Mountain Bridge from here.

The Back Forty Trail brings you out onto the yellow-blazed Pond Loop again, only about 400 feet to the east of where you left it. (If you want to skip the Back Forty portion—it is a bit hilly and might be difficult for children—just stay on the Pond Loop.) Turn left. This portion of the Pond Loop is an old farm road. Notice how it is somewhat sunken, broad, and lined by old stone walls on both sides. The stone walls tell us that the land here was once cleared for fields. Now, some hundred years later, mixed deciduous trees grow here instead. Forest animals such as deer, raccoons, possums, and ruffed grouse are common again. Were it not for the traces left behind, it would be hard to tell that a farm was ever here.

After about ten minutes on the old road, you'll come to another T intersection, this time with the red-blazed Hemlock Springs Trail. Turn left onto this trail. In less than ten minutes you'll come to some overgrown old stone foundations—all that's left of the house and outbuildings of the farm. This is a good place to wander around a bit, tracing out the arrangement of the old buildings. Look for a branch of Brinton Brook and an interesting balanced rock formation in the woods nearby.

Continue on the Hemlock Springs Trail (ignore the turnoff to one end of the Laurel Rock trail on your left after a few minutes). Brinton Brook flows along roughly parallel to the path. It can be wet here in the spring, but conveniently placed steppingstones take you over the worst spots. After about fifteen minutes, you'll come to a lovely little spot called Split Rock Spring. Willard Brinton improved on nature a bit here by diverting some of the natural flow of the spring into piping that leads out from a beautiful rock formation. He also built a charming stone bench that makes a pleasant place to sit and take a breather. If you're visiting in the spring or early summer, relax here for a few minutes and listen for the beautiful, flutelike *ee-o-lay* song of the wood thrush (*Hylocichla mustelina*), which abounds here. Look in the undergrowth and low tree branches for a rusty-headed bird slightly smaller than a robin, with strong pink legs and distinct dark spots on a white breast.

This delightful stone bench at Split Rock Spring in the Brinton Brook Sanctuary was built decades ago by the original owner, Willard Brinton.

The other end of the Laurel Rock Trail branches off to the left just past Split Rock Spring. Stay on the Hemlock Springs Trail and follow it into a thick grove of hemlock trees. These trees unfortunately are infested with the wooly adelgid, an insect that has attacked many hemlocks in the region, and many appear to be in poor condition or even dead. Once past this depressing sight, the Hemlock Springs Trail soon rejoins the Pond Loop. Turn left and follow the grassy Pond Loop along a sunny, south-facing slope. You'll arrive back at the parking lot in about ten minutes.

Hours, Fees, and Facilities

Brinton Brook Sanctuary is open daily from dawn to dusk. There is no fee. There are no facilities. No pets are allowed.

Getting There

Heading north on Rte. 9 from Croton-on-Hudson, exit at Senasqua Road. Turn left (north) onto Senasqua Road and follow it for 0.9 mile. You'll pass the Sky View nursing home on your left. After another 0.3 mile you'll see a discreet wooden sign on the right with some family names and the abbreviation SMRAS. Make a sharp right here just past the stone wall. Follow the narrow road 0.3 mile to the small dirt parking lot. Please note that private residences share the road. In the unlikely event that the lot is full, don't park anywhere else—come back another time instead.

For More Information

Saw Mill River Audubon Society, Inc.
275 Millwood Road
Chappaqua, NY 10514
914-666-6503

Cranberry Lake Natural Environment Park

Valhalla

- **1 mile**
- **about 1 hour**
- **easy**

An easy walk through woodlands and a bog.

The name of this gem of a park is a bit misleading. There is indeed a cranberry bog near the lake, but you can't really get to it. Nonetheless, a visit to Cranberry Lake Natural Environment Park takes you through some varied and very pretty terrain. The park itself covers only 142 acres, but right next door to the east is the Kensico Reservoir, which is part of the New York City watershed. To the south and west, the park is bordered by the White Plains watershed. Nearby are Rye Lake and Silver Lake Preserve, part of the Westchester County park system. With so much other undeveloped land around it, Cranberry Lake is very quiet and seems considerably larger than it really is. For a park so close to residential and business areas, there is surprisingly little—almost no—traffic noise.

This walk will take you to Cranberry Lake, around the bog at its southern end, and back along the other side of the lake. It's easy walking on clearly marked trails with lots to see—ideal for kids.

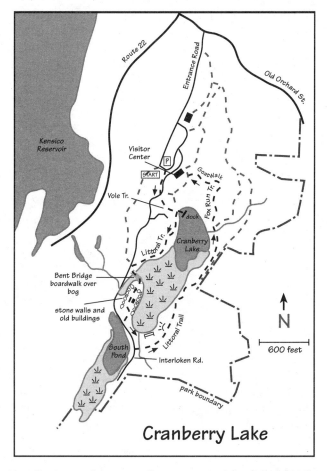

Cranberry Lake

Begin at the very pleasant visitor center near the parking lot. Look for the yellow-blazed trail to the right, leading off into the woods. After just a couple of minutes, turn left onto the white-blazed trail, also whimsically called the Vole Trail. If you're visiting near dusk, look around here for the meadow vole, or field mouse, a small nocturnal rodent found in grasslands, open woods, and forest edges. About 3.5 to 5 inches long, with a tail that is another 1.5 to 2.5 inches long, meadow voles are brown on top and gray below. You might easily confuse the meadow vole with the deer mouse, another small rodent common in this habitat. Deer mice have similar coloring, but they are somewhat larger, with much longer tails that are between 2 and 5 inches long. What's the difference between a vole and a mouse? Not much, if you're a predator such as a fox, coyote, or owl. To a naturalist, however, the differences are clear. Voles and their close relatives lemmings are stocky and rounded; there is little distinction between their bodies and their heads. Mice have similar bodies, but their heads are more defined. Voles have small, beady eyes; mice have larger, rounder eyes. Voles have small, rounded ears almost hidden in the fur on their heads; mice ears are much more visible. Vole tails are relatively short; mice have proportionately longer tails.

Follow the Vole Trail downhill for another few minutes to a boardwalk, which leads to a dock projecting out into ten-acre Cranberry Lake. Rare for this part of the world, Cranberry Lake is a natural formation. It is a **glacial scour**, created some 20,000 or more years ago when the last glacier scooped out a deep, steep-sided depression as it advanced. A smallish body of water with little or no natural drainage creates the ideal situation for a bog to develop—and from here, you can look across the lake and see how it gives way to a large bog at the southern end. In fact, the bog is somewhat larger that the lake itself.

After enjoying the sights from the dock, backtrack along the boardwalk and look for the blue blazes of the Littoral Trail that circles the lake. Turn left. The trail skirts along the edge of the lake for a bit and then heads uphill and runs along a wooded ridge overlooking the lake. The views looking out from here are quite nice. Notice the many large, gray boulders scattered about here and throughout the park. The same glacier that formed the lake dropped these huge rocks here as it retreated some 12,000 years ago.

Continue following the blue trail for another ten minutes or so. As you look out to your left, you'll see that the open water of the lake is giving way to the thick

A beautiful little cascade runs down from the woods at Cranberry Lake. Nearby benches make this a great spot for lunch.

vegetation of the bog. In a few more minutes the blue-blazed trail joins the red- and yellow-blazed trails—all three run together for a bit. Turn left and then left again to go onto Bent Bridge, a long boardwalk that takes you across a portion of the bog. Pause along here to get a close look at the characteristic vegetation.

Once you've crossed the Bent Bridge, stay on the trail as it passes some old foundations on the left. These may be the remains of an old root cellar. You'll see also some old stone fences. In a few more minutes you'll arrive at Interlaken Road. Turn left and follow this dirt road. There are some nice views out over South Pond to your right. After just a couple of minutes, look on your left for the resumption of the blue-blazed trail. There's a charming little cascade in a shady glen right here. The split-log benches here are a good spot to take a rest.

As you continue on, a blue sign points you to the left to an overlook. Follow the trail for about twenty yards, then follow the blue arrow to your right to a junction with the red-blazed trail known as the Long Way. Follow the red blazes for another minute to reach the overlook on your left. (If you miss the red blazes, don't worry— just stay on the blue-blazed trail.) The elevation here is 437 feet—you get a very nice view out over the lake and bog. Contrast the low-lying bog vegetation with the upland woods you are in now.

Continue on the red-blazed trail downhill for another two minutes. Cross a small boardwalk over a wet area and continue for just another minute. You'll meet up again with the blue-blazed trail here. Follow it as it leads down to the lake level through a grove of beeches and over a small wooden bridge. Ignore the yellow-blazed trail known as Deer Run that branches off to your right just after the bridge. After another twenty yards or so, look for the orange-blazed trail known as Fox Run and make a right onto it. Follow Fox Run for another few minutes, until you come to Goat Walk on your left—this white-blazed path is between two upright log segments and leads directly back to the visitor center in just a few more minutes.

Bog Plants

The water in a bog is generally cold, still, oxygen-poor and acidic. One of the few plants that thrives in this environment is sphagnum moss (*Sphagnum capillaceum*). Look for a pale green moss with branching stems and pointed leaves; it grows to a height of about 1.5 inches. Because the water is so cold and has so little oxygen, the dead undergrowth of the moss doesn't decay. Instead, it forms thick rafts of organic debris. And because dead sphagnum moss can absorb up to a hundred times its weight in water, the debris forms hummocks that stick up from the water and become a support for other plants. From Bent Bridge, you can easily see several common **bog plants**.

Leatherleaf (*Chamaedaphne calyculata*) is an evergreen, shrubby plant that grows to about four feet high. Its leathery, alternate leaves are oblong and yellowish underneath. From March to July, it flowers with numerous white, bell-like blossoms that hang down from the tips of the upper branches. Later the flowers form small, upturned cups called rattleboxes because the seeds rattle around inside them. Bog rosemary (*Andromeda glaucophylla*) is another leathery, evergreen shrub. Its narrow, toothless, alternate leaves are dark green above and whitish underneath. Bog rosemary grows to about three feet tall. From May through July, it flowers with small white or pink blossoms. Later, reddish brown seed capsules appear. The seeds are a valuable wildlife food. Bog rosemary is not related to the common culinary herb; it gets its name from a superficial resemblance of the leaves. You wouldn't want to eat this plant—it has evolved an effective chemical defense against attack. The leaves contain a very bitter, poisonous substance that makes them very unattractive to insects and wildlife.

Swamp loosestrife (*Decodon verticillatus*) is another shrubby bog plant. It is deciduous and can grow as high as eight feet tall. It's very easy to identify: the lance-shaped leaves grow in threes up the arching stem. In July and August, tufted, deep-pink blossoms appear in the upper leaf axils, where the leaf joins the stem. Purple loosestrife (*Lythrum salicaria*) is a different plant altogether. This European invader bears spikes of vivid purple flowers. More a swamp plant, purple loosestrife is a fast-growing pest that takes over pastures and crowds out native wetlands plants, yet provides little of value to birds or wildlife.

Wild cranberry (*Vaccinium oxycoccus*) grows at Cranberry Lake as well, of course, but it tends to be deep in the bog where you can't see it. If you do spot a delicate, creeping vine, look for smooth, alternate, dark-green glossy leaves. Wild cranberry blossoms from June to August with clusters of pink, bell-like flowers at the tips of the stems. In the autumn, bright red berries form. Wild cranberries are only about two-thirds the size of the familiar Thanksgiving cranberry, a different species that is harvested commercially in managed bogs.

Hours, Fees, and Facilities

Cranberry Lake Natural Environment Park is open from 9:00 A.M. to 5:00 P.M. Wednesday through Sunday. There is no fee. Restrooms, water, and picnic tables are at the visitor center. No dogs are allowed.

Getting There

Take the Bronx River Parkway just past exit 27; look for the yellow signs for Rte. 22. Head north on Rte. 22 (also called Mount Kisco Road) for 1.3 miles (you'll get a glimpse of the Kensico Dam on your left) to Old Orchard Street. Turn right and follow Old Orchard Street 200 feet to the park entrance on the right. Follow the park road for 0.3 mile to the parking area. Drive carefully on the Bronx River Parkway—this narrow, winding road has some unexpected traffic lights, and many motorists ignore the posted speed limit.

On Sundays in the late spring and summer the Bronx River Parkway is closed to cars so bike riders may enjoy the scenic road. Instead, take the Cross Westchester Expressway (Rte. 287) to the intersection with Rte. 22 (also called Broadway) in White Plains. Follow Rte. 22 north about 2 miles to the intersection with the Bronx River Parkway and follow directions as above.

For More Information

Cranberry Lake Natural Environment Park
Old Orchard Street
North White Plains, NY 10603
914-428-1005

Ward Pound
Ridge Reservation
Cross River

- **3.3 miles**
- **2 hours**
- **moderate**

A walk through the woods to a cave and a view.

The largest and oldest park in Westchester County, Ward Pound Ridge Reservation covers 4,700 acres of beautiful rolling countryside—nearly six square miles. The land that is now the park was once thirty-two different farms. In 1925, the newly formed Westchester Parks Commission purchased the farms and set the land aside as a nature sanctuary and as a recreational and educational area. The original name of the area was Pound Ridge, so called because the Indians who once lived here were said to conduct hunting drives that forced the deer up against a high, long ridge—impounding them. The Ward part was added in 1938 in honor of William Ward, a leader among the reservation's founders.

If you can, visit this park on a day when the Trailside Nature Museum is open—especially if you have kids with you. This small but excellent nature center has interesting displays of the natural history and Native American heritage of the park. The museum also houses the Delaware Indian Resource Center. Outside the museum

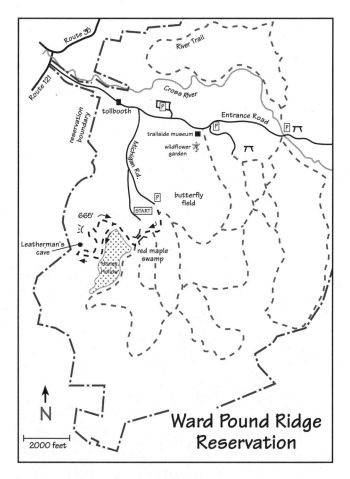

Ward Pound Ridge Reservation

2000 feet

is the half-acre Luquer-Marble Memorial Wildflower Garden. It contains more than 100 species of labeled wildflowers.

The terrain at Ward Pound Ridge is extremely varied, ranging from deep hollows to ridges that rise up more than 800 feet. There are hemlock gorges, dry uplands, wetlands, ponds, and two rivers, all connected by thirty-five miles of trails. Many of the old farm roads are now used as hiking and cross-country skiing trails.

There are so many trails and places of interest in Ward Pound Ridge Reservation that it's sometimes hard to decide which way to go. In the spring, the wildflowers along the white-blazed River Trail near the Kimberly Bridge picnic area are truly spectacular. For a good all-season walk that combines historic and scenic interest, though, I think my first choice would have to be the trail to the Leatherman's Cave. (See below for more about the Leatherman.)

The Leatherman's Cave at Ward Pound Ridge Reservation is really more a rock shelter. It doesn't extend back much beyond what is visible here.

This walk begins in the parking area at the end of Michigan Road, the first right after driving through the tollbooth. If you're interested in **butterflies**, however, you may never get started. Ward Pound Ridge Reservation is famous among butterfly-watchers as one of the best places in the entire New York metro region, and the area around this parking lot is one of the best places within the park. The field full of milkweed and dogbane near the eastern end of the parking lot is particularly productive, especially in late June and July. Many hairstreak and skipper species can be spotted then, along with a number of other species.

To start your walk to the Leatherman's Cave, look to the right of the parking circle for two white posts connected by a cable; there's also a sign for the Boone Trail. Walk past the posts and bear to the right when the trail forks almost at once. Look for the red and green metal arrows that indicate the red/green cross-country-ski trail. As you walk along, the trail becomes a short, elevated causeway that takes you through a small red maple swamp with dry feet. (This useful piece of trail building was done in 1933 by Civilian Conservation Corps [CCC] workers. The CCC also built the lean-to camping shelters and picnic areas.) After the causeway, the trail starts to head uphill through woodlands in a few minutes. Take the right fork here to stay on the red/green ski trail; when the trail forks again just a little way up the hill, stay on the left.

The trail soon levels off. You'll see a smaller, unblazed trail leading off uphill to your left—ignore it and stay on the red/green trail. Keep an eye out now for white-painted square blazes. When the trail starts heading downhill again, look for a double white blaze and a wooden sign for the Leatherman's Cave. Turn right here, leaving the red/green trail. Follow the white blazes for the next twelve minutes or so as the path climbs up a short, steep hill and then winds back and forth a bit. Look again for double white blazes. Turn left onto a narrow path that goes steeply downhill. This path leads you down and through Honey Hollow, so called because a local farmer kept bees there a hundred years ago. Many reminders of the old farms are still here in the form of old stone walls, foundations, and cellar pits.

In about ten minutes you'll come to a large trail. Turn right here and follow the trail as it descends a small hill, paralleled by an old stone wall. After you go down a small hill, look for a white arrow and sign pointing you uphill through a gap in the stone wall to the Leatherman's Cave and Overlook. Follow the trail for about thirty feet to a fork. Take the left fork and climb a short distance up the steep hill. Look for a massive boulder on your right at the base of a towering ridge. The Leatherman's Cave—really more of a shelter formed by an overhang among the jumbled rocks—is beneath the boulder.

From the Leatherman's Cave, backtrack to the fork. Take the right fork this time and follow the white blazes. The trail starts out along the base of the ridge and then turns left to take you up to the overlook, a short, steep climb that zigzags a bit toward the end. It only takes about ten minutes, however, to arrive at **spectacular views** from an elevation of 665 feet. To your left is the valley, to your right is the Cross River Reservoir, built in 1905 as part of the New York City water system. On a clear day, you can see right across the Hudson River.

A typical rock formation at Ward Pound Ridge Reservation. The stone slabs are made of granitic gneiss; water freezing and expanding in the cracks causes the rock to fracture into blocks.

To start the return walk, follow the white blazes straight ahead. The trail soon bends away to the right in a wide arc, descends into a small dip, and then curves to the left. In another few minutes you'll come to a large intersection marked with a white arrow. Follow the arrow and turn right here. You'll come to the Honey Hollow path in another few minutes. Turn onto the path and retrace your steps back to the trailhead.

Who Was the Leatherman?

From about 1858 to his death in 1889, a mysterious but gentle wanderer, dressed entirely in heavy leather garments of his own making, was a familiar sight to people living in upper Westchester and Connecticut between the Hudson and Connecticut Rivers. The Leatherman, as he was called, walked continuously on a never varying circuit, covering exactly 365 miles in exactly thirty-four days. Much speculation surrounded the Leatherman. No one knew his age or where he had come from. The Leatherman rarely spoke—perhaps because he couldn't speak English—and communicated by crude sign language. He seemed illiterate but carried a French Bible, leading many to believe he was from France or perhaps Quebec. Because he was harmless and so predictable in his appearances, people left food out for him or invited him in to eat. Although he accepted the food, the Leatherman would never sleep indoors. Instead, he traveled from one rock shelter or cave to another, never staying more than a night. The Leatherman's Cave in Ward Pound Ridge Reservation is one of the places the Leatherman was known to visit. In his day, the view looking south out from the cave would have been over fields and pastures, not the woodlands that have grown up since then.

Hours, Fees, and Facilities

Ward Pound Ridge Reservation is open daily from 9:00 A.M. to dusk. The park office is open daily from 9:00 A.M. to noon and from 1:00 P.M. to 5:00 P.M. The Trailside Nature Museum is open Wednesday to Sunday, 9:00 A.M.

to 5:00 P.M. The entrance fee is $6 per car. Restrooms and water are available at the park entrance, at the Meadow picnic area, the Kimberly Bridge picnic area, and the Trailside Nature Museum. Dogs are allowed on leashes only.

Getting There

Take NY Rte. 686 to exit 6 (Cross River/Katonah/Rte. 35). At the exit turn east onto Rte. 35 and follow it for 4.1 miles to Rte. 121. Turn right (south) onto Rte. 121 and follow it for 0.2 mile. Look for the reservation entrance on the left just over the bridge. Follow the park road for 0.7 mile to the tollbooth. The Trailside Nature Museum is another 0.8 mile on the park road.

For More Information

Ward Pound Ridge Reservation
Box 461
Cross River, NY 10518
914-763-3493

Trailside Nature Museum
914-763-3993

Marshlands Conservancy
Rye

- **1.5 miles**
- **1.5 hours**
- **easy**

An outstanding saltwater marsh on the Long Island Sound.

Public access to the Long Island Sound in Westchester County and Connecticut is restricted mostly to a few small recreation beaches. The Marshlands Conservancy offers the rare opportunity to get down to the natural shoreline. This enjoyable Westchester County park contains 143 acres of mixed terrain, including woodlands, a meadow, and a pond, but the real attraction is the extensive salt marsh on the Sound. Unspoiled in itself despite surrounding development and heavy recreational boating in Milton Harbor, the Marshlands Conservancy is a great place to observe the dynamics of life in a salt marsh. If at all possible, try to time your visit to coincide with low tide (call the park). The park is also one of the most productive sites in all Westchester for bird-watching: more than 230 species have been seen here.

To get to the salt marsh, start at the trail near the picnic tables to the right of the shelter building (look for a metal 3 on a fence post). Follow the roped wood-chip trail into the woods. After a few minutes the trail turns right and crosses a small wooden bridge to come out on

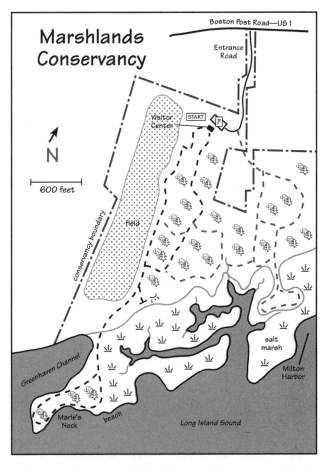

the edge of a long, narrow field. A wide, mowed path runs along the length of the field. A century ago this was a wheat field; during World War II it was an airstrip.

Since then, the field has been allowed to grow naturally into an **extensive meadow**. To keep the field from reverting back to woodlands, it is mowed every year to cut off seedlings of such invasive trees as black cherry, locust, and sumac. The field is full of wildflowers and grasses, including thistles, orange butterfly weed (rare for the area), goldenrod, sunflowers, milkweed, boneset, and many others. Naturally, there are a lot of butterflies here—where there are wildflowers and open fields, there are butterflies. This is great spot for seeing monarchs, American ladies, painted ladies, and common buckeyes.

The trail takes you along the edge of the meadow for another ten or twelve minutes. When the trail forks, bear left into the woods onto a short path leading to a viewpoint looking out over the salt marsh, Milton Harbor, and a few islands scattered near the marsh. Looking down, you see the **classic salt-marsh terrain**. It's flat and irregular, with inlets from Milton Harbor meandering through it. Most of the area is covered with grasses of different heights, and clumps of trees or shrubs stick up here and there where the ground is a bit higher. At low tide, the marsh is fringed with exposed mud flats. The high-tide line will be very apparent from above—it's where the grass gets shorter. In any salt marsh in the Northeast, two related types of grass are the predominant vegetation. The tall grass that lines the seaward side of the marsh and the inlet channels is called *Spartina alterniflora*, otherwise known as cordgrass (the name *Spartina* actually comes from the Greek for cord) or thatch grass. Ranging in height from three to six feet or even higher, cordgrass is coarse and tough—it has to be to withstand twice-daily high tides. The low-growing

Looking out over the salt marsh and Milton Harbor from a viewpoint at the Marshlands Conservancy. At low tide, the streams that meander through the marsh are very visible.

grass that is found higher up in the marsh, where the salt water reaches only twice a month at the lunar high tides, is *Spartina patens*, sometimes called salt hay. *Spartina patens* doesn't grow any higher than two feet. It is much finer in texture than cordgrass, so fine that it bends easily. If you look more carefully at the areas of *Spartina patens*, you'll see that they have been blown by the wind and twisted by the tide into hummocks or "cowlicks."

Backtrack from the overlook and turn left when you reach the field trail again. In about ten yards you'll see a log bench. Bear left and follow the graveled path as it leads downward into the woods. In a few minutes you'll be on the salt marsh in an area called Marie's Neck. The path here is a low dike. On your right is a small bay called Greenhaven Channel; on your left is the salt marsh. If it's low tide, **mud flats** will be exposed on the marsh. If you look carefully, you'll see zillions of little holes in the mud. Tiny fiddler crabs (*Uca pugnax*) live in these burrows, feeding on algae and decaying plant and animal life. One of the male fiddler crab's front claws is enormous and shaped like a fiddle—hence the name. In the summer breeding season, watch the male go through his elaborate courtship ritual, raising and lowering the fiddle claw and bobbing his body. It's sometimes hard to see the fiddler crabs at first, because they are very well camouflaged. Once you see the first one, however, you'll soon see lots of them scurrying around and popping in and out of their holes.

As the path continues, you can easily see the two different *Spartinas* on the marsh side. You also may hear the loud, frequent buzzy noises and musical rattles of the marsh wren, which nests among the cordgrass. The sharp-tailed sparrow, on the other hand, prefers to nest near the ground in the shelter of *Spartina patens*. This is the small, nondescript brown bird that flushes from the grass as you walk by, flies weakly for a little way, and then drops back down. Listen for its faint, high trill.

The path is lined with wildflowers and lots of poison ivy—be careful. In a few more minutes the trail forks to make a loop around the wooded tip of Marie's Neck. Turn to your right and follow the path. After a couple of minutes look on your right for a side path leading directly down to the water's edge. At low tide, steppingstones are exposed here. This is a great place to explore. The ebbing tide leaves behind pools filled with tiny fish, crabs, scallops, and other small sea creatures. Interesting salt-adapted plants are also easy to spot along here. One of the most interesting is *Salicornia*, a stubby plant with water-swollen stems that grows in sandy areas right by the water. This plant goes by a variety of colorful common names, including chicken toes, saltwort, salt-marsh pickle, glasswort, and marsh samphire. The reasons for the names become obvious when you look at the plant. It does resemble a chicken foot in shape; it tastes slightly salty and was made into pickles by early settlers; and it is slightly translucent because of the water in the stems. The name marsh samphire comes from its resemblance to a European plant named for Saint Pierre (Peter)—"samphire" by the time the English colonists were done mangling it.

At low tide, you can continue around the tip of Marie's Neck along the shore; at high tide, follow the trail. After you've rounded the tip of the neck, you'll find a small, sandy beach littered with boulders. Look out over Milton Harbor to see gulls, ducks (rafts of them in the winter), cormorants, and other seabirds. You might spot an osprey—there's a nesting platform in the salt marsh.

The **beach area** is fun to explore—kids love to climb on the rocks. To return from here, don't walk through the salt marsh. Look for the trail near the bench on the beach and follow it straight ahead. A few minutes' walk brings you back to the dike; to return from there, retrace your steps. If you'd prefer to return through the woods, retrace your steps as far as the meadow trail. Take the second right and then the first left. The walk back from here takes about fifteen minutes.

Hours, Fees, Facilities

The Marshlands Conservancy is open daily except Sunday from 10:00 A.M. to dusk. This is a popular park, especially with birders in the springtime and early autumn. The park also offers an extensive schedule of nature walks and the like, so it can be a little crowded, though not unpleasantly so, on weekends. There are no fees. Restrooms and water are available at the nature museum. No pets are allowed.

Getting There

Take I-95 (New England Thruway) to exit 19 (Rye). Follow the Playland Parkway access road for 0.5 mile to US 1 (Boston Post Road). Turn right (south toward Mamaroneck) onto US 1 and follow it for 1.2 miles. The entrance is on the left just past the Rye Golf Club. Follow the entrance road for 0.3 mile to the parking area.

For More Information

Marshlands Conservancy
Rte. 1
Rye, NY 10580
914-835-4466

Anthony's Nose
Bear Mountain Bridge

- **2.5 miles**
- **2 to 3 hours**
- **moderate, though quite steep for the first half-mile**

*Glorious views up and down the Hudson River
from the east bank.*

Anthony's Nose is a steep, 900-foot mountain on the eastern bank of the Hudson River in the dramatically beautiful portion known as the **Hudson Highlands**. The Bear Mountain Bridge across the Hudson is at the foot of the mountain. Anthony's Nose is on 2,000 acres of land owned by Camp Smith, where the New York State National Guard trains. The rifle ranges at Camp Smith are used also by local law enforcement personnel. Because of the weapons activity at Camp Smith, hikers must always remain on the blazed trails. Do not bushwhack off the trail into the woods, and do not go onto any of the woods roads and unmarked trails—these areas are closed to the public and you will be considered a trespasser. The New York–New Jersey Trail Conference sells a good map of the east Hudson trails region, including Anthony's Nose.

The hike to the top of Anthony's Nose can be an oddly noisy experience, but it's worth it for the incredible view at the top. Traffic noise from the Bear Mountain

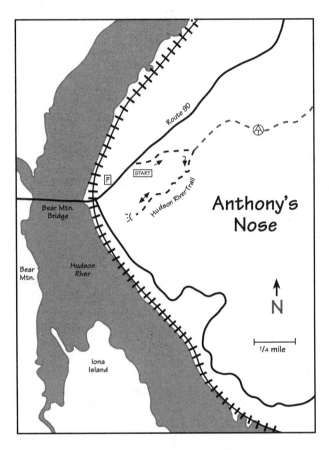

Bridge is a constant, and often you can hear the rattle of rifle fire and the heavier chatter of machine-gun fire from the ranges at Camp Smith. You also might hear the whistle of a train on the MetroNorth/Amtrak rails that run along the riverbank. Anthony's Nose is a popular spot for day hikes, so you are likely to encounter other walkers on the trail.

On your walk to the top of Anthony's Nose you will be on two different trails. The walk starts on the Appalachian Trail (AT) and continues to the top on the Hudson River Trail (HRT). The HRT is a multiuse trail on both sides of the river. On the western bank, it will be eventually a path leading from the confluence of the Hudson and Mohawk Rivers all the way to the New York–New Jersey border. On the eastern bank, it will lead from the Troy Dam to the Westchester–Bronx border. Much of the trail, which is still under development, utilizes such existing trails as the Croton Aqueduct Trail in Westchester, although some new trails will be cut. A major portion was opened recently in the New Jersey Highlands. When negotiations and trail building are complete, the Hudson River Trail will cover some 300 miles.

To begin climbing Anthony's Nose, look for the green Appalachian Trail marker with the hiker symbol. It's on the eastern side of Rte. 9D just before the bridge entrance. (Be very careful of traffic while walking on Rte. 9D.) As you turn off Rte. 9D onto the trail, you'll immediately see some stone steps cut into the mountainside on the left. The path is marked here with white Appalachian Trail blazes. After following it for a few minutes, look for a sign pointing you to the Viewpoint Trail (0.4 mile) and the Hemlock Springs Campsite (1.4 miles). Follow the trail as it runs up the foot of the mountain through woods made up mostly of oak and hickory trees with a thick understory of mountain laurel. Although it is steep and quite rocky, the trail is also very clear and well maintained, with stone and log steps to help you up the hardest places. Take your time and be careful, especially in the autumn. The many acorns that litter the trail can be like so many ball bearings as you scramble along. As if you didn't already know from all the climbing, the presence of so many oaks—particularly chestnut oaks—indicates that you are on a steep and windy mountain ridge that is part of a **dry upland**. The chestnut oak (*Quercus prinus*) grows well in the thin, dry, acidic soil that is characteristic of this terrain. To spot a chestnut oak, look for broadly oval leaves about five to six inches long with rounded, regular waves around the edges (not the lobes usually associated with oak leaves). The acorn is long, with a smallish cap.

After about twenty-five to thirty minutes of steady climbing, you will emerge at a fork in the trail. Look for a double white blaze on a small oak tree here. The AT continues on to the left, leading to the Hemlock Springs Campground. To get to the top of Anthony's Nose, turn right onto the Hudson River Trail. Thankfully, this part of the trail follows an easy, fairly level woods road. The trail theoretically is blazed in blue from here to the summit, but the blazes, if any, are hard to find. The trail is broad and obvious, however, and there's no real need for guidance. Follow it through pleasant, open woods with sunny patches for another ten minutes or so. You'll pass a lovely little pond on your left. Carry on for another ten minutes until you come to a blue-blazed boulder on the right side of the path. The word NOSE in blue letters lets you know that you're on the right trail, but it's hardly necessary—you're almost there. Follow the path as it curves around granite boulders to the right, the left, and then the right again. In another minute, you're at the top. The view up and down the entire length of the Hudson Highlands is fantastic. This is a great place to see migrating

The view looking west across the Hudson River to Bear Mountain from the top of Anthony's Nose.

hawks soaring past at eye level in the autumn. Wander around among the bare rocks at the summit, checking out the view in different directions and enjoying the steady breeze. Watch out, though—there are some steep drops.

To return, follow the same route back.

In 1996, the New York–New Jersey Trail Conference was given permission to create a footpath through Camp Smith to Anthony's Nose. This new portion of the Hudson River Trail begins at the former Toll House on Rte. 6/202 south of the Bear Mountain Bridge and continues north parallel to the Hudson for approximately three miles to the top of Anthony's Nose. The trail has eight magnificent viewpoints, but it also has some very steep climbs and a number of dangerous cliffs—it is not for beginners. If you'd like to get a trail map, contact the New York–New Jersey Trail Conference.

Who Was Anthony?

Whenever a mountain is called something like Anthony's Nose, you know there will be several different explanations of the name, all equally believable (or unbelievable). According to some historians, the mountain was named by the Spanish/Portuguese explorer Estevan Gomez, who entered the Hudson in 1525 and explored some way up it. Because he entered the river on St. Anthony's Day (January 17), he called it the Rio San Antonio; Anthony's Nose supposedly represents that of the saint. This story has always seemed not only far-fetched but faintly blasphemous to me. I prefer the equally far-fetched tale that the steep, triangular slope down to the water resembled the famously prominent nose of a pre-Revolutionary Dutch river captain named Anthony. The mountain is definitely not named for General Anthony Wayne, although this part of the river was tremendously important during the American Revolution.

The Bear Mountain Bridge spanning the Hudson was built in 1924. The river span is 1,632 feet long; the entire bridge is 2,258 feet long. At the time, it was the world's longest suspension bridge.

The Geology of the Hudson Highlands

The Hudson Highlands is the formal designation for the very scenic, narrow, mountainous section of the Hudson River stretching from Peekskill in the south some fifteen miles north to Beacon. The Highlands mountains begin with Dunderberg in the south and end at Storm King. Geologically speaking, this portion of the river is a fjord: a narrow, steep-sided, glacier-carved, drowned river valley. (The original river valley is as deep as 1,000 feet below sea level and extends into the Atlantic about 150 miles beyond New York Bay. When the glacier retreated, the sea level rose and "drowned" the valley.) The fjord is the southernmost in the entire northern hemisphere. The Hudson is very narrow and deep here: only three-eighths of a mile across and up to 165 feet deep.

As you look out from the top of Anthony's Nose, you can see the glacial history of the Hudson River spread in front of you. Directly across the river, at the base of Bear Mountain, you can see Iona Island and a large channel that separates it from the western shore. Bald eagles sometimes winter on Iona Island. You can also see a flat terrace on the side of Bear Mountain; the famous Bear Mountain Inn stands here and is clearly visible. The river originally followed a fault zone and flowed in the channel west of Iona Island; the terrace of Bear Mountain, now some 160 feet above the water, is the ancient riverbed. During the Wisconsin glacial period that ended some 12,000 years ago, the ice carved a new, straighter channel and forced the river to the east. Before the glacier, Anthony's Nose extended across the current channel. As the glacier and then the river plowed through, what is now Iona Island was detached from Anthony's Nose by the new river channel.

The mountains of the Hudson Highlands are part of a northeast-trending belt of low mountains called the Reading Prong. This mass extends northeastward from Reading, Pennsylvania, and includes the New Jersey Highlands and the Ramapo Mountains; on the eastern side of the Hudson, the Reading Prong extends to include the Housatonic Highlands of western Connecticut, the Berkshire Mountains of Massachusetts, and the Green Mountains in Vermont. The Hudson Highlands consist of granite and other metamorphic rocks that are very ancient—as old as a billion years in places. Anthony's Nose consists largely of Canada Hill granite (named for where it was first classified in nearby Hudson Highlands State Park), which is about 800 million to 900 million years old. The bare boulders at the summit are made of this granite. Look for a coarse-grained, whitish rock with many sparkly bits of biotite mica in it. If you look carefully, you'll see that the mica is aligned in layers. You also can see bits of light-colored feldspar, white quartz, and lens-shaped pods of a pale-green mineral called epidote in the granite.

Hours, Fees, and Facilities

The Hudson River Trail through Camp Smith is open year-round during daylight hours only. There are no fees and no facilities. Pets are allowed on leashes only.

Getting There

The trailhead is on Rte. 9D just to the north of the Bear Mountain Bridge. Parking is in pullouts on either side of the road above and below the trailhead. Be very cautious of traffic when walking from your car to the trailhead.

For More Information

Park Superintendent
Hudson Highlands State Park
914-225-7207

Clarence Fahnestock Memorial State Park

Carmel

- **Pelton Pond walk, about 1 mile, about 1 hour, easy**
- **Appalachian Trail/Three Lakes walk, about 2.5 miles, 2 to 3 hours, moderate**

Iron mining and the Appalachian Trail in a vast park.

The largest park in Dutchess or Putnam County, Clarence Fahnestock Memorial State Park covers more than 6,530 hilly acres in the Hudson Highlands. The original 3,600 acres of the park were donated to the state of New York in 1929 by Dr. Ernest Fahnestock as a memorial to his brother Clarence, who was killed in France near the end of World War I. The additional acreage was acquired in the 1960s. Some 4,000 additional pristine acres in the Hubbard-Perkins Conservation Area adjoining the northeast portion of the park were acquired in 1991 by the Open Space Institute, a nonprofit land-preservation organization. (Helen Hubbard, whose property comprises a major portion of this area, was the sister of Ernest and Clarence.)

In 1995, the Open Space Institute acquired Glynwood Farm, a 957-acre estate nearly surrounded by the Hubbard-Perkins area. About 700 acres of the property will become part of the park.

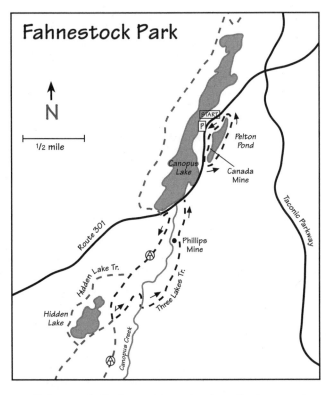

Fahnestock Park

Fahnestock Park is managed primarily for camping and outdoor recreation, so this is a great place for hiking. It's also excellent for fishing—Stillwater Pond is stocked with brook and rainbow trout every year. Canopus Lake, Pelton Pond, John Allen Pond, and Duck Pond are great sites for bass, perch, sunfish, and pickerel. There's a nice swimming beach complete with picnic area, changing rooms, and other facilities at Canopus Lake.

There are numerous lovely trails in Fahnestock Park. I've selected two walks that show off the park's natural beauty and its history without being too rugged or long. The Appalachian Trail runs for several miles through the park. In my opinion, this is the most beautiful part of the AT in all of New York State. A good map of the region is available from the New York–New Jersey Trail Conference. Ask for map 3 covering the east Hudson trails.

Pelton Pond

The interpretive trail that circles Pelton Pond is short (less than a mile), easy, and quite revealing of the natural and human history of the area. The walk starts at the west end of the parking lot, near the entrance from Rte. 301—look for the wooden sign with a carved outline of the pond. Follow the stone steps up to the stone shelter and terraced overlook at the northern end of the pond. From here, you can see that the pond was made by damming a ravine. Most of the charming, site-appropriate stone structures around Pelton Pond were built by Civilian Conservation Corps workers in the 1930s. They built the steps and shelter, along with fifty-six stone fireplaces in the picnic area, the other camping and picnic areas throughout the park, and five dams, including the dam on Pelton Pond. Actually, there was always a pond here; the dam just made it bigger. In the 1800s, the locals called it Poison Pond, because the high iron content of the water made it undrinkable. The name was changed to Pelton Pond (nobody knows who or what Pelton was) by the CCC.

From the shelter terrace, turn west (right) and follow the trail through the CCC fireplaces. The trail is pretty obvious all the way around the pond, but just in case, the main trail is blazed with yellow plastic disks helpfully printed with the words TRAIL MARKER. On your left will be some short side trails that lead down to the edge of the pond. Continue for a few minutes until you see a side trail on your right. Follow this path for a short distance to the long, east-west cut of the old Canada Mine, which runs roughly parallel to Rte. 301. The rusty stains on the walls of the cut tell you that this was once an **iron mine**. The Precambrian gneiss that makes up the bedrock of Fahnestock Park consists mostly of granite with many deposits of magnetite iron ore. This high-quality ore was mined up until the 1880s in several places throughout what is now the park. It was taken to the West Point foundry at Cold Spring, about eight miles away, for smelting. The route was via the Cold Spring Turnpike, now known more prosaically as Rte. 301. The mine shaft is interesting, but be careful about exploring it—look out for loose and falling rocks.

Backtrack to the main trail and continue for five minutes or so on the embankment along the pond's shore. Look along here for striped maple (*Acer pennsylvanicum*) trees. Also called moose maple, moosewood, and goosefoot maple, the smallish striped maple tree has large, hairless, finely toothed leaves and green bark with white streaks. Other trees around the pond include numerous eastern hemlocks (*Tsuga canadiensis*). Look for drooping, twiggy branches with flat, double-ranked needles about half an inch long. The trail here cuts across the neck of a little peninsula that juts out into the pond. After a couple more minutes the trail leads down to a small cove. To explore a bit on the peninsula, look for a side trail on the left. The main trail leads on and a bit upward toward the dam through a stand of black birches. The path crosses the dam and then turns back east through a shady area full of hemlocks and mountain laurel. A few minutes after you pass a small beach, a bridge takes you over the narrow inlet stream of the pond. As the path continues close to the shore, look on your right for dramatic stone ledges; in a few minutes, some stone steps help you descend. Look for a lovely stone bench near here. Continue to follow the path for about seven minutes longer as it circles around the tip of the pond. You'll see a low stone structure with an unusual, trapezoidal shape—this is an old pump house, built in CCC days. The trail soon makes a sharp left. In another minute or two you'll come upon the rest rooms and a water fountain, gifts from the CCC. If you look on the ladies side (north) of the rest rooms, you can see the cut of the Canada Mine continuing on into the woods for another quarter-mile. From here, the path takes you back to the parking area in another few minutes.

The Appalachian and Three Lakes Trails

One of the most enjoyable walks I know, this loop takes you along the side of a beautiful hemlock gorge, down to the creek that runs through it, and back up the other side. It begins near the parking pullout on Rte. 301, across from the south end of Canopus Lake. Look for the familiar green Appalachian Trail sign on the road. The AT portion of this trail is blazed in white paint.

Almost immediately after starting along the trail, turn right at the Y junction. Follow the trail down past Canopus Creek, tumbling here from a culvert leading from the lake across the road. The trail, which is clearly marked and easy to follow, if a bit rocky, continues onward through hemlock woods. You are walking on a ridge along the side of the gorge—note the tumbled boulders on your right and the drop down on your left. The ridge at this point and for the next half-mile or so is actually the old rail bed from the **iron mining operations** here. The narrow-gauge tracks carried ore cars pulled by mules. As you continue on this portion of the trail until it intersects with the Hidden Lake Trail, you'll see occasional reminders of the rail bed in the form of old stone retaining walls and abutments and some raised portions of the trail. Iron mining in this part of the park was abandoned by 1873. Looking at the heavily wooded gorge today, it's hard to imagine that much of the timber was cut down during mining days. (The abundance of rain and the relatively temperate climate of the Northeast allow forests to regenerate much faster than in, say, the US West.)

The trails leads in and out of dense stands of mountain laurel. One-flowered wintergreen (*Pyrola uniflora*) grows on the ground beneath the laurels. Look for three small, flat, shiny green, rounded leaves growing close to the ground. Some members of the wintergreen family, such as Indian pipe (*Monotropa uniflora*), are actually saprophytes, or root parasites. Because these plants lack chlorophyll, they have a pinkish or reddish color. One-flowered wintergreen is not a parasite. In fact, it is green all year round—hence the common name. In the spring, it sends up a single pinkish flower with five petals on a long stem. Wintergreens in general prefer cool forests, and one-flowered wintergreen is no exception—it is

Joe, Dagmar, and Leo (lower left) on the trail at Fahnestock State Park. The trail here is an old railroad bed that hugs the side of a ravine.

found in cool woodlands throughout the Northeast. Because of their elevation in the Hudson Highlands, the woods here at Fahnestock are not just cool, they're downright cold. In the winter, what falls as icy rain south and north of the region often falls as snow here. In the early spring, there's usually still snow on the ground here long after it has melted everywhere else.

After another ten minutes, you'll come to a small stream. Look for a double white AT blaze and three yellow plastic disks on an oak tree on your left. The yellow blazes indicate the start of the trail to Hidden Lake. (To make this enjoyable side trip of about 1.5 miles, follow the yellow blazes. The trail roughly parallels Hidden Lake; bear left where the trail curves around its tip. At the T junction, turn left onto the blue-blazed Three Lakes Trail and follow it for about fifteen minutes to the X junction with the AT. Follow directions below from there.) Stay on the AT for another twelve minutes as it winds through another stand of mountain laurel. Just as the stand ends, you will arrive at an X junction with the blue-blazed Three Lakes Trail. Turn left (north) onto the Three Lakes Trail. After a few minutes the trail heads downhill and makes a broad switchback down toward the creek at the bottom of the gorge. The trail here is not well blazed, but it's still fairly easy to follow. If you end up bushwhacking a bit, just aim toward the marshy area of phragmites that is below. You should easily see the blazes again in the hemlock stand at the southern end of the marshy area. From here, the trail enters its most beautiful portion. It drops down sharply through shady, **cool hemlock woods** and then runs parallel to Canopus Creek for a bit. In about five minutes you'll come to a stream crossing. If the water is low, you can try going across on the boulder-sized steppingstones. If you prefer, cross on the flattened log or on the charming stone bridge that is another legacy of the CCC. On the other side, notice how the creek briefly disappears under a jumble of rocks. The trail parallels the creek again briefly and then bears off to the right into the woods and climbs up and away. (For the rest of the way back, you'll be walking parallel to the Appalachian Trail on the opposite edge of the gorge.) As you gradually ascend the other side of the gorge, such deciduous trees as hickories and oaks—hardwoods that prefer drier, sunnier locations—

start to appear again. Some ten to fifteen minutes after crossing the stream, you'll come to an intersection on your right with an old, unmarked woods road. Since this road will take you quickly out of the park into private property, stay on the blue-blazed Three Lakes Trail. In another ten minutes or so, the trail will take you near the old Phillips Mine on your left. This iron mine site has a deep shaft that is hard to find and dangerous once you do find it—stay away. Another fifteen minutes' walk brings you back out to Rte. 301. To avoid clambering over the guardrail, stay in the woods. Turn left and walk on the trail parallel to the road for a couple of minutes to reach the AT trailhead where you began.

Hours, Fees, and Facilities

Fahnestock Park is open from dawn to dusk year-round. The park office on Rte. 301 opposite Pelton Pond is open daily from 8:00 A.M. to 4:30 P.M. Some access roads (not the ones mentioned here) are closed in winter. There are no fees for day hikers. Restrooms, water, and picnic areas are available at Pelton Pond and at the beach facility on Canopus Lake. Pets are allowed on leashes only. Fahnestock Park has extensive campgrounds and wilderness camping areas; group cabins are available at the Taconic Outdoor Education Center. Call for information about reservations and fees.

Getting There

From the Taconic State Parkway, go east on Rte. 301 (Cold Spring Road) for 0.6 mile to the parking area on the left at Pelton Pond. Continue on for another 0.9 mile to the roadside pulloffs on the left for the Appalachian Trail. Be careful not to block the road and be careful walking on Rte. 301. If the pulloffs are full (they might be on a nice weekend day), use the parking areas at the south end of Canopus Lake. From Rte. 9 in Carmel, head west on Rte. 301 (Cold Spring Road) for about 6 miles to the AT trailhead on the right; continue on 0.9 mile to reach the parking area at Pelton Pond on your right.

For More Information
Clarence Fahnestock Memorial State Park
Taconic Region
Office of Parks, Recreation, and Historic Preservation
Box 308
Staatsburg, NY 12580
914-225-7207

Taconic Outdoor Education Center
914-265-3773

Campsite reservations
800-456-CAMP

Orange and Rockland Counties

Harriman State Park
Orange/Rockland Counties

- **3.8 miles**
- **3 hours**
- **moderate**

Old iron mines in one of the metropolitan region's largest, oldest, and most popular parks.

Only thirty-five miles from New York City, Harriman State Park is one of the most popular recreation areas in the metropolitan region. The park is huge, covering 46,647 acres in the Ramapo Mountains of the Hudson Highlands. Especially in the summer, the numerous campgrounds, picnic areas, swimming beaches, and fishing lakes are heavily used. Though the recreational areas in the park don't really cover that much ground, most people stay within them. The trails at Harriman State Park are remarkably tranquil.

The only real problem a walker faces in this vast park is selecting a trail from the extensive network that reaches into every corner. There are forty-three well-marked

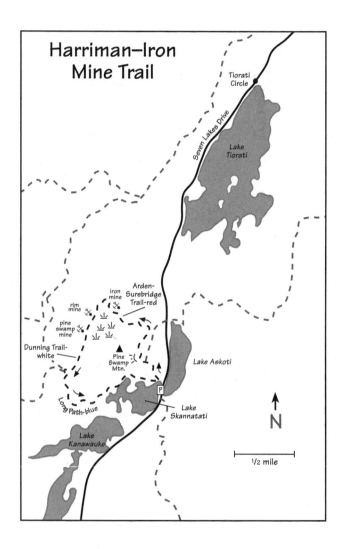

Harriman–Iron
Mine Trail

Tiorati
Circle

Seven Lakes Drive

Lake
Tiorati

Arden-
Surebridge
Trail-red

iron
mine

rim
mine

pine
swamp
mine

Dunning Trail-
white

Pine
Swamp
Mtn.

Lake Askoti

P

Lake
Skannatati

Long Path-blue

Lake
Kanawauke

N

1/2 mile

trails covering 225 miles, as well as an additional fifty-six unmarked trails covering 103 miles more. Only in Harriman would there be a trail intersection called Times Square. It's very easy to put together some good if somewhat long loops here, particularly with the help of the excellent maps published by the New York–New Jersey Trail Conference (maps 3 and 4 for Harriman and Bear Mountain State Parks). The loop described below is designed to take in beautiful scenery and some of the history of the park.

The loop begins in the parking area at Lake Skannatati. This lake is one of thirty-six—almost all manmade—in Harriman and Bear Mountain parks. When the lakes were planned, historic English-language names were proposed, but in many cases Major Welch (see below) discarded the names in favor of Native American names in the Algonquian language of the Indians who once lived here. Lake Skannatati, which was completed in 1938, is said to mean "the other side." Lake Askoti across the road, completed in 1937, is said to mean "this side."

A small brown sign at the northern end of the lot tells you that this is the hikers' parking area. The Arden–Surebridge Trail, blazed with a red triangle on a white circle, begins here just to the left of the sign. (Ignore the blue blazes of the Long Path.) Follow the trail into the woods straight ahead and then immediately turn right. The trail begins a steady upward ascent for the next twelve minutes or so as you climb toward a ridge at the top of Pine Swamp Mountain. You come then to the only difficult part of this walk: the trail goes up and over a large, jumbled rock formation. You'll have to scramble up the steep trail here for a few minutes. Once you're over the rocks, the going is much easier. Turn left and follow the clear trail for another few minutes past the junction with the Red Cross Trail. You'll soon come out onto gorgeous views from about 1,100 feet up (the parking lot is about 900 feet above sea level).

From here, the trail leads downhill through pleasant, open woods for another twenty minutes. As you get down to the lower, cooler, and moister valley, eastern hemlocks start to appear. The trail takes you through several nice stands of them as it skirts the edge of Pine Swamp. Over the next fifteen minutes or so, the trail climbs gradually up again. After you go over a small rise, look around on your right for old stone foundations. This was once the site of an iron mining camp.

Continue on the trail for another seven or eight minutes. As the trail bears to the left, it climbs up over a small hill. Look more closely—the hill is made of small pieces of crushed rock. It's really a pile of tailings from the **iron mines** that are straight ahead. Be extremely cautious—there are no signs or barriers by any of the mine cuts. Do not let children run ahead on the trail in this area. The cuts into the rock usually end in deep, water-filled shafts. You'll see one cut immediately in front of you from the trail; two others are nearby.

After exploring here, continue on the Arden–Surebridge Trail, ignoring the woods road that leads off to the right. The trail turns quickly to the left. In another minute or so you'll see another very large mine cut into the rock on your right. Steppingstones then take you over a runoff stream (often dry). In another few minutes you'll come to the intersection with yellow-blazed

Dunning Trail. Turn left onto the trail, which is an old woods road (the continuation of the woods road you saw earlier). In another ten minutes or so you'll come to the large cut of the Pine Swamp Mine on your left. This mine, which dates back to the 1830s, is one of the largest in the park. It is here that two friends and I had a very close brush with disaster. As we came out from exploring the cut, a boulder perched high on the wall overhead came crashing down where we had been just two seconds before. Ever the eloquent, articulate writer, my response was a shocked "Holy smoke!" Interestingly,

Guy Smith inspects the boulder that nearly cut short some promising literary careers at the old Pine Swamp iron mine in Harriman State Park.

three palm warblers arrived within moments to feed, with their characteristic bobbing motion, on the insects and grubs revealed in the earth where the rock had been.

Continue on the Dunning Trail for another twenty minutes. When you see Pine Swamp on your left in a few minutes, look on your right for a huge, overgrown hill of mine tailings. If you want to take your chances with poison ivy, bushwhack up the hill. You'll come to a rocky cliff above a deep, water-filled mine shaft. Off to the left is the entrance to a cavelike mine shaft. It's a rough climb to get up to the cave—prudent hikers won't do it.

When you see both blue and yellow blazes on some trees straight ahead of you on the trail, you have arrived at the junction with the Long Path, which runs with the Dunning Trail for about 250 feet here. Do not continue on to those blazes! Instead, look immediately to your left. You'll see the blue blazes for the Long Path leading away downhill as a narrow trail through the woods. This is the correct path. It's easy walking from here as you follow the Long Path up and down (mostly down) through open oak woods, mountain laurel, and high-bush blueberries (fruiting in August) on your way back to Lake Skannatati. About ten minutes into this portion of the trail, it skirts a huge rock ledge on your left for a while—very dramatic but slightly unnerving if you've just nearly been done in by a falling rock. About fifteen minutes later the trail crosses a rocky stream on a bridge of steppingstones. From here, the trail takes you back to the parking area in another twenty minutes.

Harriman History

Harriman and Bear Mountain State Parks are part of the Palisades Interstate Park Commission (PIPC). The PIPC was formed in 1901 to preserve the Hudson Palisades from destruction by quarrying. The mandate of the commission soon extended farther north to the magnificent and historic scenery of the Hudson Highlands. Inconclusive discussion was galvanized in 1909, when New York State proposed building a new prison near the current site of the Bear Mountain Inn. George Perkins, a wealthy banker who was the head of the PIPC, and railroad magnate Edward H. Harriman, who owned a very large estate in the area, proposed a plan to extend the jurisdiction of the PIPC into the highlands. Harriman planned to donate nineteen square miles of his estate, along with $1 million to purchase additional land, if the state would give up its plans to build the prison. Harriman died without seeing his plan adopted. On October 29, 1910, his son W. Averell Harriman presented the deed and a check to the PIPC.

Technically speaking, Harriman State Park and Bear Mountain State Park are separate entities, even though they adjoin each other and are administered jointly by the PIPC. For all practical purposes, though, the two parks form one unit that shares a common history. The parks in 1909 were very different from their appearance today. The forests had been repeatedly cut in the 1800s for mining, charcoal, lumber, and cordwood. By 1890, mining and charcoal production had pretty much ended, but wood cutting for cordwood was still a major source of employment for local workers. The mountains were bare or covered with early second-growth woods. There were few roads or blazed trails. From 1912 to 1940, Major William A. Welch, the first general manager of the parks, supervised the construction of twenty-three lakes, 100 miles of roads, and numerous other structures and amenities, including the Bear Mountain Inn. Additional lakes, roads, and improvements were built in the 1930s by CCC workers. Many of the hiking trails in Harriman were cut in the 1920s and 1930s by volunteers inspired by Raymond H. Torrey. Editor of the outdoor page of the *New York Evening Post* for many years, Torrey also wrote a popular weekly column about hiking and conservation. He wrote the first edition of the *New York Walk Book* in 1923. Torrey was a moving force behind the trails at Harriman, the organization of the New York–New Jersey Trail Conference, and the creation of the Appalachian Trail.

The parks were opened to the public in 1913. In 1914, more than a million people visited them; by 1917, the number was up to 2 million. In 1995, nearly 1.7 million people visited Bear Mountain alone; another 2.7 million visited Harriman State Park, for a combined total of about 4.4 million visitors. By contrast, Yellowstone National Park, which covers 2.2 million acres, had about 3.1 million visitors in 1995.

Hours, Fees, and Facilities

Harriman State Park is open every day from dawn to dusk. Entrance is free, but there are parking fees in some areas (not Lake Skannatati). Do not park on the roads. Restrooms, water, pay phones, and a seasonal food concession are found at Tiorati Circle, 2.6 miles to the north on Seven Lakes Drive. (Tiorati means "blue like the sky.") Pets are allowed on leashes only.

Getting There

Take the Palisades Interstate Parkway to exit 18. This is the end of the road, so the exit leads you into the Long Mountain traffic circle. Follow the circle almost completely around to Seven Lakes Drive (don't get onto Rte. 6 by mistake). Follow Seven Lakes Drive for 3.8 miles to Tiorati Circle. Continue past Tiorati Circle for 2.6 miles. The turnoff to the parking area at Lake Skannatati is at a sharp angle on the right—start looking for it as soon as Lake Askoti comes into view on your left.

From Rte. 17 or I-87 (New York State Thruway), take Rte. 6 at Harriman and head east for approximately 7 miles to the Long Mountain traffic circle. Follow directions as above.

It is disgracefully difficult to get to Harriman via public transportation. Buses are not allowed in the park. International Bus Lines goes directly to the Bear Mountain Inn (see separate entry). The Short Line bus stops at the "Welcome to Harriman Park" sign on Rte. 17 in Arden; tell the driver you want to get off there.

For More Information

Harriman State Park
Bear Mountain, NY 10911
914-786-2701

Bear Mountain State Park
Orange/Rockland Counties

- 3.7 miles
- 2 hours
- moderate

A climb to the top of Bear Mountain along the original section of the Appalachian Trail.

Bear Mountain State Park and Harriman State Park are effectively one unit of the Palisades Interstate Park system (see the discussion of Harriman and the Palisades for more information). Officially, the Bear Mountain part is the 5,067 acres that encompass Popolopen Torne, Bear Mountain, West Mountain, Iona Island, and Dunderberg Mountain.

Bear Mountain itself is a massive chunk of pinkish gray Storm King granite looming 1,305 feet above the Hudson River. The picturesque Bear Mountain Inn, built in 1915, lies on a terrace formed by the ancient course of the river at the base of the mountain. Hessian Lake, a banana-shaped glacial scour that is one of the very few untouched natural bodies of water in the park, is behind the inn. The nearby Trailside Museum and Zoo is well worth a visit for its excellent displays on the geology, natural history, and human history of the region. Fort Clinton, a Revolutionary War site, is also preserved near here.

Only about forty-five miles from New York City, Bear Mountain is a popular destination for family and

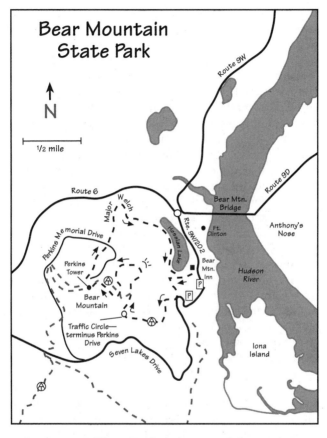

Bear Mountain
State Park

↑
N

1/2 mile

Route 9W

Route 6

Major Welch

Perkins Memorial Drive

Perkins Tower

Bear Mountain

Traffic Circle—
terminus Perkins
Drive

Seven Lakes Drive

Hessian Lake

Rte. 9W/202

Bear Mtn.
Inn

P

P

Route 9D

Bear Mtn.
Bridge

Ft.
Clinton

Anthony's
Nose

Hudson
River

Iona
Island

group outings. The area directly around the inn is managed as a very active recreation area. Ball fields, picnic
areas, a swimming pool, and a skating rink are all here,
along with huge parking lots to accommodate the over-
flow crowds on summer weekends. Try to time your

visit to avoid the peak periods. Even when the recreation areas are busiest, however, the trails—especially the more strenuous ones—are fairly quiet.

The very first segment of the Appalachian Trail was opened in Bear Mountain in 1923 (see below). To follow this historic trail to the top of Bear Mountain, walk on the asphalt path past the southern side of the Bear Mountain Inn to a junction with three other paved paths (Major Welch, Suffern–Bear Mountain, and Cornell Mine). Look for a helpful sign and the rectangular white blazes of the Appalachian Trail here. For a little while, the AT and the yellow-blazed Suffern–Bear Mountain Trail run jointly. Follow the blazes uphill and straight ahead on the asphalt. The trail quickly curves to the left and goes past the skating rink on your left. Continue on for about ten minutes more. Soon after you pass an old ski jump the trail turns into a wide dirt path, somewhat sunken with use. A few minutes after this, the Suffern–Bear Mountain trail splits off to the left and the Appalachian Trail turns to the right. For the next twenty minutes or so, the trail is clear and easy to follow as it takes you steadily upward through open woods, mountain laurel, and high-bush blueberries.

After passing under some power lines, the trail comes out onto an old and unused asphalt road. Turn right here and follow the road for fifty yards to a traffic circle. The circle is the terminus of Perkins Memorial Drive, the vehicular route to the top of Bear Mountain. Turn left and follow the road (note the white blazes on the boulders). In about ten minutes magnificent, sweeping views up and down the Hudson come into sight.

To continue on the Appalachian Trail, look for the double blazes on a large rectangular boulder and on a tree to your left (if you come to a dirt road on your left you've missed the turnoff—backtrack). The trail from here to the summit is more strenuous. In about five minutes, it crosses Perkins Memorial Drive again and then continues on to the summit in another fifteen minutes.

If you prefer a more leisurely route, and/or if you are hiking on a slow-traffic day, simply follow winding Perkins Memorial Drive for the next thirty minutes or so, admiring the many glorious views on the way. You can also easily see the pink granite of the mountain exposed in many places along the road. Remember that the traffic here is two-way.

The view from Perkins Drive looking south toward Iona Island.
The causeway across the island carries Conrail freight tracks.

The five-story Perkins Tower at the top of Bear Mountain was built in 1934 to replace an earlier fire tower. It was named for George Walbridge Perkins, the first president of the Palisades Interstate Park Commission and the man often called the father of the state park movement. The views from the tower and the surrounding area are impressive. Restrooms, water, and picnic areas are available here.

To the south you can see Iona Island and Dunderberg Mountain; Anthony's Nose is directly across the river. To the north is West Point. The mountains include Black Rock, Crow's Nest, and Storm King—the northern end of the Hudson Highlands. In 1962, Consolidated Edison planned to build a huge new hydroelectric power plant on Storm King Mountain. This monstrosity, which would have caused massive destruction of some of the most scenic parts of the Hudson Highlands, aroused a vocal wave of public protest. In many ways, the Storm King controversy was the beginning of the modern conservation movement. The legal and legislative battle went on for seventeen years before the plan finally was defeated.

The Appalachian Trail continues on from here, following Perkins Memorial Drive downhill for a bit and then branching off to continue southwest through Harriman State Park in the general direction of the Delaware Water Gap.

To return to the inn, backtrack the way you came— the trail is a lot easier going down. Alternatively, you could return via the Major Welch Trail down the west slope of the mountain. This trail is blazed with red dots on a white rectangle. It starts just past Perkins Tower where the road leads downhill. Look on the right side of the road for a sign with the word INN on it and an arrow. This trail is very narrow, steep, and rocky at first. Later on, it's just very narrow and steep as it descends 900 feet in about a mile. The trail levels off and follows a contour about 400 feet up along the mountain for about a quarter of a mile. It then leads down to the paved path at the north end of Hessian Lake; from there it is a blessedly flat and easy walk of just under half a mile back to the inn.

The closest I've ever come to getting hurt on this rough trail was seeing a woman sprain her ankle by stumbling over a twig on the paved path by Hessian Lake. Still, be very careful if you take this route. Follow the Major Welch Trail only if you are in reasonably good condition, are wearing sturdy hiking shoes, and wish to become intimately familiar with the Storm King granite. Do not take this trail if you are alone or if the weather is wet or icy.

The Appalachian Trail

In 1921, Benton MacKaye was working for the US Department of Labor. His job was to find ways to create jobs through the wise use of natural resources. An avid hiker with an abiding belief in the spiritual values of the outdoors, MacKaye was well suited for his work. Working with two friends who were prominent architects, MacKaye proposed a footpath that would run from Maine to Georgia along the entire Appalachian Mountain chain. The idea was published in an article in the American Institute of Architects' journal in 1921. Major William A. Welch, the general manager of Bear Mountain State

Park, was immediately very enthusiastic, particularly since the idea fit well with the trail system he was building in the park. The very first section of the Appalachian Trail was a 16-mile path that ran from the foot of Bear Mountain to the top and then westward on through the park to Arden. It was officially opened on October 19, 1923. The full 2,025 miles of the trail were completed in 1937. The Bear Mountain portion is not only the oldest section of the trail, but also contains the lowest elevation—the path is only 120 feet above sea level at the Trailside Museum just west of the Bear Mountain Bridge.

Any discussion of the Appalachian Trail must pay tribute to the many selfless volunteers who negotiated land-use agreements, planned and cut trails, built shelters, made maps, and maintained trails over the decades. In 1984, the Appalachian Trail came under the jurisdiction of the National Park Service, but much of the operation and maintenance of the trail is still done by local volunteers and organizations under the umbrella of the Appalachian Trail Conference.

Hours, Fees, and Facilities

Bear Mountain State Park is open daily from dawn to dusk. There is a small seasonal parking fee. Restrooms, water, pay phones, and food are available year-round at the Bear Mountain Inn. Restrooms and water are available at Perkins Tower.

Getting There

From the Palisades Interstate Parkway, take exit 19 for Perkins Memorial Drive and Bear Mountain. Follow Seven Lakes Drive approximately 2 miles to the Bear Mountain Inn; numerous signs point the way clearly. From the Bear Mountain Bridge, follow the clear signs pointing south to Rte. 9W/202 and from there to the Bear Mountain Inn; total distance is under half a mile. From Rte. 17 or I-87 (New York State Thruway), take Rte. 6 at Harriman and head east for approximately 9 miles to the Bear Mountain Bridge traffic circle. Follow the circle around to Rte. 9W south and follow directions as above.

International Bus Lines goes directly to the Bear Mountain Inn. In the warmer months, you can get here on the cruise boats of the Hudson River Day Line from Pier 83 at West 42d Street and the Hudson River in Manhattan. A mooring area for small craft is to the south of the large dock at Bear Mountain.

Black Rock Forest Preserve and Consortium

Cornwall, Orange County

- **about 2 miles**
- **about 1.5 hours**
- **moderate**

*Hiking through a serene restored forest
in the Hudson Highlands.*

Warning: Hunting is allowed in the preserve. This site is closed to hikers during deer season from mid-November to mid-December.

Black Rock Forest Preserve covers some 3,750 wooded acres in the Hudson Highlands, about fifty miles north of New York City. To the northeast the preserve borders on the Storm King Mountain section of the Palisades Interstate Park; to the east and south it abuts the extensive property owned by the United States Military Academy at West Point. More than a dozen peaks within the preserve rise to over 1,400 feet, offering spectacular views in all directions. Large and beautiful as the site is, it gets little use, perhaps because it is quite close to the more popular Harriman and Bear Mountain parks. A detailed map of Black Rock Forest is available from the New York–New Jersey Trail Conference (trail map 7, west Hudson trails).

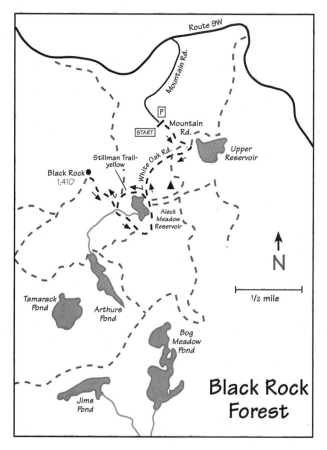

In the late 1800s, the land that is now Black Rock Forest had been cut over and turned into struggling farms. At the end of the century, James Stillman, a wealthy banker and associate of William Rockefeller, purchased the land. In 1911, he gave a portion of it to his son, Dr. Ernest Stillman, a research physician, as a wedding present. Over the years, the Stillmans purchased additional land, always with the goal of restoring the forest to health. In 1928, Dr. Stillman established the forest as a research and demonstration site; he donated it to Harvard University in 1949. Forty years later, having done little with it, Harvard transferred the property to a consortium of fourteen public and private research and educational institutions located in the lower Hudson valley and New York City. Among the institutions now part of the consortium are the American Museum of Natural History, New York University, and the Brooklyn Botanic Garden. The forest is now maintained as a site for education and scientific research, with the goal of providing a model for careful resource management.

Many years of loving management have paid off handsomely in Black Rock Forest. Wild turkeys, once extirpated from the area, are now abundant. When coyotes found their way to the preserve in the early 1980s, they filled the last ecological niche—that of major predator—still open in the forest. The coyotes now are well established and play an important role in limiting the white-tailed deer population. Their presence makes Black Rock Forest a healthy, fully mature ecosystem.

Since the forest takes its name from Black Rock, a rocky outcropping that reaches 1,410 feet, the trail to the top seems an appropriate one for a visit here. Don't be scared off by the height of the peak—the entire preserve is part of a raised Precambrian granite plateau that is already some 800 feet above sea level. The vertical rise you cover will be about 600 feet, spread out over about a mile.

The route begins in the parking area on Mountain Road. At the start of the dirt road leading into the woods (the continuation of Mountain Road), note the sign welcoming you to Black Rock Forest Preserve. Also note the fire hazard indicator. Forest fires are an ever-present danger in the Hudson Highlands. When the risk is high, the preserve is sometimes closed. Fires of any sort are prohibited at all times.

Follow the dirt road past the locked gate. Continue on through the woods, admiring the stream burbling on your right and the numerous glacial boulders strewn about on either side. In about fifteen minutes you'll come to two small buildings—one of red brick and another of stone—on your right; on your left will be the raised banks of the Upper Reservoir. This reservoir, along with several other ponds in the forest, is part of the water supply system for the municipalities of Cornwall and Highland Falls. The buildings, no longer in use, were also part of the system.

Mountain Road intersects here with another dirt road, White Oak Road (the gate shown on some maps has been removed). Turn right onto White Oak Road and continue onward. In about ten minutes on either side of the road you'll see some trees with blue numbers spray-painted onto them and some blue stakes planted firmly into the ground. This is not the start of a trail—it's a **forestry experiment**. Black Rock Forest Preserve is a scientific site as well as a recreational area. You may notice other markers of various sorts here and there throughout the area. In 1994, there were a dozen ongoing research studies being conducted in the preserve. One study that looks at tree growth and tree population dynamics in the preserve has been going on since 1931.

Continue on the road for a few more minutes, passing through a fragrant stand of evergreens, until you come to a large sign on the right reading "Nature Trail." Follow the arrow to the right. The Aleck Meadow Reservoir will be straight ahead, just beyond the gate. The Nature Trail is marked by a series of numbered posts and by some labeled trees. This is a good place to refresh your tree identification skills: look for labels indicating red oak, white ash, eastern hemlock, tulip poplar, American beech, and others.

Follow the trail to the right, around the reservoir and past the dam at its northern end. The stepped spillway goes under the trail and emerges as a beautiful stream tumbling over boulders down a hemlock-lined ravine.

Just past the stream, start looking on your right for the yellow rectangular blazes of the Stillman Trail (the Nature Trail and the Stillman Trail are the same here). Earlier hikers may have bushwhacked some paths to avoid the muddy area at the intersection, but the blazes are clear and you should find them easily. Follow the Stillman Trail for another ten minutes as it climbs gently upward. At post 4 of the Nature Trail, the route intersects another path blazed in white (this is Black Rock Hollow Trail). Stay on the Stillman Trail and turn left here. Almost immediately you will see a dirt road ahead—it's White Oak Road again. The Stillman Trail will turn abruptly right again and start climbing more steeply upward through mountain laurel. Another ten minutes of this brings you to post 7 and another turn to the right. In a few more minutes you'll start to catch glimpses of

Black Rock, the high point in the forest, is a type of basalt that really is dark gray. The view from the top is fabulous in all directions.

Black Rock through the trees. The trail is getting steeper, but you're almost there. Five more minutes and a bit of a scramble brings you to the top. What an amazing, unobstructed view in all directions! Looking due east across the Hudson, you can see three counties— Dutchess, Putnam, and Westchester. Looking south down the Hudson River you get a magnificent view of the Hudson Highlands, including the Bear Mountain

Bridge and West Point; looking north you can see Storm King, the Beacon-Newburgh Bridge, and beyond. To the west are Schunnemunk Mountain, the Shawangunks, and the Catskills in the distance. Closer at hand, note the sturdy pitch pines growing out of the rocky soil below the summit.

To return, backtrack to post 5—the point closest to White Oak Road. Go onto the road and turn left. Follow the road for about ten minutes until it forms a T junction with Mountain Road. Turn left again; another ten minutes brings you back to the gate at Aleck Meadows Reservoir. Turn left onto the road and follow it back to the Upper Reservoir and from there back to the parking area.

Hours, Fees, and Facilities

Trails are open daily from dawn to dusk. Admission and parking are free. There are no facilities. Pets are allowed on leashes only.

Getting There

The entrance to Black Rock Forest Preserve is a little tricky to find. Coming from the north on Rte. 9W, pass Quaker Street and continue on for about 1.5 miles. Note a roadside pullout with a sign saying "Black Rock Forest Preserve Boundary." Do *not* stop here. Start looking carefully to your right—the entrance you want is coming up, but it's easy to miss if you're not watching for it. After 0.3 mile, turn right onto a narrow road that angles off sharply through a gap in the white traffic barrier. This is Mountain Road, although there is no street sign; an inconspicuous wooden sign tells you that it is the preserve entrance. Follow Mountain Road for 0.3 mile; at the T junction turn right (even though the sign says it is a dead end) and go another 0.7 mile to the parking area. If you are coming from the south on Rte. 9W, go past Mountain Road and the entrance to Storm King School. Make a U-turn through the next convenient opening in the divided highway barrier, head south on Rte. 9W to Mountain Road, and follow directions as above.

For More Information

Forest Manager
Black Rock Forest Preserve
Box 483, Continental Road
Cornwall, NY 12518
914-534-4517

Connecticut

Audubon Center in Greenwich
Greenwich

- **1.5 miles**
- **1.5 hours**
- **easy**

An enjoyable stroll around a quiet lake.

Tucked away in the wooded ridges of northwestern Connecticut, the Audubon Center in Greenwich contains 485 acres divided into two major tracts. The main Audubon Center consists of 280 acres of open woodlands, meadows, ponds, and streams. Several interesting trails wind through this part of the property and cover a variety of habitats, including a lake, a red maple swamp, and an old pasture. The smaller portion of the center is the 127-acre Audubon Fairchild Garden less than a mile away. The garden was established in the early 1900s by Benjamin Fairchild as an example of naturalistic landscaping. It is noted for its wildflowers and pharmaceutical plants (here usually one and the same). Eight miles of enjoyable trails wind through the garden and woodlands.

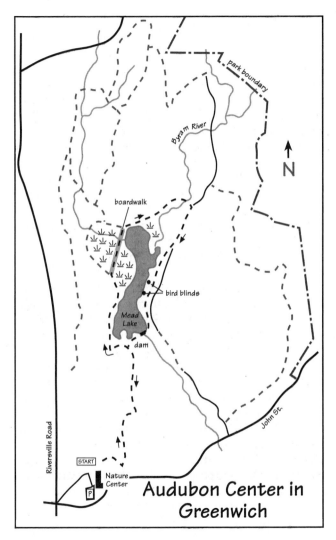

boardwalk

Byram River

park boundary

N

bird blinds

Mead
Lake

dam

Riversville Road

START

Nature
Center

P

John St.

Audubon Center in
Greenwich

The Audubon Center in Greenwich is the local chapter of the National Audubon Society. The center offers a wide variety of courses, workshops, and events for children and adults. In the summer, the center offers the Audubon Ecology Workshop, a residential program for adults that is attended by people, including many teachers, from all over the country. There is an excellent nature bookstore in the interpretive center.

For an enjoyable and easy walk that is well suited for both adults and children, try the Lake Trail around Mead Lake at the Audubon Center. A boardwalk takes you through a large, swampy area at the northern end of the lake, giving you a comfortably dry-shod look at the profusion of life there. Two bird blinds on the eastern edge of the lake give you a good look at the avian life on and near the lake. More than 160 bird species have been recorded here.

All the trails through the center start near the large interpretive building at the entrance. Look for an asphalt path just to the left of the backyard habitat exhibit. The signs for the various paths are quite clear; the paths themselves are obvious, well kept, and easy to follow.

Follow the path straight ahead for a minute or two; the asphalt is quickly replaced by grass. In another few minutes you'll see a sign for Mead Lake. Follow the arrow and turn right into the woods. Follow the trail through the open woods for about fifteen minutes until you arrive at the southern tip of the lake. The trail loops around the lake, so it doesn't really matter which way you go. For the purposes of this walk, however, follow the sign pointing to the boardwalk and turn left. Just after you do, look carefully in the moist, mossy areas along this short part of the trail (before it turns to the right) for round-leaved sundews (*Drosera rotundifolia*). This carnivorous plant, a relative of the Venus' flytrap, has flat, maroon-colored, hairy leaves that exude glittering drops of a clear, sticky substance. Flies are attracted to the sticky fluid and get fatally stuck. They are then digested slowly by enzymes in the fluid; the nutrients are absorbed by the leaves. Sundews grow in acid, boggy or sandy areas that are poor in minerals. Instead of getting the nutrients they need from the soil, they get them from the bodies of the flies.

The trail turns to the right and runs parallel to the lake for about ten minutes until it arrives at the Ronald C. Simjian Memorial Boardwalk on the right. This is a good place to see some of the **aquatic plants** growing in the lake. Waterlilies, blue flag, cattails, pickerelweed, arrowhead, water milfoil, and water plantain all grow here. So does another carnivorous plant, common bladderwort (*Utricularia vulgaris*). The leaves and stems of these plants drift just below the water and send up small, spurred flowers on a long stalk. The small leaves are finely dissected (divided into deeply cut segments) and have tiny pouches, or bladders, on them. Each bladder has a mouth fringed with sensitive hairs. When insect larvae, fish fry, or other minuscule creatures blunder into the bladder, its mouth closes and the bladderwort digests the contents. Bladderwort needs to get its minerals from living creatures because it has no roots and can't get nutrients from the banks or bottom of the lake. The boardwalk is also a good spot to look for birds, turtles, and frogs and to see the territorial activities of dragonflies and damselflies (see below).

Waterlilies bloom in the summer on placid Mead Lake. An easy walking trail surrounds the lake.

When the boardwalk comes to an end, turn right to continue on the lake trail (signs point you back toward the interpretive center). In about five minutes, you'll come to the first of two **bird blinds** on the lake. This one overlooks a marshy area. A little farther on is the second bird blind, which overlooks a more open portion of the lake. Both blinds are well placed for observing different kinds of birds. From the first blind, you're more likely to see insect-eating birds that like damp areas, such as thrushes, warblers, sparrows, and flycatchers. From the second blind, you're more likely to see birds of the shore and open water, such as waterfowl and wading birds.

The trail continues on and takes you over the old dam that forms the lake (it was once used to power a sawmill). From there, turn right to retrace your steps back to the interpretive center.

Dragonflies and Damselflies

The boardwalk on Mead Lake is an outstanding place for observing the insect order Odonata, or dragonflies and their close relatives, damselflies. These insects are the most ancient of the flying insects. Fossils of ancestral forms can be dated back to the Carboniferous period, 350 million to 280 million years ago. At that time, some dragonflies had wingspans of twenty-six inches!

Dragonflies and damselflies have two pairs of large, membranous, many-veined wings; long bodies; huge eyes; and short, bristlelike antennae. The wings can be moved independently, so these insects can fly both forward and backward. Unlike most other flying insects, they can't fold their wings. Dragonflies generally rest with their wings held horizontally; damselflies rest with their wings held together vertically above the body. Dragonflies are fabulous fliers that zoom around rapidly and directly; damselflies fly more weakly. These insects usually are found near water because they spend the first part of their lives there. As both larvae and adults, dragonflies and damselflies are formidable mosquito-eaters.

Dragonflies are very territorial—something that can be seen easily from the boardwalk here. The dragonfly stakes out his territory, usually a spot near water that is appropriate for laying eggs. After he has mated with a female, he allows only that female to lay eggs in the spot. All others are chased away. Depending on the species, the territory can be fairly large, extending for several yards in each direction, or as small as a single water plant. The male dragonfly perches in a prominent spot at one end of the territory, then patrols to the other end, often hovering for a few moments at a time along the way. Intruding males and nonmated females are chased away very aggressively.

Several dragonfly species are common on Mead Lake. One that is very easy to spot is the white-tail dragonfly (*Plathemis lydia*). This dragonfly has a flat, white abdomen and a large black band across each wing. The males are very territorial and often fly out from a perch to attack other males. The green darner (*Anax junius*) is another common dragonfly here. It's big—usually three inches long with a four-inch wingspan—and has a green thorax and a narrow, purplish abdomen. The wings are clear. Look for green darners zooming back and forth ten or fifteen feet above the water. A common damselfly at Mead Lake is the circumpolar bluet (*Enallagma cyanigerum*). Slender and delicate, this damselfly has alternating black and bright blue stripes on its long, slim abdomen; the wings are clear. The red bluet (*Enallagma pictum*) is also very common; it has a brilliant red abdomen and clear wings. Red bluets sometimes land on observers, but they are harmless.

Hours, Fees, and Facilities

The Audubon Center in Greenwich is open year-round Tuesday through Sunday from 9:00 A.M. to 5:00 P.M. It is closed Mondays and holiday weekends. The Fairchild Garden is open daily from dawn to dusk. Admission is $3.00 for adults and $1.50 for children and senior citizens; free to Friends of the Audubon Center and members of the National Audubon Society. Restrooms and water are available at the interpretive center. No pets are allowed.

Getting There

Take I-684 (Hutchinson River Parkway) to exit 3N (Rte. 22 North/Bedford). Go north on Rte. 22 for 0.3 mile to the first traffic light. Turn right onto Rte. 433 and follow it for 2.2 miles to the stop sign at John Street. Turn left here at an acute angle for the entrance to the center. To reach the Fairchild Garden from the Audubon Center, turn south onto Riversville Road (a helpful sign points you in the right direction) and follow it for 1.0 mile to North Porchuck Road. Turn left onto North Porchuck Road and follow it for 0.5 mile to the entrance on the right.

For More Information

Audubon Center in Greenwich
613 Riversville Road
Greenwich, CT 06831
203-869-5272

Lucius Pond Ordway–Devil's Den Preserve
Weston

- **2.8 miles**
- **2 hours**
- **moderate**

A hike through rugged, wooded ridges and fabulous scenery.

The largest nature preserve in southwestern Connecticut, the Lucius Pond Ordway–Devil's Den Preserve is owned by The Nature Conservancy. The preserve covers 1,660 acres of woodlands, wetlands, and rock ledges, accessible on about twenty-one miles of well-maintained trails. The terrain here is very typical of the region. A **rugged series of north-south ridges**, separated by valleys, is the dominant feature. The ridges are bare, rocky, and dry. You can see how the Wisconsin glacier scraped the area bare; the glacial till that fills the valleys provides only thin, rocky soil. The trees on the slopes are mostly mixed hardwoods, including large numbers of red and white oaks and some fairly large black birches. Evergreens are scarce. There are some white pines and a few eastern hemlocks; pitch pines can be found on the ridge tops. In the wetter areas in the valleys, red maple is common. Wildflowers abound here from early spring through the autumn. Far more than 400 species have been identified, including cardinal flower, pink lady's

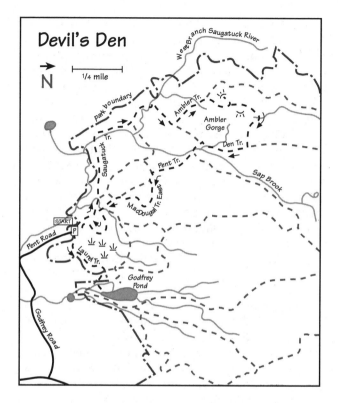

slipper, Indian pipe, Indian cucumber vine, and Dutch-man's-breeches.

The west branch of the Saugatuck River runs through the western edge of the preserve; a number of smaller streams that are tributaries of the Saugatuck run through the valleys. Saugatuck is said to mean "tidal river" in the Algonquian tongue of the Native Americans who once lived here. The Saugatuck does indeed form a tidal estuary where it empties into Long Island Sound at Westport to the south.

The brooding rock ridges and mature forest at Devil's Den give it a primordial feel that is actually somewhat at odds with the history of the site. An Indian rock shelter on the Harrison Trail near Godfrey Pond was in regular use 5,000 years ago. Archaeologists have studied sixteen other Native American sites within the preserve. Old stone walls here and there throughout the preserve are the remnants of old farms. In 1769, the pond was dammed and its level raised thirty feet to provide water power for a mill. You can still see the ruins of that mill at the southern end of the pond. Another mill was operated here by the Godfrey family until 1897. Looking at the preserve today, it's hard to imagine that it was heavily logged from the late 1800s through the turn of the century for charcoal production. The remains of more than fifty old charcoal-burning pits and associated structures dot the preserve. A demonstration site on Laurel Trail shows a typical charcoal mound and explains the process used to make this old-fashioned, wasteful fuel.

The original 1,350 acres of the preserve, along with a generous endowment, were donated to The Nature Conservancy by the late Katherine Ordway, a Weston resident. Additional acres from twenty-four contiguous tracts have been added over the past twenty-five years. The Devil's Den part of the name was given to the area by the charcoal burners of a century ago. It supposedly comes from a hoof-print-shaped depression on a rock somewhere in the preserve, although no one has ever been able to tell me exactly where.

The hiking trails at Devil's Den are blazed in yellow; in places, a hiking trail also has red blazes, indicating cross-country ski trails. White blazes in some places indicate that the trail is also part of the Saugatuck River Trails System. Trail intersections are marked by numbered signposts that correspond to the free trail map available at the parking lot.

If you want an easy walk that kids will enjoy, take the Laurel Trail for the popular 1.1-mile loop around Godfrey Pond. For a very quiet, beautiful, but occasionally challenging walk that takes you past some dramatic scenery and to some sweeping vistas, by all means take the route to Ambler Gorge. Despite the preserve's reputation for spring wildflowers, I think the best way to get the maximum scenic effect is to do this walk on a crisp, clear day in early October. The trees will be in full autumn color, and you're likely to see migrating hawks sailing south from the ridge tops.

The trail starts behind the parking area on the exit road. Look for a broad dirt path paralleling an old stone wall; there will be yellow and red blazes here. In a few minutes, you'll come to signpost 3; turn left here and follow the trail over a small stone bridge. In just another few minutes you'll come to a five-way intersection marked by signpost 17. Follow the sign that points to the right for the Saugatuck Trail. The trail becomes somewhat narrower here but remains clear and easy to follow; it is still blazed in red and yellow. Follow the Saugatuck Trail for about ten minutes; you will cross some small wooden bridges over streams and marshy areas. The bridges here and elsewhere thoughtfully have been covered with chicken wire to help you keep your

Rugged cliffs, slabs of tumbled rock, and bridges over rushing streams are part of the rugged beauty at Devil's Den. Joe Buff admires the scenery on the Ambler Gorge trail.

footing even in wet weather. The trail now starts to get hillier, but wooden steps help you over the harder parts. A bridge takes you over a gorgeous stream that is the west branch of the Saugatuck. The trail then bears to the right to run parallel to the river for the next fifteen minutes. It gets narrower and a little rocky here, but it is still easy to follow. Soon after you cross another bridge over the river, look for signpost 14 at a Y intersection. Go straight ahead to stay on the Saugatuck Trail. You'll cross the river on yet another bridge in about five minutes. A

Mountain laurel blooms in profusion at Devil's Den.

few minutes after that, the trail skirts some private property and bears to the right. You'll come upon signpost 12 shortly thereafter. This is the intersection with the Ambler Trail, blazed in yellow and white. Turn left onto the Ambler Trail and follow it as it climbs upward. In about ten minutes you'll come to another trail intersection at signpost 46. Bear right to stay on the Ambler Trail. Here the trail climbs steeply up through thick mountain laurel past a **towering rock ledge** on your left. Just past the ledge, the trail turns sharply left and leads immediately to signpost 45. Turn left here for a stunning view out to the west; note the pitch pines clinging to the barren ridge. Return to the main trail and go straight ahead past signpost 45 for another steep few minutes along the crest of the ridge until you arrive, a bit out of breath, at another magnificent vista, this time looking east. The ridge to the east is Deer Knoll, at 485 feet the highest point in the preserve. If you look south from either viewpoint on a clear day, you can see Long Island Sound. You're no more than 450 feet above sea level here, and only about 150 feet above the parking lot, but somehow it seems much higher.

To begin the return walk, continue on the trail as it descends past a dramatic escarpment with a jumble of massive boulders at its base. A log bridge takes you over Ambler Brook, a small stream that flows through the valley. In about five minutes you'll arrive at a memorial sign dedicating the gorge to the Ambler family. Continue on the trail to signpost 44. Turn right here onto the broad, grassy Den Trail, blazed in red and white. The going is now much easier. Five more minutes brings you to signpost 10 and a sign directing you back to the parking lot. Turn left here onto Pent Trail, cross the bridge over Sap Brook, and go straight ahead past signposts 8, 7, 6, 19, 5, and 3 until you arrive back at the parking lot in about ten minutes.

Hours, Fees, and Facilities

The trails at Devil's Den are open daily from sunrise to sunset. The gate to the parking lot is locked at sunset, so be sure you're back at your car by then. Visitors are asked to sign in at the map shelter in the parking lot. Entrance to the preserve is free, but donations are requested. There is a pay phone in the parking lot but there are no restrooms and no water. No pets are allowed.

Getting There

Friends who live in nearby suburban Connecticut tell me they've never been here because they've never been able to find the entrance. They just don't know where to look. Take the Merritt Parkway to exit 42 (Weston/Westport) and turn right at the traffic light onto Rte. 57 north. Follow Rte. 57 for five miles to Godfrey Road. Turn east (right) onto Godfrey Road and follow it for 0.5 mile to Pent Road. Turn left onto Pent Road and follow it for 0.6 mile until it dead-ends in the entrance to the preserve's parking lot. Follow the driveway another 0.3 mile to the lot.

For More Information

Lucius Pond Ordway–Devil's Den Preserve
Box 1162
Weston, CT 06883
203-226-4991

Northern New Jersey

Palisades Interstate Park
Alpine section

- 2.5 miles
- 3 hours
- moderate

Down, along, and up the cliffs of the Palisades.

The sheer red-brown cliffs of the Palisades on the western bank of the Hudson River are a rare and unusual geological formation. Their most striking feature is what gives the formation its name: massive vertical columns that resemble a palisade, or defensive fence made of stakes (like the cavalry forts in westerns). Today the Palisades form a very long, very thin ribbon park. Roughly eleven miles long but only about a quarter of a mile wide on average, Palisades State Park covers 2,472 acres. There are two major trails running the length of the park. The Shore Trail runs along the Hudson River at sea level, while the Long Path runs along the cliff. Five widely separated trails connect the two.

There are lots of good long walks in the Palisades. Because the park is so long and thin, it's a little harder to make a shorter but still interesting loop. I think the walk

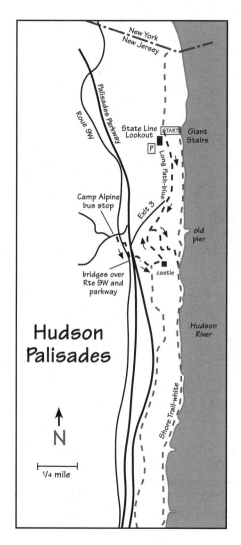

Hudson
Palisades

N

1/4 mile

outlined here gives you a good taste of the history, geology, and ecology of the Palisades.

This walk begins at the State Line Lookout, also known as Point Lookout, about ten miles north of the George Washington Bridge. Before starting your walk, admire the view from the terrace. At 532 feet, this is the **highest spot in the Palisades**. The big city directly across the Hudson is Yonkers.

From the parking lot, head south toward the river. Turn right to follow an old road for a few minutes. This road turns into the access road you drove in on; look here for the blue blazes of the Long Path. Follow the blazes along the road for another ten minutes. You'll come to a tree with a large blue double blaze and a sign warning you to stay on the trails. Turn left here and follow the trail into the woods. In a few minutes the trail begins a steep descent down a winding series of stone steps. Note the many tumbled slabs of rock here—stay on the trail! If the weather is wet or icy, don't go on this trail at all.

In a few minutes you'll cross a small stream on stepping-stones. On the other side, the trail forks. The left fork leads down to the river via the Forest View Trail. The right fork leads steeply up more stone steps to the Long Path along the cliffs. Take the right fork and follow the trail for five minutes or so until a turreted stone building appears. This is the Women's Federation castle, erected in 1929 as a monument to the volunteer effort that helped establish the park (see below). There's nothing in the castle and you can't go into it, but even so, judging from the amount of broken glass on the ground, this spot is a favorite among the beer-drinking youth of

New Jersey. The view is pretty good, though, and in the spring you can see pussy's-toes (also called everlasting) blooming here. This woolly wildflower has clusters of small, white, silky flowers that look a little like dandelions that have gone to seed.

To continue the walk, backtrack to the intersection with the Forest View Trail. This time, turn right to continue carefully down a series of switchbacks and steps. The trail here isn't particularly well marked, but it's very obvious. As you go down, note how the woods change. Near the ridge, which is dry and windy, the trees are mostly oak and hickory. As you descend into the cooler and moister conditions farther down, sugar maple, tulip tree, beech, hemlock, birch, and ash appear and get larg-

The Women's Federation castle commemorates the volunteers who helped preserve the Palisades as a park.

er the farther down you go. At the bottom, some of the maples and tulips are huge—they could easily be a couple of hundred years old. Your descent should take about twenty-five to thirty minutes—don't rush it. Just before you reach the river, the trail passes between two boulders. Ignore the side trail here that leads off to some picnic tables and continue straight ahead. In a few more minutes you'll see the blue blaze of the Long Path and the white blaze of the Shore Trail on a boulder. At this point you've reached the Shore Trail and can go either left (north) or right (south). I think the trail is little more interesting to the north, so turn left.

For the next few minutes, the path goes through a wide, grassy area that has some nice picnic tables. Note the cattail marsh along the water's edge and the old stone dock protruding into the river. In the spring, paulownia trees (*Paulownia tomentosa*) bloom here with purple blossoms. These lovely trees, also called princess trees or empress trees, are escapees from the garden of one of the estates that once lined the Palisades.

Continue on the trail for another ten minutes or so as it turns close to the river. When the path is blocked by a jumbled mass of fallen rock slabs from an old landslide, you've reached the Giant Stairs—almost directly below the State Line Lookout. To continue on the Shore Trail, you'd have to clamber over this rugged area—I don't recommend it. Instead, turn back and explore downriver as far as you want, always remembering that you'll have to retrace your steps on the way back. If you carry on south for two miles you'll reach the Alpine boat basin.

Return to your starting point via the Forest View Trail. To make the climb a little easier, take it slowly and stop to bird-watch along the way. This is a good area for seeing forest birds such as red-eyed vireos, wood thrushes, and scarlet tanagers. You might spot a worm-eating warbler in the thick, undisturbed woods near the river. I've also seen black-and-white warblers, ovenbirds, and yellow warblers here.

Palisades Geology and History

The Palisades were formed some 190 million years ago, when a sill of magma (molten rock) was squeezed up between layers of sandstone and shale and slowly solidified there, still covered by the sedimentary rock. As the thousand-foot-thick magma cooled, it contracted while under pressure from the weight of the overlying sediments. As a result, the rock fractured into polygonal vertical columns intersected by horizontal joints. Millennia later, the softer overlying sedimentary rock eroded away to expose the harder rock underneath. The Hudson River wore away the sandstone to the east, exposing the eastern flank of the formation.

Because the magma of the **Palisades** cooled slowly over a period of hundreds or possibly thousands of years, the rock is made of a complex mixture of minerals that sometimes appear in distinct layers that resemble strata. The rock is referred to generically as diabase, meaning a type of coarse basaltic rock in which different minerals can be seen distinctly. The vertical columns of the Palisades are scored by horizontal faults. Weathering causes the rock to break up into massive, blocky slabs that resemble steps. For this reason, the rock is sometimes called traprock, from the Swedish word *trapp*, or stairs. Fallen slabs and boulders form a talus layer at the foot of the Palisades that extends almost halfway up the cliff face.

The Palisades formation actually begins on Staten Island, but runs underground until it rises from the earth near Weehawken in New Jersey. It extends northward for nearly forty more miles before descending below ground again near Haverstraw in New York's Rockland County.

Palisades diabase is very durable, which makes it valuable for use as a building material (it was used to build many of the brownstones in New York City) and for road construction. Because of this, and because the cliffs are conveniently placed for cheap and easy water transport, the diabase was quarried extensively in the latter half of the nineteenth century. Appalled by this uncontrolled destruction, members of the New Jersey

The sheer cliffs of the Palisades as seen from the State Line Lookout. Note the vertical fracturing of the rock.

Federation of Women's Clubs fought for legislation to protect the Palisades from further damage. In 1900, their goal was achieved when the Palisades Interstate Park Commission (PIPC) was established. With money from the states of New York and New Jersey and donations from private philanthropists, fourteen miles of shoreline and cliff were purchased. In the 1930s the Civilian Conservation Corps (CCC) built trails and structures in the park that remain today. Most of the land on the cliff tops was occupied by large estates. During the real estate boom that followed the completion of the George Washington Bridge in 1931, however, it became apparent to the commissioners that the cliffs were in danger of commercial development (one glance at the towering apartment buildings of Fort Lee tells you they were right). Through purchase, donation, and condemnation, the cliff tops were incorporated into the Palisades Interstate Park; the mansions were torn down to recreate a natural environment. Today, all of the Palisades is part of one continuous park that includes Tallman Mountain, Blauvelt, Hook Mountain, High Tor, Rockland Lake, Harriman, and Bear Mountain State Parks. The Palisades Interstate Park Commission owns almost 2,500 acres in New Jersey and more than 81,000 acres in total; the parks are in five counties and two states. (For more about the history and attractions of the PIPC parks, see the walks in Harriman and Bear Mountain parks, pages 241 and 250.)

Nature lovers in the region hope that Sterling Forest, a 19,000-acre tract of unspoiled woods that straddles the New York–New Jersey border, will be added soon to the PIPC's holdings. The land is now owned privately by a Swiss insurance company that has threatened to develop it into a huge commercial and residential complex. The land is an environmentally sensitive watershed area that provides drinking water to some 2 million people in New Jersey. A portion of the Appalachian Trail runs through it, and limited hiking by permit is allowed (call 914-351-5714 for information). The best way to see Sterling Forest is to hike with one of the many groups that regularly visit the area. Check with the New York–New Jersey Trail Conference for scheduled trips.

The state of New Jersey already has purchased some of the forest. Recently, the governors of both states have pledged millions toward the purchase price of the rest. The federal help needed to complete the purchase, however, is still controversial and uncertain. As of this writing, Sterling Forest remains threatened.

The scenic, forty-two-mile Palisades Parkway connects the parks by road. By foot, the parks are connected by the Long Path, a hiking trail that starts at Fort Lee in the Palisades and extends 236 miles to the town of Ashland 12 miles north of Catskill Park. Maintained by the New York–New Jersey Trail Conference, the Long Path was first proposed in the 1920s. The first section of the trail was built in Palisades State Park in the 1930s, but serious work on the trail didn't begin until the early 1960s. In 1971 the Long Path was declared a National Recreation Trail. Work to extend the Long Path farther north to the Mohawk River and into the Adirondack Mountains is ongoing.

Hours, Fees, and Facilities

Palisades State Park is open dawn to dusk year-round. A seasonal parking fee of $3 per car is charged at some parking areas. Restrooms, water, and pay phones are available year-round at the State Line Lookout; there is also a seasonal restaurant. Seasonal facilities are available at the Englewood and Alpine areas on the shore. Pets are permitted on leashes only.

Getting There

From the George Washington Bridge, follow signs for the Palisades Interstate Parkway (PIP). It's more direct from the upper level of the bridge. Follow the PIP north for 7.5 miles to exit 3 for Point Lookout. Follow the lookout road for 0.5 mile to the parking area. Parking at the lookout is restricted to two hours.

The Red & Tan bus line from the George Washington Bridge terminal in Manhattan runs up and down Rte. 9W, a busy local road that closely parallels the Palisades Interstate Parkway (commercial traffic and buses are not allowed on the PIP). Tell the driver you want to get off at the Camp Alpine stop, also known as the Boy Scout Camp stop. Walk south about thirty yards to the footbridges over Rte. 9W and the PIP. Follow the trail more or less straight ahead for about ten minutes until you reach the Women's Federation castle (don't turn right onto the Long Path), then follow directions as above.

For More Information

Palisades Interstate Park Commission
Box 155
Alpine, NJ 07620
201-768-1360

Cheesequake State Park
Matawan

- **3.5 miles**
- **2 hours**
- **moderate**

*A variety of habitats, from pine barrens
to rare white cedar swamp.*

Only thirty miles from New York City, Cheesequake
State Park is one of the most accessible New Jersey state
parks. The park's 1,274 acres lie near Raritan Bay in the
Atlantic coastal region of the state. This is a **transitional
zone** between New Jersey's southern and northern vegetation types. Among the habitat types you can see here
are open fields, salt marshes, freshwater marshes, a
white cedar swamp, pine barrens, and typical northeastern hardwood forest.

Despite its size, there are only three significant hiking trails through the park. The longest and most interesting is the green trail, which goes through several different habitats, including a typical pine barrens forest
and a white cedar swamp. This trail, while very enjoyable, can be wet in places, especially in the spring. It can
also be very buggy in the spring and summer.

Start in the parking area a little past the main
entrance to the park. Look for the well-marked trailhead
near the stop sign and water fountain. Follow the yellow

Cheesequake State Park

disks into the woods. After just minute or two you'll see the return portion of the yellow trail on your right. Ignore it and keep going down the shallow steps of the broad path you started on. In a few more minutes you'll come to the well-marked junction with the green/red trail. Turn left and follow the blazes as the path leads you along a small stream and then to a modern new nature center. Note how the upland forest has quickly given way here to a boggy area full of skunk cabbage, ferns, and sphagnum moss.

From the nature center, follow the green arrow around the left side of the building to get back on the very obvious red/green trail. In about five minutes, at marker 5, the terrain changes again. The soil is dry and sandy; pitch pines and blackjack oak (*Quercus marilandica*) are found here. This is a little sample of a **pine barrens**. (For a really big example, visit the Pine Barrens region of southern New Jersey—it covers 960,000 acres, or about one-quarter of the state's total land area.) You might not realize that the blackjack oaks are oaks at all, since their leaves have only three very blunt lobes, instead of the more numerous, deeper, and pointier lobes found on leaves from the more familiar red, white, or pin oaks. The leaf resembles a rounded triangle and is much broader at the tip than at the base.

Follow the trail as steps made from old railroad ties lead you down to a bridge over a stream. The terrain changes to open, mixed woodland with a lot of shrubs. Sweet pepperbush (*Clethra alnifolia*) is very common here. The shrub puts up a stalk of small white blossoms in the spring; later, the blossoms turn into small seed capsules resembling peppercorns. High-bush blueberry shrubs (*Vaccinium corymbosum*) are also common. It's interesting to note that cultivated blueberries, which are an important crop in New Jersey, were developed from this plant.

Continue on the trail for another five minutes or so as the trail crosses Perrine's Road, a sandy, unpaved park road that has almost no traffic. The trail splits here; follow the green blazes to the right and continue

This section of the boardwalk through the freshwater swamp at Cheesequake State Park is built around some large red maple trees.

onward for another ten minutes. The trail changes to railroad tie steps and steppingstones that take you to a boardwalk through a freshwater swamp. The boardwalk opens out into a very pleasant viewing platform with a bench built around some red maple trees. This is a good spot for a rest and some bird-watching. Look especially for nuthatches and downy woodpeckers hunting for insects on the trunks and branches of the red maples and black willows that are the predominant trees here. In the summer, ruby-throated hummingbirds can be spotted feeding on the nectar of the orange jewelweed flowers. In the summer you might also spot basking spotted turtles.

From the boardwalk a series of railroad tie steps leads you up again. Bear to the right to follow the green arrow. In just a few minutes more you descend again to another long boardwalk. This time the **freshwater swamp** is subtly but significantly different. The dominant tree here is the eastern or Atlantic white cedar (*Chamaecypris thyoides*). This tree is easily recognized: it has scalelike needles and produces numerous small, globular cones. Why does white cedar grow here and not in the swampy area a hundred yards away? The reason is that here a layer of clay, washed down from the glacial moraine to the north, lies just underneath the surface. The impermeable clay traps moisture, while accumulated dead leaves make the soil very acidic. The thick needles of the cedars form a dense canopy that shades the understory. Shrubs that can withstand the shade and acid soil here include high-bush blueberry, swamp azalea, and sweet bay magnolia. This sort of habitat is ideal for great horned owls. They're hard to spot, but listen for their resonant hoots (anywhere from three to eight at a time) late in the afternoon.

After leaving the boardwalk, continue on for another fifteen minutes or so on the gently rolling trail until you reach another unpaved road. This is Museum Road; look for a conveniently placed resting bench here. A large signboard points you across the road to continue on the green trail. Just past the road is a stand of very large eastern white pines (*Pinus strobus*) that are between 100 and 150 years old. Look for long, pointed needles in clumps of five; the cones are long with tightly overlapping scales. In the nineteenth century, most of the old-growth white pines in the Northeast were logged, so a stand with trees this large is a bit unusual.

As you continue on for the next fifteen minutes or so, the trail leads through a typical and very beautiful **hardwood climax forest**. The well-drained soil here supports large trees, including red oak, white oak, American beech, and pignut hickory. In the understory, look for shrubs such as spicebush, mountain laurel, and viburnum. In the spring, this area is very productive for wildflowers. In May, look along the trail near here for dense patches of pink lady's slipper. This orchid (*Cypripedium* family) has a downy stem, three sepals, and three petals. One of the petals resembles an inflated pouch, or, more fancifully, a delicate slipper.

Continue to follow the green markers, ignoring any side trails. Some huge old tulip trees indicate the start of a flood plain area. The small stream nearby sometimes floods after heavy rains, depositing nutrients that enrich the soil. Tulip trees seem to thrive on being flooded a few times a year. The same flooding that makes the trees grow well may make walking a bit wet. Follow the trail blazes even when they seem to be taking you along a stream bed. In a few more minutes you'll cross a small bridge over the real stream.

The trail then skirts a small pond on the left and reaches another boardwalk in about five more minutes. The boardwalk takes you over a very pretty spring-fed stream that flows over a sandy bottom. Five minutes later, you arrive at another intersection with Perrine's Road—and another bench. Turn left here to follow along the road briefly past the Gordon Field Scout campsite; the red trail will rejoin the green here on your left. The green/red trail turns off the road again to the right and runs along the edge of Gordon Field more or less parallel to Museum Road for another ten minutes; then it joins the road and takes you back to your starting point in about ten minutes more.

During this walk you may have been wondering how the park got its unusual name. Cheesequake seems to be what the Leni Lenape Indians called the area, but nobody seems to know what the word actually means.

Hours, Fees, and Facilities

Cheesequake State Park is open during daylight hours every day. From Memorial Day to Labor Day the entrance fee is $5 per vehicle. The park is free on Tuesdays except holidays. Restrooms, water, pay phones, and free maps are available at the park office just inside the main entrance. Pets are allowed on leashes only.

Getting There

Take the Garden State Parkway to exit 120 (Matawan/ Laurence Harbor). If you are coming from the north, stay in the local (right) lanes. The exit is marked with brown Cheesequake signs, as is the route to the park. As you exit, you will pass through a park-and-ride parking area leading to Matawan Avenue. Turn right onto Matawan and follow it for 0.2 mile to the traffic light.

Turn right at the light onto Cliffwood Avenue and follow it for 0.4 mile to the traffic light. Turn right at the light onto Gordon Avenue and follow it 0.8 mile to the park entrance. To reach the trailhead, follow the park road past the tollbooth for another 0.2 mile to the parking area.

For More Information

Cheesequake State Park
Matawan, NJ 07747
908-566-2161

Scherman-Hoffman Sanctuaries
Bernardsville

- **2.5 miles**
- **2 hours**
- **moderate**

*Enjoyable trails wind through dogwoods
and along the Passaic River.*

These twin sanctuaries are operated by the New Jersey
Audubon Society (NJAS; see below). The 125 acres of the
Scherman section were donated to NJAS in 1965. In 1973
and 1975, the Hoffman family donated adjacent land.
The Hoffman house, barn, and outbuildings were donated in 1981; the house is now the sanctuary office, bookstore, and education center. All told, the sanctuaries now
cover 260 acres of diverse terrain. In addition, the New
Jersey Brigade section of nearby Morristown National
Historical Park borders the sanctuaries on the north, providing additional protected land that helps attract birds
and wildlife to the area.

There are three well-marked trails through the sanctuaries. The walk described here links all three for a thor-
ough look at the varied terrain.

Start at the northern end of the parking lot near the
Hoffman building. Follow the clear signs for the Field
Loop trail. This easy loop takes you along open fields

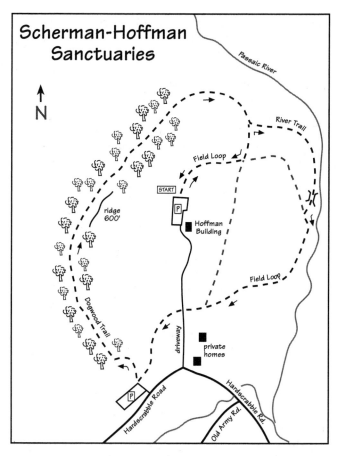

full of wildflowers and butterflies; the fields are mowed periodically to keep them from being taken over by shrubs and saplings. You might see deer grazing in the meadows here. After a few minutes, the Field Loop intersects the Dogwood Trail. Turn left here onto the Dogwood Trail and follow it for just a minute or two until it intersects with the River Trail. Turn right onto the River Trail and follow it as it leads you down to the Passaic River. Here only a mile or so from its headwaters, the Passaic is a broad, shallow stream; the water gurgles as it flows over the rocky stream bed. Amazingly, this is the same river that pours out of the first Watchung Mountains at Paterson some thirty miles to the north to form the Great Falls of the Passaic, a spectacular example of water power.

Follow the trail for another ten minutes or so as it leads along the **tree-shaded, fern-lined river**. In the spring, this is a good spot to look for warblers. Some twenty-five species occur here regularly during migration between May 5 and May 20. There are sixty resident bird species here, including pileated woodpecker, eastern bluebird, worm-eating warbler, and Louisiana waterthrush (which is, despite its name, a warbler).

The River Trail soon crosses a wooden bridge and rejoins the Field Loop. Turn left and follow the Field Loop as it curves away from the river. In about ten minutes it joins the Dogwood Trail, near some private homes. (If you want to cut your walk short here, continue straight ahead for another minute to the sanctuary entrance road. Turn right to return to the parking lot in just a few minutes.)

To continue on the Dogwood Trail, go straight ahead. The trail almost immediately crosses the road you drove in on and then leads down to another parking area off Hardscrabble Road. From the back of the lot, the red-blazed Dogwood Trail leads off again into the woods.

This part of the trail is uphill and can be slightly strenuous—the trail makes several switchbacks as it climbs up the sunny southern slope of a steep, wooded hill. Look along here for the flowering dogwood trees (*Cornus florida*) that give this trail its name. These lovely little trees rarely exceed thirty feet in height. Because they grow well in partial shade, dogwoods thrive here in the shadow of the taller oaks, hickories, tulip trees, and sugar maples. Flowering dogwoods bloom in May with beautiful white flowers. By the autumn, the flowers have developed into bunches of red berries. The common English name dogwood goes back many centuries. It

The Passaic River, here only about a mile from its source, is a rocky stream burbling through the woods.

refers to the berries, which were considered to be inferior and unfit for human consumption—in other words, fit only for dogs. (Some dogs, anyway—mine won't touch them.) Actually, the berries are an important bird and wildlife food in the winter. You can spot a dogwood easily by its broad, oval leaves—they taper at both ends and the prominent veins curve to follow the margin. The leaves turn brilliant scarlet in the autumn.

In about fifteen minutes you'll be at the top of the hill, about 600 feet above sea level. Here, where the vegetation thins out, you can see blocky chunks of billion-year-old **bedrock gneiss** protruding from the ground. The rounded boulders are glacial erratics that were left here much more recently—only 12,000 years ago, when the Wisconsin glacier receded. Chestnut oaks grow on this dry, rocky ridge—look for wavy-edged leaves about five inches long.

From the ridge top the trail winds gradually downhill to the north. In another fifteen minutes or so the path intersects the River Trail on the left. Stay on the Dogwood Trail for another few minutes until it intersects the Field Loop. Turn right and follow the Field Loop back to the parking lot.

If the Hoffman building is open, pay a visit to the excellent bookstore (they carry my birding books), look at the very interesting exhibit on New Jersey birds, and enjoy the displays of wildlife art and photography.

The New Jersey Audubon Society

A number of states have independent Audubon organizations that are separate and distinct from the well-known National Audubon Society. This confusing situation dates back to the start of the popular conservation movement in the late 1800s, when numerous organizations using the Audubon name arose. Many eventually coalesced into the National Audubon Society, but some remained unaffiliated as state societies. The New Jersey Audubon Society, founded in 1897, remains a large, independent organization with its own extensive education and conservation programs, five nature centers, and nineteen sanctuaries. As you might expect from an organization with Audubon in its name, birds are important to the NJAS. The organization sponsors the famed World Series of Birding every spring and maintains the Cape May Bird Observatory at Cape May Point—by universal acclaim one of the finest spots in the country for bird-watching.

Wildlife conservation and habitat preservation in general are the larger interests at NJAS, however. The organization works very hard—and often very successfully—to foster environmental awareness and a conservation ethic among the citizens of New Jersey. A big part of the environmental effort is accomplished through outstanding education programs for both children and adults.

Hours, Fees, and Facilities

The trails at the sanctuaries are open daily from 9:00 A.M. to 5:00 P.M. The Hoffman Building is open Tuesday through Saturday, 9:00 A.M. to 5:00 P.M., and on Sunday from noon to 5 P.M. There are no fees. Restrooms and water are available at the Hoffman building. No pets are allowed.

Getting There

Take I-287 to exit 26B (Bernardsville and Rte. 202). Follow Rte. 202 south for about half a mile; look for the small NJAS signs. Turn right onto Childs Road. After 0.2 mile, turn right onto Hardscrabble Road and follow it for 1.0 mile to the entrance on the right. Follow the driveway 0.2 mile more to reach the Hoffman building and parking lot. If you prefer to start your walk from the Scherman parking lot, continue on Hardscrabble Road for 0.1 mile longer; the lot is on the right. Do not park on the street if the lot is full.

For More Information

Scherman-Hoffman Sanctuaries
New Jersey Audubon Society
11 Hardscrabble Road
Box 693
Bernardsville, NJ 07924
908-766-5787

Great Swamp National Wildlife Refuge
Morristown

- **1.2 miles**
- **1 to 2 hours**
- **easy**

*Rare turtles, wood ducks, and a range
of terrains in an unusual refuge.*

The Great Swamp National Wildlife Refuge covers more than 7,200 acres of swamp woodland, hardwood ridges, cattail marshes, streams, ponds, bogs, and grassland. The adjoining Lord Stirling Park covers 430 acres of similar terrain on the western edge of the refuge. Among the varied habitats of these two sites you can see hundreds of different plants, more than 222 bird species, 39 reptiles and amphibians, and 32 different mammals—all only twenty-six miles west of Times Square.

The Great Swamp was created some 25,000 years ago, when the Wisconsin glacier reached its southernmost point just to the north of it. As the glacier advanced, it pushed a huge pile of sand and gravel ahead of it. When the glacier slowly withdrew over thousands of years, it left the pile behind as a huge ridge called a terminal moraine. The ridge blocked the outlet of an ancient, preglacial river basin. Water from the melting glacier backed up in the basin behind this natural

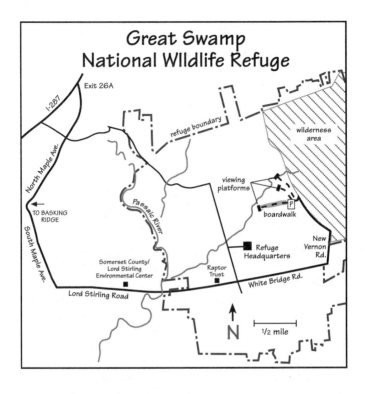

Great Swamp
National Wildlife Refuge

Exit 26A

I-287

North Maple Ave.

refuge boundary

wilderness
area

TO BASKING
RIDGE

South Maple Ave.

Passaic River

viewing
platforms

P

boardwalk

New
Vernon
Rd.

Refuge
Headquarters

Somerset County/
Lord Stirling
Environmental Center

Raptor
Trust

White Bridge Rd.

Lord Stirling Road

N

1/2 mile

dam, forming Glacial Lake Passaic, a huge body of water that was thirty miles long, ten miles wide, and up to 200 feet deep. The lake lasted for about four thousand years, laying down a thick layer of clay that reached 80 feet in places. Eventually, as the glacier retreated even farther, it uncovered a second outlet to the river basin at what is now called Little Falls Gap. The lake waters drained out along the valley of the Passaic River. The lake disappeared gradually and was replaced by extensive marshes and swamps that remain in part to this day. (Vegetation determines the difference between a swamp and a marsh. Swamps mostly have such shrubs as buttonbush and arrowwood and such moisture-loving trees as red maple and black willow. Marshes mostly have grasses, sedges, and such rushes as cattails and phragmites; saltwater marshes have *Spartina* grasses.) The clays underlying the swamp are above the water table. Water levels here are controlled solely by precipitation and the flow of two streams that run through the area.

Great Swamp National Wildlife Refuge

In the mid-1800s, some of the land in the Great Swamp was drained for farming, but by the beginning of the 1900s, most of the farms were gone and the land was reverting to its natural state. Some drainage projects in the 1920s and 1930s didn't have much of an impact, and the land was seen as basically worthless. In 1959, however, a new use was proposed: a major airport. The local residents and conservationists nationwide strenuously opposed the idea. Volunteers raised more than a million dollars to purchase nearly 3,000 acres, which were then donated to the Department of the Interior. These acres formed the nucleus of the refuge; additional land has been added over the years.

Today the Great Swamp National Wildlife Refuge is divided into two areas. The eastern half of the refuge was designated as a Wilderness Area in 1968; development and motorized vehicles are forbidden. Almost eight miles of hiking trails run through this part of the

Two sturdy boardwalks with viewing areas accommodate visitors to the Great Swamp. Typical swamp vegetation such as ferns can be seen easily here.

refuge. These trails allow a true wilderness experience, but they tend to be very wet.

Fortunately, you can get a very good look at the swamp from the two excellent boardwalk trails in the western half of the refuge. This section is managed actively to maintain optimum habitat for a wide variety of wildlife. Water levels are regulated, grasslands and brush are mowed periodically, shrubs are planted, and nesting boxes for bluebirds and wood ducks are provided. This is nature-watching at its easiest, with just one problem: bugs. Mosquitoes, ticks, and deerflies are abundant from May to September. To minimize discomfort and the chance of getting Lyme disease from deer ticks, apply insect repellent containing DEET liberally; wear long sleeves, long trousers tucked into socks, and closed shoes; and check yourself carefully for ticks after your visit. Because the boardwalks are so accessible, the refuge can be crowded on weekends. If you visit on a weekend, try to arrive as early in the morning as possible.

To get onto the boardwalks, park at the Wildlife Observation Center. Boardwalk A is directly ahead from the short entrance path. This boardwalk is 0.4 mile long and ends in an observation blind; it has several wider observation areas along the way. Boardwalk B begins to the right, a little way past the restroom structure. It is only 0.2 mile long; it too ends in an observation blind. Near the start of this boardwalk a short trail with some boardwalk sections leads off through the woods. A ten-minute walk along the trail brings you to yet another observation blind. The blinds are fairly elaborate, with slanted viewing windows and carpeting to muffle the sound of footsteps. To see the most wildlife, move and speak quietly and stay back a bit from the windows. Don't stick your arms or head out the window—you'll spook the animals.

You can see an incredible amount of life on these short walks. The largest breeding population of eastern bluebirds in New Jersey is found in the refuge; note the nesting boxes that have been placed near open areas. One of the largest breeding populations of **wood ducks** in the entire mid-Atlantic region also is found here. Look for them especially from the blind at the end of boardwalk B. Wood ducks are very beautiful and rather shy; you're most likely to see them early in the morning in the springtime from the end of March to the middle of May. They nest in tree cavities, which are in short supply here. Fortunately, the wood ducks nest happily in the larger boxes on poles that you see scattered throughout the refuge.

The diverse habitats of the refuge attract a wide variety of migratory and residential birds. The best season for seeing such waterfowl as ducks and marsh and

The Great Swamp on a rainy spring day. The shallow ponds are a great place to spot turtles and frogs.

such waterbirds as herons, bitterns, rails, and gallinules is in the early spring, before the marsh vegetation grows high enough to hide them. The best time to see warblers and other songbirds is in May.

Early in the morning or late in the afternoon, especially in the spring, you're quite likely to see a muskrat or two from the boardwalks. Muskrats play an important role in keeping the marsh areas open. They pull up marsh vegetation by the roots for food and to build their conical houses.

A number of interesting amphibians and reptiles are found in the refuge. **Eight different turtle species** can be seen here. The most common is the eastern painted turtle, the stinkpot or musk turtle, and the spotted turtle. The uncommon eastern mud turtle is found in quiet, shallow water. The uncommon wood turtle, a threatened species, is found in a range of habitats here, although it prefers moist woods. This turtle has bright, orange-red skin and a heavy, keeled carapace (shell) with deep concentric grooves. Adults are fairly large, reaching seven to nine inches in length. For turtle fans, the real prize is the rare bog turtle, an endangered species that is one of the rarest in the eastern United States. The bog turtle is the smallest turtle in the world; its narrow carapace is only three to four inches long. Look for the large orange spot on each side of the head. You might spot it in swampy areas, bogs, and slow-moving streams.

Twelve different snakes, including the very rare earth snake, inhabit the refuge. From the boardwalk, however, you are most likely to see the northern water snake. You might also spot the eastern ribbon snake and the eastern garter snake.

Of course, frogs abound here. The most common are northern spring peepers, green frogs, and northern leopard frogs. Less common but still very abundant are wood frogs, bullfrogs, New Jersey chorus frogs, gray tree frogs, and northern cricket frogs. Upland chorus frogs and pickerel frogs are uncommon here, but dedicated frog hunters will be able to find them in the appropriate habitats.

Lord Stirling Environmental Education Center

The 430 acres of the Environmental Education Center at Lord Stirling Park, owned by Somerset County, were opened in 1971. The park has more than eight miles of well-marked trails, including some extensive sections of boardwalk through marsh and swamp. Aside from the trails, this park is worth a visit to see the education building. This attractive modern structure, opened in 1977, was the first solar-powered public building in the country.

The Raptor Trust

Located on the road between Great Swamp National Wildlife Refuge and Lord Stirling Park, the Raptor Trust is a private, nonprofit organization devoted to the preservation and well-being of birds of prey. The large avian rehabilitation center here takes in injured and orphaned wild birds of all species. The goal is always to release the birds back into the wild. A number of birds that were too seriously injured to be released are on exhibit here—a rare opportunity to look an owl or hawk in the eye.

Hours, Fees, and Facilities

The trails and boardwalks in the Great Swamp National Refuge are open daily from dawn to dusk. The refuge headquarters on Pleasant Plains Road is open Monday through Friday from 8:00 A.M. to 4:30 P.M. and on some Sundays in the spring and fall. There are no fees. Restrooms and water are available at the Wildlife Observation Center. Pets are allowed on leashes only and only in the parking area.

Getting There

Take I-287 to exit 26A (Basking Ridge). The exit leads you onto North Maple Avenue; follow it east for 0.7 mile to the traffic light. Turn left at the light (note the sign for the refuge) onto Madisonville Road and follow it for 0.5 mile to Pleasant Plains Road. Follow Pleasant Plains Road for 3.2 miles to White Bridge Road. Turn left (east) and follow White Bridge Road for 1.1 miles to New Vernon Road. Turn left (north) and follow New Vernon Road for 1.2 miles to the Wildlife Observation Center entrance on your left.

To get to the Raptor Trust from the Wildlife Observation Center, return to White Bridge Road and turn right (west). Follow White Bridge Road for 1.2 miles to the entrance on your right.

To get to Lord Stirling Park from the Wildlife Observation Center, return to White Bridge Road and turn right (west). Follow White Bridge Road for 2.1 miles to the entrance on your right. (White Bridge Road is also called Lord Stirling Road near the park.)

For More Information

Great Swamp National Wildlife Refuge
Pleasant Plains Road
RD 1, Box 152
Basking Ridge, NJ 07920
201-425-1222

Lord Stirling Park Environmental Education Center
190 Lord Stirling Road
Basking Ridge, NJ 07920
908-766-2489

The Raptor Trust
1390 White Bridge Road
Millington, NJ 07946
908-647-2353

Wawayanda State Park
Highland Lakes

- **3 miles**
- **2 hours**
- **moderate**

*Hiking on old woods roads in a rugged area
of outstanding scenic beauty.*

Warning: Hunting is permitted in parts of this park. Check with the park office if you plan to hike in the remoter areas during hunting season.

Wawayanda State Park is vast. It covers more than 13,000 acres across two counties in northern New Jersey along the New York border. This area, known geologically as the New Jersey Highlands province, is an extension of the Hudson Highlands and has the same climate—it's cold and snowy here in the winter. The terrain is rugged and rocky, with dense woods, a large swamp, lakes, and wetlands. It's just possible that you might see a bear.

The name Wawayanda is said to mean "water on the mountain" in the Algonquian language of the Lenape Indians who once lived here. There are more than 40 miles of trails winding through Wawayanda. Most are well-blazed old woods roads. Some of the roads date back to iron mining days, but most are a legacy of the 1940s, when the area was heavily logged

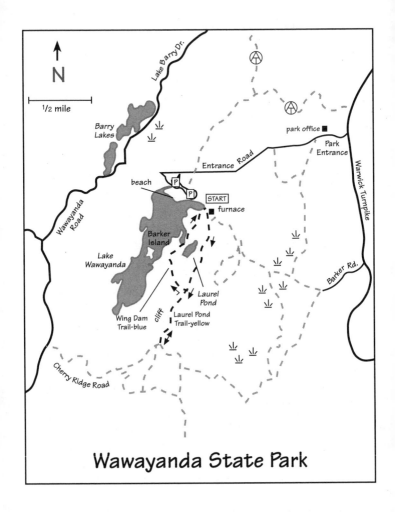

Wawayanda State Park

for mine props by the New Jersey Zinc Company. The land was purchased by the state in 1961. A narrow, very rocky, and isolated 19.6-mile stretch of the Appalachian Trail also goes through the park. The New York–New Jersey Trail Conference publishes a good map of this park. Ask for trail map 21 showing north Jersey trails.

The walk described here will take you on an interesting loop past remnants of the area's iron-mining history and along the edge of the Wawayanda swamp natural area. It starts in the parking lot at 225-acre Wawayanda Lake, once called Double Pond because it was actually two lakes separated by a narrow strip of land. Sometime in the mid-1800s, the Thomas Iron Company built an earthen dam at the northeastern end of the lake (near the parking lot); a wing dam was added on the eastern shore. The two dams raised the water level nearly eight feet and drowned the land separating the ponds. The original intent was to provide water power for the nearby iron furnace (see below). Today this lovely lake is managed chiefly for fishing and recreation, with a swimming beach, boat rentals (blessedly, no motors allowed), and picnic grounds. If you like to hike and your family doesn't, this is a good place to go.

Follow the gravel road that leads east (to your left when looking at the lake) through a picnic area away from the lake. In about five minutes you'll pass the stone wing dam on your right; in another minute you'll cross a wooden bridge over the spillway from the dam. Shortly after this you'll come to an unusual tall structure that is the old iron furnace (see below).

Continue straight ahead past the furnace and past the turnoff for the group campsite on your left. You're looking for the Laurel Pond Trail, marked by square yellow paint blazes. The trail begins just after you cross another small bridge and enter the woods. The trail is a slightly sunken old woods road that is fairly broad but somewhat eroded and stony.

In about ten minutes you'll see an unmarked side trail on your right. This short trail leads down through cool, shady hemlocks to Laurel Pond, a pristine little ten-acre pond. This is an enjoyable spot to explore. The pond is bordered by mountain laurel and rhododendrons; a virgin stand of tall hemlock trees grows at the southeast end.

To continue, backtrack to the Laurel Pond Trail and turn right. The trail begins to climb steadily here as it

A stand of tall hemlock trees is at the southeastern end of Laurel Pond.

goes through a lovely area of **mixed woodland**. Continue for another twenty minutes or so until you come to a bare, rocky area on your right. The trail here is about 1,375 feet above sea level. You haven't actually climbed that high, though—the parking lot at Lake Wawayanda is about 1,100 feet above sea level.

As you continue along the trail for another few minutes, you'll come to the triple blue blazes of the Wing Dam Trail on your right. For now, ignore this turnoff and continue on the Laurel Pond Trail as it takes you along a dramatic ridge past some magnificent granite outcroppings. There are some nice views here looking out over the Wawayanda Plateau.

After another twenty minutes, the trail ends at the unmarked T intersection with Cherry Ridge Road. Turn around and backtrack to the triple blue blazes. Turn left onto the Wing Dam Trail, which is a narrow hiking path, not a woods road. The trail leads upward for a few minutes to the top of a bare, rocky ridge and then goes mostly downhill through the woods for another twenty minutes. This part of the walk is particularly enjoyable. The trail is well marked, very clean and quiet, and virtually deserted even on a summer Saturday.

The Wing Dam Trail eventually turns into another graveled woods road. You'll pass some side trails on your left as you walk along here. These lead down to the eastern shore of Lake Wawayanda—they're fun to explore.

In another five minutes you'll start to see Lake Wawayanda through the trees on your left. A few minutes after that you'll come out of the woods at a wooden bridge that leads over the outflow stream of the wing dam that gives the trail its name. Follow the trail for another few minutes until you come to three large rocks that block the road. The three blue blazes on the rock at the right tell you this is the end of the trail. From here, go straight ahead and follow the road around to the left to return. You'll be back at your car in about five minutes.

The Old Iron Furnace

In the nineteenth century, iron mining and smelting were important industries in the Hudson and New Jersey Highlands (see the walks in Harriman State Park and Fahnestock State Park). The old iron furnace preserved at Wawayanda was built in 1846. It is thirty-seven feet high and thirty feet wide. The furnace is open at the top. A charging bridge once led from the hill behind the furnace to the top. Cartloads of crushed iron ore, mixed with limestone and charcoal, were dumped into the top. Water channeled from Lake Wawayanda, which was dammed for the purpose, turned a water wheel that pumped a giant bellows attached to the furnace. The molten iron was tapped from the bottom of the furnace and run into trenches and shallow pits in the sand floor. The molded iron in the pits resembled piglets lined up along a sow's belly—hence the term "pig iron." Running at full capacity, the furnace could make eight tons of pig iron a day. To do so, it needed charcoal, which was obtained by cutting and burning the surrounding woods. The Wawayanda furnace remained operative, with some pauses, from 1853 to 1867. By 1857, cheaper, hotter-burning coal in Pennsylvania had become the fuel of choice for making iron and

The old iron furnace was built in 1846; it is thirty-seven feet high and thirty feet wide. The encircling steel cables are part of the modern preservation effort.

steel; new, more efficient blast furnaces were built farther west. The Wawayanda furnace grew increasingly obsolete and finally closed forever.

While it operated and for several decades after, the furnace was the focal point of a large village. By 1900, however, the area was largely abandoned. Ghostly traces still survive near the furnace site. Look around for the old sluices to the water wheel and for old stone walls. The foundations of many buildings, including a large mule barn that burned down in 1985, still can be found in the woods that have grown up over the decades.

Hours, Fees, and Facilities

Wawayanda State Park is open daily from 8:00 A.M. to dusk. There is a seasonal entrance fee of $5 per vehicle on weekdays; on weekends and holidays, the fee is $7. Restrooms, water, pay phones, and free maps are available at the park office just past the tollbooths daily from 8:00 A.M. to 4:30 P.M. Restrooms are available seasonally at the swimming beach on Lake Wawayanda. Pets are allowed on leashes only.

Getting There

Take I-80 westbound to Rte. 23 north. Follow Rte. 23 for 17 miles to Union Valley Road (County Road 513). Look for the brown Wawayanda sign here. Make a right and follow Union Valley Road northeast for 7.6 miles. At the light in Milford, follow the Wawayanda sign and bear left to stay on Union Valley Road for 1.0 mile longer. At White Road follow the Wawayanda sign and bear left. Stay on White Road for 0.3 mile to Warwick Pike. There is no Wawayanda sign here, although there ought to be. Instead, follow the sign for Upper Greenwood Lake and turn left onto Warwick Pike. Follow this road for 4.3 miles to the park entrance on your left. Follow the park road for 2.7 miles to the Lake Wawayanda parking area. Go through the first parking area to the second near the boathouse.

For More Information

Wawayanda State Park
Box 198
Highland Lakes, NJ 07422
201-853-4462

Walks and Highlights

Region	Walk	Page Number	Difficulty Level	Distance	River
New York City	Central Park	1	easy	3	
	Riverside Park	12	easy	1.5	✔
	Fort Tryon Park	20	moderate	1.5	✔
	Inwood Hill Park	29	moderate	1.5	✔
	Van Cortlandt Park	38	easy	1.0	
	Pelham Bay Park	48	easy	1.5	
	NY Botanical Garden	56	easy	1 to 3	✔
	Prospect Park	63	easy	3	
	Brooklyn Botanic Garden	72	easy	1.5	
	Jamaica Bay NWR	78	easy	1.7	
	Clay Pit Ponds	86	easy	1.0	
	High Rock Park	94	moderate	4.0	
Long Island	Sands Point	101	easy	2 to 3	
	Planting Fields	109	easy	1 to 3	
	Caumsett S.P.	116	easy	4 to 5	

Lake or Pond	Swamp/ Marsh	Beach	Scenic Vista	Unusual Plants	Special Geology	Birds/ Animals	Public Trans.
✔				✔			✔
			✔				✔
			✔	✔	✔		✔
			✔		✔	✔	✔
✔	✔						✔
	✔	✔			✔	✔	✔ seasonal
				✔			✔
✔			✔		✔	✔	✔
✔				✔			✔
✔	✔	✔				✔	✔
✔	✔				✔		✔
✔	✔		✔		✔		✔
		✔	✔		✔		
				✔			
	✔	✔	✔		✔	✔	

Region	Walk	Page Number	Difficulty Level	Distance	River
Long Island	Caleb Smith Park	124	easy	2.25	✔
	Sunken Meadow S.P.	131	easy	2	✔
	Bayard Cutting Arboretum	137	easy	1 to 2	✔
	Connetquot River S.P.	145	easy	2	✔
	South Shore Nature Center	152	easy	2	
	Fire Island	160	easy	2.5	
West-chester	Teatown Lake	170	easy/mod.	1.6/1.6	
	Rockefeller S.P.	178	easy/mod.	1.3/2.6	✔
	Croton Point	185	easy	2	✔
	Brinton Brook	193	easy	2	✔
	Cranberry Lake	200	easy	1	
	Ward Pound Ridge	208	moderate	3.3	
	Marshlands Conservancy	216	easy	1.5	
	Anthony's Nose	223	moderate	2.5	✔

Lake or Pond	Swamp/ Marsh	Beach	Scenic Vista	Unusual Plants	Special Geology	Birds/ Animals	Public Trans.
✔							✔
	✔	✔	✔		✔		
				✔			
						✔	
	✔			✔		✔	
		✔		✔	✔	✔	
✔			✔				
✔						✔	
		✔	✔				
✔						✔	
✔	✔			✔	✔		
✔			✔			✔	
	✔	✔		✔		✔	
			✔		✔		

Region	Walk	Page Number	Difficulty Level	Distance	River
West-chester	Fahnestock S.P.	231	easy/mod.	1/2.5	✔
Orange/ Rockland Counties	Harriman S.P.	241	moderate	3.8	
	Bear Mountain S.P.	250	moderate	3.7	
	Black Rock Forest	258	moderate	2	
Conn.	Greenwich Audubon	266	easy	1.5	
	Devil's Den	274	moderate	2.8	✔
New Jersey	Palisades Park	282	moderate	2.5	✔
	Cheesequake S.P.	292	moderate	3.5	✔
	Scherman-Hoffman	300	moderate	2.5	✔
	Great Swamp	307	easy	1.2	
	Wawayanda S.P.	317	moderate	3	

Lake or Pond	Swamp/ Marsh	Beach	Scenic Vista	Unusual Plants	Special Geology	Birds/ Animals	Public Trans.
✔							
✔	✔		✔		✔		✔
			✔				✔
✔			✔				
✔							
✔			✔				
			✔		✔		✔
✔	✔			✔	✔		
						✔	
	✔			✔	✔	✔	
✔			✔		✔		

Appendix A
Useful Names and Addresses

General

Appalachian Mountain Club
5 Joy Street
Boston, MA 02108
617-523-0655

Appalachian Mountain Club
New York–North Jersey Chapter
202 East 39th Street
New York, NY 10016
212-986-1430

Long Island Greenbelt Trail Conference
23 Deer Path Road
Central Islip, NY 11722
516-360-0753

The Nature Conservancy
Long Island Chapter
250 Lawrence Hill Road
Cold Spring Harbor, NY 11724
516-367-3225

New York City Audubon Society, Inc.
71 West 23d Street, Room 606
New York, NY 10010
212-691-7483

New York–New Jersey Trail Conference
232 Madison Avenue
New York, NY 10016
212-685-9699; e-mail: nynjtc@aol.com

Westchester Trails Association
c/o Sandra Harrison
10 Franklin Avenue, #1A
White Plains, NY 10601

New York State

Office of Parks, Recreation, and Historic Preservation
Empire State Plaza
Albany, NY 12238
518-474-0456

Camping and Cabin Reservations
800-456-CAMP

Long Island Region
Box 247
Babylon, NY 11702
516-669-1000

New York City Region
915 Broadway
New York, NY 10010
212-387-0271

Palisades Region
Bear Mountain, NY 10911
914-786-2701

Taconic Region
914-889-4100

Department of Economic Development
Division of Tourism
One Commerce Plaza
Albany, NY 12245
800-CALL-NYS
518-474-4116

Department of Environmental Conservation
50 Wolf Road
Albany, NY 12233
518-457-2500

New York City
Central Park Conservancy
The Arsenal, Central Park
New York, NY 10021
212-315-0385

City Parks Foundation
The Arsenal, Central Park
New York, NY 10021
212-360-1399

The Historic House Trust of New York City
830 Fifth Avenue, Room 203
New York, NY 10021
212-360-8282 or 212-360-3448

National Association for Olmsted Parks
7315 Wisconsin Avenue, Suite 504E
Bethesda, MD 20814
202-362-9511

New York City Parks and Recreation
830 Fifth Avenue
New York, NY 10021
212-360-1305

Borough Offices
Bronx Parks
Ranaqua
Bronx Park
Bronx, NY 10462
718-430-1800

Brooklyn Parks
Litchfield Villa, Prospect Park
Brooklyn, NY 11215
718-965-8900

Manhattan Parks
16 West 61st Street
New York, NY 10023
212-408-0201

Queens Parks
The Overlook
Forest Park
Kew Gardens, NY 11415
718-520-5900

Staten Island Parks
Stonehenge
Clove Lakes Park
Staten Island, NY 10301
718-390-8000

New York City Urban Park Rangers
24-hour information line: 800-201-PARK
Bronx: 718-548-0912
Brooklyn: 718-287-3400
Manhattan: 212-772-0210
Queens: 718-699-4204
Staten Island: 718-667-6042

Staten Island Greenbelt Administrator
High Rock Park
200 Nevada Avenue
Staten Island, NY 10306
718-667-2165

Orange County

County Tourism Office
800-762-8687

Rockland County

County Tourism Office
914-638-5800

Westchester County

Department of Parks, Recreation, and Conservation
19 Bradhurst Avenue
Hawthorne, NY 10532
914-593-PARK
914-593-2600

New Jersey

Department of Environmental Protection and Energy
Division of Parks and Forestry
CN 404
Trenton, NJ 08625

Skylands Region (Region 3)
RD 1, Box 999
Rte. 23
Franklin, NJ 07416
201-827-6200

Gateway Region (Region 2)
434 Freehold-Englishtown Road
Freehold, NJ 07728
908-462-5868

Appendix B
Public Transportation Information

New York City Transit
718-330-1234

Port Authority of New York Bus Terminal
212-736-4700

Staten Island Transit
718-979-0600

Rockland County Bus Information
914-634-1100

Suffolk County Bus System
516-360-5700

Westchester County Transit
BEE-LINE Bus System
914-682-2020

Gray Line Buses
212-397-2600

International Bus Services
201-529-3666

Red & Tan Line Buses
212-279-6525

Short Line Buses
800-631-8405; 212-736-4700

Long Island Railroad
718-217-LIRR

MetroNorth
212-532-4900; 800-638-7646

Bibliography

Albright, Rodney and Priscilla. *Short Nature Walks on Long Island*, 4th ed. Old Saybrook, Ct.: Globe Pequot Press, 1993.

Anderson, Katherine S. and Peggy Turco. *Walks and Rambles in Westchester and Fairfield Counties*, 2d ed. Woodstock, Vt.: Backcountry Publications, 1993.

Barbour, Anita and Spider. *Wild Flora of the Northeast*. Woodstock, N.Y.: Overlook Press, 1991.

Barlow, Elizabeth. *The Forests and Wetlands of New York City*. Boston: Little, Brown, 1971.

Benyus, Janine M. *The Field Guide to Wildlife Habitats of the Eastern United States*. New York: Simon & Schuster, 1989.

Boyle, Robert H. *The Hudson River: A Natural and Unnatural History*. New York: W. W. Norton, 1979.

Cronon, William. *Changes in the Land*. New York: Hill and Wang, 1983.

Dann, Kevin and Gordon Miller. *30 Walks in New Jersey*. New Brunswick, N.J.: Rutgers University Press, 1982.

Drennan, Susan Roney. *Where to Find Birds in New York State*. Syracuse, N.Y.: Syracuse University Press, 1981.

Dunwell, Frances F. *The Hudson River Highlands*. New York: Columbia University Press, 1991.

Glassberg, Jeffrey. *Butterflies through Binoculars: A Field Guide to the Butterflies in the Boston–New York–Washington Region*. New York: Oxford University Press, 1993.

Graff, M. M. *Central Park and Prospect Park: A New Perspective.* New York: Greensward Foundation, 1985.

Graff, M. M. *Tree Trails in Central Park.* New York: Greensward Foundation, 1970.

Guide to the Long Path. New York: New York–New Jersey Trail Conference, 1992.

Harrison, Marina and Lucy D. Rosenfeld. *A Walker's Guidebook.* New York: Michael Kesend Publishing, 1988.

Ingersoll, Ernest. *Handy Guide to the Hudson River and Catskill Mountains.* Reprint of 1910 edition. Astoria, N.Y.: J. C. & A. L. Fawcett, 1989.

Kick, Peter, Barbara McMartin, and James M. Long. *50 Hikes in the Hudson Valley, 2d ed.* Woodstock, Vt.: Backcountry Publications, 1994.

Kieran, John. *A Natural History of New York City.* New York: Fordham University Press, 1982.

Kulik, Stephen, et al. *The Audubon Society Field Guide to the Natural Places of the Northeast: Inland.* New York: Pantheon Books, 1984.

Maslow, Jonathan Evan. *The Owl Papers.* New York: Vintage Books, 1988.

Myles, William J. *Harriman Trails: A Guide and History.* New York: New York–New Jersey Trail Conference, 1994.

New York State Atlas and Gazetteer. Freeport, Maine: DeLorme Mapping Company, 1988.

New York Walk Book. New York: New York–New Jersey Trail Conference, 1971.

Scheller, William G. *Country Walks near New York,* 2d ed. Boston: Appalachian Mountain Club, 1986.

Schuberth, Christopher. *The Geology of New York City and Environs.* New York: American Museum of Natural History, 1968.

Scofield, Bruce. *Circuit Hikes in Northern New Jersey.* New York: New York–New Jersey Trail Conference, 1992.

Scofield, Bruce, Stella J. Green, and H. Neil Zimmerman. *Fifty Hikes in New Jersey.* Woodstock, Vt.: Backcountry Publications, 1988.

Smith, Richard M. *Wild Plants of America.* New York: John Wiley & Sons, 1989.

Symmers, Divya. *Country Days in New York City.* Castine, Maine: Country Roads Press, 1993.

Teal, John and Mildred. *Life and Death of the Salt Marsh.* New York: Ballantine Books, 1969.

Turco, Peggy. *Walks and Rambles in Dutchess and Putnam Counties.* Woodstock, Vt.: Backcountry Publications, 1990.

Van Diver, Bradford B. *Roadside Geology of New York.* Missoula, Mt.: Mountain Press Publishing, 1985.

Venning, Frank D. *Wildflowers of North America.* New York: Golden Press, 1984.

Weidensaul, Scott. *Seasonal Guide to the Natural Year: Mid-Atlantic.* Golden, Co.: Fulcrum Publishing, 1992.

Williams, Deborah. *Natural Wonders of New York.* Castine, Maine: Country Roads Press, 1995.

Zim, Herbert S. and Hobart M. Smith. *Golden Guide to Reptiles and Amphibians.* Racine, Wisc.: Western Publishing, 1987.

About the Author

Sheila Buff grew up on Long Island and now divides her time between Brooklyn and northern Dutchess County. The author of numerous books on a wide variety of topics, her favorite subjects are natural history and the outdoors. Among her books in those areas are *Birding for Beginners, The Birder's Sourcebook, The Gardener's Sourcebook,* and *The Birdfeeder's Handbook.*

Howard Rosenzweig

About the AMC

The Appalachian Mountain Club pursues an active conservation agenda while encouraging responsible recreation. Our philosophy is that successful, long-term conservation depends on firsthand experience of the natural environment. AMC's 71,000 members pursue interests in hiking, canoeing, skiing, walking, rock climbing, bicycling, camping, kayaking, and backpacking, and—at the same time—help safeguard the environment.

Founded in 1876, the club has been at the forefront of the environmental protection movement. As cofounder of several leading New England environmental organizations, and as an active member working in coalition with these and many other groups, the AMC has successfully influenced legislation and public opinion.

The most recent effors in the AMC conservation program include river protection, Northern Forest Lands policy, Sterling Forest (NY) preservation, and support for the Clean Air Act. The AMC depends upon its active members and grass-roots supporters to promote this conservation agenda.

The AMC's education department offers members and the general public a wide range of workshops, from introductory camping to intensive Mountain Leadership School taught on the trails of the White Mountains. In addition, volunteers in each chapter lead hundreds of outdoor activities and excursions and offer introductory instruction in backcountry sports.

The AMC's research department focuses on the forces affecting the ecosystem, including ozone levels, acid rain and fog, climate change, rare flora, habitat protection, and air quality and visibility.

Another facet of the AMC is the trails program, which maintains more than 1,400 miles of trail (including 350 miles of the Appalachian Trail) and more than 50 shelters in the Northeast. Through a coordinated effort of volunteers, seasonal crews, and program staff, the AMC contributes more than 10,000 hours of public service work each summer in the area from Washington D.C. to Maine.

In addition to supporting our work by becoming an AMC member, hikers can donate time as volunteers. The club offers four unique weekly volunteer base camps in New Hampshire, Maine, Massachusetts, and New York. We also sponsor ten-day service projects throughout the United States, Adopt-A-Trail programs, trail days events, trail skills workshops, and chapter and camp volunter projects.

The AMC has a longstanding connection to Acadia National Park. Working in cooperation with the National Park Service and Friends of Acadia, the AMC Trails Program provides many opportunities to preserve the park's resources. These include half-day volunteers projects for guests at AMC's Echo Lake Camp, ten-day service projects, weeklong volunteer crews in the fall, and trail days events. For more information on these public service volunteer opportunities, contact the AMC Trails Program, Pinkham Notch Visitor Center, P.O. Box 298, Gorham, NH 03581; 603-466-2721.

The club operates eight alpine huts in the White Mountains that provide shelter, bunks and blankets, and hearty meals for hikers. Pinkham Notch Visitor Center, at the foot of Mt. Washington, is base camp to the adventurous and the ideal location for individuals and families new to outdoor recreation. Comfortable bunkrooms, mountain hospitality, and home-cooked, family-style meals make Pinkham Notch Visitor Center a fun and affordable choice for lodging. For reservations, call 603-466-2727.

At the AMC main office in Boston and at Pinkham Notch Visitor Center in New Hampshire, the bookstore and information center stock the entire line of AMC publications, as well as other trail and river guides, maps, reference materials, and the latest articles on conservation issues. Guidebooks and other AMC gifts are available by mail order 800-262-4455, or by writing AMC, P.O. Box 298, Gorham, NH 03581. Also available from the bookstore or by subscription is *Appalachia*, the country's oldest mountaineering and conservation journal.

General Index

Alphabetical Listing of Areas